THE CULT AT THE END OF THE WORLD

THE CULT AT THE END OF THE WORLD

The Terrifying Story of the Aum
Doomsday Cult, from the Subways of
Tokyo to the Nuclear Arsenals of Russia

DAVID E. KAPLAN &
ANDREW MARSHALL

Crown Publishers, Inc.
New York

Published by Crown Publishers, Inc.,
201 East 50th Street, New York, New York 10022.

Random House, Inc.
New York, Toronto, London, Sydney, Auckland

Originally published in Great Britain by
Hutchinson Random House (UK)

Crown is a trademark of Crown Publishers, Inc.

Manufactured in the United States of America

Library of Congress Cataloging-in-Publication
Data is available upon request.

ISBN 0-517-70543-5

10 9 8 7 6 5 4 3 2 1

First American Edition

CONTENTS

AUTHORS' NOTE

Readers may find portions of the book difficult to believe. This is, however, the true story of an extraordinary group. The events and characters described have been carefully drawn from interviews, court documents, law enforcement reports, statements by cult members, and extensive coverage by Japan's largest news organizations. Based on these sources, the authors have recounted certain scenes and conversations. In those cases, we have relied as much as possible on primary material, such as eyewitness accounts and police confessions.

Japanese names are rendered in the Western style, with the surname last. Currency amounts are given in U.S. dollars at conversion rates current at the time noted.

ACKNOWLEDGMENTS

This book could not have happened were it not for the generous efforts of many people. Our friends, colleagues, and sources helped us time and again to piece together a story that gave both its authors more than one bad dream.

Fellow journalist Abigail Haworth was a walking encyclopedia on Aum whose perceptive advice was invaluable. From the beginning, her talents as a writer and editor gave a huge project impetus and direction.

Hiroshi Suto did everything we could have asked of him, and more. His many talents included research, translation, and trouble-shooting of every sort. We were fortunate to have had such a terrific assistant. Likewise, John Sweeney came through every time we asked, which was too often. John's myriad talents – librarian, journalist, Asia scholar – led us to a gold mine of information on everything from mind control to mass destruction.

In Moscow, we were helped enormously by Vladimir Galin, one of Russia's finest journalists. In Australia, Stan Correy made a great and much appreciated contribution. And in Tokyo, our thanks go to Kyoko Goto and Mark Schreiber.

We are especially grateful to those in law enforcement and elsewhere in government, most of whom, for professional reasons, cannot be named. We were helped by officials from no fewer than ten agencies in five countries; their contribution was invaluable. Thanks much to Bill Fitzpatrick of the Australia Customs Service and his colleagues at the Australian Federal Police in Canberra. Also of great help were John Sopko, Richard F. Kennan and the staff of the U.S. Senate Permanent Subcommittee on Investigations.

In Japan, the authors thank the many people who contributed on matters large and small: Chuk and Kara Besher, David Bong, Dave Butts, Tom Caldwell, Glenn Davis, Mary-Anne Dyer, Yoshiyuki Kono, Richard Lloyd Parry, Michio Matsui, Melanie Mortimer, Emiko Terazono, and Margaret Scott. Also, much thanks to our pal Greg Starr and the talented staff at *Tokyo Journal*. And to Brian Haverty in Sydney, *domo arigato* for taking pictures and bearing witness.

To piece together Aum's far-flung story, the authors were helped by friends and colleagues around the world. Our gratitude goes out to Alec Dubro in Washington, D.C.; Charles Piller in San Francisco; Joe E. Rand in Los Angeles; Peter Erickson in San Diego; John Morearty in Stockton; Manfred Redelfs and Joachim Schröder in Germany; Doreen Johnstone and Bridget King in Nairobi; Chris Taylor in Taipei; Rainer Schmidt in London; Iain Milne at the Royal College of Physicians of Edinburgh; and in Moscow, Nataly Lesskis, Sergei Evdokimov, Vladimir Koudria, Father Oleg Stenyaev, and the members of the Youth Salvation Committee.

Andrew Marshall thanks Tim Hulse at British *Esquire* for commissioning his original story on Aum, and Chika Miyatake for helping on it. Similarly, David Kaplan thanks his colleagues at Nippon Television, with whom he did his first reports on the cult: Toshiya Sugimoto, Hisao Adachi and Dea Athon Diamant.

Our agents did a first-rate job putting together a complex deal in near-record time, and we much appreciate their efforts. Thanks to Leslie Breed and Gail Ross, Michael Meller, Abner Stein, and Howard Yoon. We also thank our editors, particularly Ann Patty, Imke Rötger, and Paul Sidey, for their patience and support.

Finally, we thank our families, who made it all possible. Andrew Marshall was lucky indeed to have the love, encouragement, and life-sustaining e-mail of the Marshall-Simpson clan. Most of all, he thanks Abi; this book is for her.

David Kaplan gives special thanks to his wife Pam, who did so much to make this book happen – juggling schedules, editing, typing notes, and helping in every other way. Much love and thanks, as well, to his daughter Adi; to his dad, who proved a terrific help on everything from the Ten Plagues to Tesla; and most of all, to his mother, to whom he dedicates this book.

PROLOGUE

Tokyo, March 20, 1995.

For nearly 400 miles the Tokyo subway system sprawls beneath this vast metropolis, a maze of concrete and steel tunneling into the night like a giant ant farm. It is the world's busiest underground railway, used by 9 million passengers each day.

It is also an ideal site for mass murder.

Commuting by train is a way of life in Japan, especially in the nation's capital. If Tokyo is the country's political, economic, and cultural heart, then the subway is its blood – pumping constantly through the veins and arteries of the world's second-largest economy, carrying the workers to their jobs and homes.

The rush hour this Monday seems much like any other morning. Tokyo's long-suffering commuters descend on elevators into a labyrinth of subterranean walkways. Announcements blare as they stand elbow to elbow on the packed platforms and then surge into the narrow trains. During hour-long commutes they are wedged like livestock into an impossibly crowded space, choking on air thick with competing aftershaves and morning-after breath.

At 7:45 a.m., five members of the Aum Supreme Truth cult blend into this massive press of humanity. The cultists board five trains at different ends of the subway system. They know the exact times and locations for each train at each station. They also know that by 8:15, all five trains will converge upon Kasumigaseki, the center of power in Japan, being home to the bureaucracies that rule over 125 million Japanese.

It is here that Aum has decided to strike a pre-emptive blow – to paralyze the Japanese state and begin its historic mission of world domination.

The operation is planned with military precision. At a hideaway near Mount Fuji, Aum's five commandos practiced by piercing vinyl bags with sharp-tipped umbrellas. As they drilled, watching over them were images of Shiva, the Hindu god of destruction and rebirth. Now aboard the trains, it is all for real: each bag holds a chemical solution that is 30 percent sarin, a nerve gas invented by the Nazis. Sarin is colorless, odorless and deadly. In minutes, perhaps seconds, it can destroy the nervous system of every living being within 100 feet.

As chilling as the plan are the murderers themselves. They are society's brightest minds – scientists, engineers, and doctors – turning their skills towards indiscriminate terror.

Aboard train one is Ikuo Hayashi, a 48-year-old cardiovascular surgeon with the morals of Dr. Josef Mengele. A graduate of the elite Keio University, Hayashi studied in the U.S. before joining the Japanese medical system. He now sits nervously on the subway's Chiyoda line, racing toward the central city.

Aboard train two is Toru Toyoda, twenty-seven, a high-flying graduate student in particle physics at Tokyo University who left his studies to join Aum. He is waiting for his Hibiya-line train to approach the city center, clutching his bags of chemicals wrapped in newspaper.

At the opposite end of the Hibiya line, aboard train three, is thirty-one year-old Masato Yokoyama, an applied-physics graduate. At the prescribed moment, he and the others will place their bags on the floor beneath their seats, puncture them, and let the sarin evaporate into a lethal gas.

Aboard train four is Kenichi Hirose, thirty, who graduated at the top of his class in applied physics at the prestigious Waseda University. Hirose planned advanced study in superconductivity before being lured into the cult. His future now rests on the Marunouchi line, speeding toward a deadly rendezvous.

Aboard train five, at the opposite end of the Marunouchi line, sits Yasuo Hayashi, thirty-seven, an electronics engineer. Like the others, Hayashi is a key member of the cult's Ministry of Science and Technology.

Each man, each train, converges inexorably on the city center. Secretaries and salarymen, bureaucrats and businessmen, students and stockbrokers shuffle on and off the airless steel cars, unaware that a cult of death is stalking their trains.

At 8 a.m., the carnage begins.

This is the story of the ultimate cult: a wired, hi-tech, designer-drug, billion-dollar army of New Age zealots, under the leadership of a blind and bearded madman, armed with weapons of mass destruction. Like scenes of an apocalyptic future in a cyberpunk novel, it is also the stuff of nightmares.

Cultists wired electrodes to their heads while chanting ancient mantras and logging onto computer nets. Methamphetamine, LSD, and truth serum ran through their veins, the product of home-made laboratories equipped with the latest gear. Those same labs worked at refining enough chemical and biological weapons to kill millions. Other cultists attempted to build a nuclear bomb, while massive facilities were built to manufacture handguns and explosives. All this activity went toward preparing for – and then unleashing – Armageddon.

Aum's story moves from the dense cities of postindustrial Japan to mountain retreats where samurai once fought, and then overseas – to Manhattan and Silicon Valley, Bonn and the Australian outback, and then to Russia. It was there, in the volatile remains of the Soviet empire, that the cult's membership exploded and its leaders found ready suppliers of military hardware, training, and, quite possibly, a nuclear bomb.

Aum leaders systematically targeted top universities, recruiting brilliant but alienated young scientists from chemistry, physics, and engineering departments. They forged relations with Japan's ruthless crime syndicates, the *yakuza*, and with veterans of the Soviet secret police, KGB, and Russian and Japanese militaries. They enlisted medical doctors to dope patients and perform human experiments that belong in a horror movie.

For years this went on, with barely a question from police or the media on three continents. Before long, Aum had become one of the world's richest, most sophisticated, and most murderous religious sects.

In a world poised between the Cold War and the new millennium, the tale of Aum is a mirror of our worst fears. Heavily armed militias, terrorist cells, zealous cults and crime syndicates all find their voice in the remarkable ascent of this bizarre sect. For years, experts have warned us: the growing sophistication of these groups, combined with the spread of modern technology, will bring about a new era in terrorism and mass murder. The coming of Aum Supreme Truth shows just how close these nightmares have come to reality.

The story of Aum is the story of its charismatic and increasingly psychopathic leader, Shoko Asahara. And Asahara's journey begins

WORLD'S RICHEST, MOST SOPHISTICATED
& MOST MURDEROUS RELIGIOUS SECTS.

one day in 1986, when a near-blind Japanese from a dirt-poor family sets off to find enlightenment.

PART ONE

GENESIS

1

RUSH HOUR OF THE GODS

The Himalayas, India, 1986. It was just as the holy men described it –
like a blinding, euphoric light snapping on inside his head. For weeks
now, he had traveled restlessly through a string of remote religious
retreats in the mystical Himalayas, to the very places the Buddha
himself had trodden 2,500 years ago. He had fasted and meditated
intensely, chanted Buddhist mantras for days without rest. He had
endured the unendurable and now it had paid off.

Shoko Asahara had finally attained enlightenment.

The Japanese looked much the same as ever. Asahara was thirty-
one years old, with a bearlike build and long hair straggling over his
shoulders. Even beneath an unruly beard, his features stood out: thick
cupid lips, an aquiline nose, a quizzical smudge of eyebrow above
each drowsy eyelid. Apart from his measured movements, nothing
indicated that he was nearly blind.

For Asahara, his Himalayan pilgrimage marked the end of a
long spiritual quest. "I had tried all kinds of practices – Taoism, Yoga,
Buddhism – and incorporated their essence into my training," he
later explained. "Finally, I reached my goal in the holy vibration of
the Himalayas. I could not have been any happier." Now Asahara
knew his true mission: "I am to walk the same path as Buddha . . ."

With enlightenment came visionary powers. Asahara claimed he
could perceive past lives and read people's minds. He could pass
through solid walls, meditate for hours underwater and levitate. "In
the future," he declared, "I will be able to fly freely through the sky."

For now, though, he took a plane. Soon, he had left the stark
natural beauty of the Indian Himalayas far behind, and arrived in the
dense, neon-lit megalopolis of Tokyo. It had been an extraordinary
journey. Shoko Asahara walked out of the Himalayas a self-
proclaimed messiah. But he had walked in as a con artist.

Shoko Asahara's first ambition was not to become a holy man.

Growing up on Japan's southern island of Kyushu, he wanted something much simpler. He wanted to be rich.

His real name was Chizuo Matsumoto. He was born in 1955, the fourth son of a weaver of *tatami*, the straw mats used as flooring in Japanese homes. His father was too poor to enjoy his own wares; their Matsumoto house was a shack with a dirt floor. With so many mouths to feed, the children often had only sweet potato to eat.

From infancy, Chizuo Matsumoto looked out upon a world of perpetual twilight. He was born blind in the left eye and partially sighted in the right. The timid, squinting boy liked to play "house" with local girls and was an easy target for neighborhood toughs. But when his parents enrolled him at a boarding school for the blind, Chizuo's partial vision gave him a big advantage over his sightless classmates. He bullied and dominated them. "He would force them to pick up his noodles and cakes, but never gave them any money," recalled one classmate. The only person who could bring out his gentler side was his older brother, who attended the same school. He was totally blind, and could often be seen holding Chizuo's shoulder for guidance as the brothers strolled through the school yard.

Chizuo wanted desperately to be a leader. He ran unsuccessfully for student-body president in elementary, junior high, and senior high school. Afterwards, he was miserable. "Why do I always lose?" he asked his classmates. One girl replied, "Because everyone's afraid of you." A dormitory roommate described living with him as "hell." Chizuo once threatened to set the dorm on fire. On another occasion, he screamed at a teacher, "I'll shoot you to death!" After each threat, the boy was chillingly dismissive. "They're just words – nothing to get upset about," he told the school counselor.

Chizuo was a difficult troublemaker to reproach. His grades were good when he applied himself. He was adept at mathematics and earned a black belt in judo at high school. But he applied his talent with numbers to scamming his classmates, and stored these ill-gotten gains along with his scholarship money and government grant for the disabled. "He was always saying, 'I've got to get rich,' " recalled one teacher. Upon graduating from senior high school, he reportedly had saved nearly $30,000.

Behind his damaged eyes, Chizuo Matsumoto dreamed of a bright future. He told friends of plans to join the nation's ruling political party, for then he would certainly reach his ultimate goal: becoming prime minister of Japan. A neighbor recalled asking Chizuo if he would attend the local university. "You've got to be kidding if you think I'd go to that place," the teenager shot back. He had his sights set on Tokyo University, the recruiting ground for Japan's elite. But despite studying hard at a Tokyo prep school, he failed the university's entrance exam. He returned home embittered, and was soon arrested for punching a fellow employee at a massage parlor.

Chizuo left again for the capital, and then his luck changed. He met a pretty college girl called Tomoko, who clearly felt the full force of the young man's charm. They were married in January 1978 and their child – the first of six – arrived just six months later. It was Tomoko, perhaps, who taught Chizuo how to harness his nervous energy. With money from her family, he established the Matsumoto Acupuncture Clinic.

The clinic thrived. Chizuo treated his customers with acupuncture and yoga, as well as with herbal cures of dubious value. One tonic, called Almighty Medicine, was simply tangerine peel in alcohol solution. Chizuo charged up to $7,000 for a three-month course of treatment. He also touted his quack remedies around Tokyo's plush hotels. Wearing a white coat and a stethoscope, he examined elderly people in their rooms and convinced them he could cure rheumatism. It was harder fooling the police. In 1982, he was arrested for fraud and fined about $1,000 – but only after the hotel scam had earned him nearly $200,000.

Chizuo Matsumoto was earning sums of money that his straw-weaving father could only dream of. But there was still a void inside him that not even cold, hard cash could fill. "For the first time, I stopped to ask myself, Why am I alive?" he later wrote. "What do I need to overcome this emptiness? I wanted to find something absolute."

Palmistry apart, Chizuo had never shown much interest in the spiritual; as a teenager, he had read political tracts by Mao Zedong. Now, with business thriving, he dabbled in geomancy and Chinese fortune-telling. In one obscure ritual, said to bring happiness and riches, Chizuo buried food and magnets in holes near his house. Eventually, the experiments bore fruit. While meditating, he felt energy throb up his spine. Afterwards he claimed he had the "psychic power" to perceive evil auras around other people.

Greatly encouraged, Chizuo began scouting around for a religion that would give him a more formal education, and found himself spoiled for choice. For by the 1980s, Japan was experiencing what one scholar memorably termed "the rush hour of the gods".

*

From its mystic origins in northern India, Buddhism began a journey across Asia that would attract millions with its teachings on the path to enlightenment. By the sixth century AD, the religion had made its way through China and Korea to Japan, where it drew a loyal following. For centuries, Japanese Buddhists coexisted peacefully with believers in Shinto, the nation's animistic nature religion. But the start of the 1868 Meiji Restoration soon saw the emergence of "State Shinto," with the Emperor himself as the central deity.

As Japan plunged into ultranationalism in the 1930s, other faiths which challenged that supremacy were swiftly crushed. The holy buildings of one deviant sect, Omoto, were dynamited into pieces less than a foot in size, so that the group would never rebuild. Other religions were snuffed out with similar brutality.

After Japan's defeat in World War II U.S. occupation authorities disbanded State Shinto and forced Emperor Hirohito to renounce his divine status. With freedom of religion now guaranteed, a plethora of fringe faiths quickly emerged; among them was a farmer's wife who declared herself the "Sun goddess" and led a group of devotees dancing in "a state of ecstasy" before bemused passers-by. One of the largest of the so-called "new religions" was the wealthy Soka Gakkai which, though founded in 1930, prospered in the postwar period; its nine million members worship a thirteenth-century Buddhist monk, Nichiren.

Then, in the 1970s, Japan's spiritual rush hour began. With the economy booming, hundreds of new religious groups set up shop to fill the void in the nation's heart. Many groups barely deserved the term "religious." One predominantly female sect, Ark of Jesus, ran a nightclub called the Daughters of Zion. By the 1980s, a hundred new religions were emerging every year. Among the proselytizers was a former Tokyo stockbroker who claimed to be the reincarnation of, among others, Socrates and Henry Ford; he set up the Institute for Research into Human Happiness, which won Japanese hearts and wallets by predicting a millennial apocalypse from which Japan alone would survive.

Into this divine traffic jam stepped the questing Chizuo Matsumoto. One Buddhist text he read was published by a Japanese religious sect called Agonshu. Established in 1969, Agonshu was in many ways a thoroughly modern cult. It recruited followers through magazine ads and used its own satellite TV station to beam out "healing psychic power." The sect demanded strict adherence to Buddhist principles, and encouraged followers to cut all contacts with families. This hardline approach was sweetened by supernatural promises, as described in cult publications like *The Psychic Power That Science Can Give You.*

Chizuo found this cocktail of fundamentalism and fantasy appealing. In 1981, he began Agonshu's central training ritual: to meditate forty minutes a day for a thousand days. It left him more dissatisfied than ever. "The peaceful state of mind I'd achieved before joining Agonshu was smashed," he recalled. But Agonshu gave Chizuo something far more important than peace of mind. It gave him a model for a cult of his own.

In early 1984 Chizuo created a new company called Aum Inc. The name Aum (pronounced "ohm") is a Hindu mantra, or chant, said to incorporate the ultimate truth of the universe. Aum Inc.'s twenty-nine-year-old president christened his first enterprise the Aum Association of Mountain Wizards. It was a fancy name for what was actually a one-room Tokyo yoga school with a profitable sideline in phony health drinks.

Ever ambitious, young Chizuo was soon in the Himalayas, searching for enlightenment. He returned home a new man, boasting of mystical powers and spiritual bliss. He had sat with Hindu holy men, spoken with the great gurus of India. Chizuo now understood that his destiny lay not in politics, but in religion. All he needed was a following, and that too would now come.

UFOs, ESP, stone circles, levitation, telepathy – no topic was too weird for *Twilight Zone* magazine. In the mid-1980s, it was one of several publications catering to a growing fascination with the supernatural among young Japanese. Its editors were overwhelmed with letters from teenagers claiming they sensed previous lives or came from other dimensions.

For Chizuo Matsumoto, *Twilight Zone* was the perfect vehicle. In 1986 the magazine ran photos of him apparently suspended in mid-air. "I can levitate for about three seconds, but the period is gradually lengthening," he told the monthly. Buddhist mystics had claimed such powers for centuries. But what Asahara called "levitation" was a relatively simple act for any yoga expert. With his legs crossed, he used his thigh muscles to propel himself momentarily from the floor. The *Twilight Zone* staffer who took the photo said Asahara landed heavily. "He was obviously in pain but tried not to show it," the photographer recalled.

Still, it was wonderful publicity. Attendance surged at Chizuo's yoga schools, and he plowed the profits back into opening new branches across Japan. Chizuo had a way with his young students. He was soft-spoken and funny, and held forth with equal authority on mystic forces or baseball. His schools were sanctuaries from the high-octane stresses of urban life; one student talked of a "homey, warm atmosphere." For many others, who had grown up in families where their workaholic parents were often absent, Chizuo was the father they never had.

They didn't know it yet, but something was wrong with Dad. While meditating on a beach on Japan's Pacific coast, a "message from God" came to Chizuo. "I have chosen you to lead God's army," the voice said. That same year, he met a radical historian during a spiritual retreat in the mountains. "Armageddon will come at the end of this century," the man warned him. "Only a merciful, godly race will survive. The leader of this race will emerge in Japan." The chance meeting and the beachside revelation ignited a firestorm in Chizuo's mind. He had been singled out to save the world.

Such a profound calling demanded a new identity. "Shoko Asahara" had a more unusual ring to it than the plain-sounding "Chizuo Matsumoto," a name better suited to corporate drudges and other nobodies-for-life. At the same time, he began cultivating a thick beard and wearing the ivory-white clothes of a holy man.

Such were the outward clues to the profound transformation he would undergo. Little Chizuo and everything he represented – poverty, blindness, failure – was gradually fading. Soon he would be buried forever in the mythic mists of an all-new Shoko Asahara.

2

GURU

Dharmsala was as busy as a town of 17,000 souls ever gets. Western tourists clambered from dilapidated buses that had ferried them to this settlement perched on a lonely spur of India's southern Himalayas. The restaurants and hotels were doing a roaring trade. Tibetan New Year was approaching, and monks in crimson robes fumbled with prayer beads as they hastened along the narrow streets. Multicolored prayer flags fluttered in the crisp mountain air.

Amid this bustle of nationalities walked the bearish figure of Shoko Asahara. It was February 1987. Months had passed since his last visit to India, and Asahara had now returned with a sacred goal. He had come to Dharmsala to receive a blessing from His Holiness the Dalai Lama, revered among 11 million Tibetan Buddhists as a living god. The Dalai Lama had fled China's brutal invasion of his homeland in 1959. Ever since, his benign presence in Dharmsala had been a magnet for Tibetan refugees, tourists and Buddhist pilgrims the world over.

Dressed in simple brown robes, the Tibetan warmly greeted Shoko Asahara in a room hung with colorful tapestries. Asahara recalled the meeting fondly. "Dear friend," the Dalai Lama began. "Look at the Buddhism of Japan today. It has degenerated into ceremonialism and has lost the essential truth of the teachings." Asahara nodded gravely. "If this situation continues," the Dalai Lama went on, "Buddhism will vanish from Japan. Something needs to be done."

Then Tibet's god-king gave his Japanese visitor a divine mission. "You should spread real Buddhism there," he said. "You can do that well, because you have the mind of a Buddha. If you do so, I shall be very pleased. It will help me with my mission."

The mind of a Buddha! Asahara was almost drunk with joy. He can perceive my level of spiritual practice and knows I'm enlightened, he thought. Afterwards, His Holiness blessed the Japanese with holy

water and then posed for a photo, which would be reprinted in Aum
books as a kind of sacred endorsement.

Such were Asahara's recollections of his memorable encounter.
The Dalai Lama, however, had a slightly different version of events.
The Tibetan leader recalled giving Asahara no special mission. In
fact, he remembered Asahara showing more interest in how to
structure a religious organization than in Buddhist thought. The
Japanese was simply one of hundreds of people His Holiness meets
each year. According to an aide to the Dalai Lama, "Asahara was
nothing special."

But he was. After his Dharmsala sojourn, Asahara's burgeoning
megalomania became obvious. "I have no intention of becoming a
charismatic leader," he told followers, but his ramblings suggested
otherwise. "With my ability to know the past, I've learned that I was
once an Egyptian chieftain," he wrote on returning from Egypt that
year. He also claimed credit for designing the pyramids in a previous
incarnation as the Egyptian architect Imhotep.

The journey to Cairo was one of several trips designed to bolster
his credentials as a mystic and religious figure. A year after finding
enlightenment in the Himalayas, Asahara returned to India with a
coterie of students. By then, he claimed, his spiritual mind had
progressed to a magical point. "I was now free to leave my physical
body, any time, anywhere," he wrote. But the pilgrims at one
Himalayan retreat were less than impressed by Asahara's entourage.
"They were very unpopular," recalled one. "Asahara preached to
experienced disciples and said they needed more training. He said to
the retreat master, 'Let's have a photo of the two of us,' and put his
arm round the master's shoulder. We were astonished."

Enlightenment, genuine or otherwise, was highly marketable.
Asahara returned to Japan and penned his first book, *Secrets of
Developing Your Supernatural Powers.* "Spiritual training that doesn't lead
to supernatural powers is hogwash!" ran an ad for the book. "The
Venerable Master will show you the secrets of his amazing mystic
powers. See the future, read people's minds, make your wishes come
true, X-ray vision, levitation, trips to the fourth dimension, hear the
voice of God and more. It will change your life!" To prove it, the
cover bore the infamous photo of Asahara in full yogic flight.

With Asahara's rise to "venerable master," the tone of Aum's
classes began to change. The aspiring prophet gave his lectures a
more redemptive, more missionary flavor. His aims now were "to
rescue people from their suffering," he declared, and "to lead the

world to enlightenment." But unlike fake herbal remedies, enlightenment was an intangible thing to sell. Asahara needed a visual sales tool.

He found this by adapting a simple yoga technique, in which the gaze of teacher and student is aligned and the two chant in unison. Asahara would simply place his hand on a student's head and "inject the yoga master's divine energy into disciples." Afterwards, students testified to extraordinary results, including miracle recoveries from road accidents, out-of-body experiences, and 90 percent win-rates at mahjong. Asahara charged students $350 each for this ritual.

Five months after his return from Dharmsala, Shoko Asahara made an announcement. His yoga schools would no longer be called the Aum Association of Mountain Wizards. They now had a new name: Aum Supreme Truth. Many students were perplexed. "Before then the group wasn't religious at all," said one. "The whole atmosphere was about enjoying yoga to develop psychic powers." Students paid a modest $40 for a three-day course, and called their instructor either "Mr. Asahara" or *sensei*, a Japanese term of respect commonly used for teachers.

With the advent of Aum Supreme Truth, everything changed. Students were told that cash donations to Aum would help their "spiritual development." They were asked to hand out Aum leaflets, buy Asahara's books, and bring more people to meetings. And they were told to call Asahara by his new title, *sonshi* – the Japanese word for "guru." For each disappointed student who deserted the fledgling sect, several more joined, lured by the guru's eclectic blend of Eastern religion and supernatural power.

Asahara was building a powerful personality cult, and a handcrafted theology to accompany it. As if shopping a vast spiritual supermarket, he pushed his cart through the world's religions, gathering bits of ritual and dogma to make his own sacred stew. At its core, Aum Supreme Truth became a familiar New Age blend of Eastern religion and mysticism. Its beliefs and rituals were drawn heavily from Tibetan Buddhism, its physical rigor from yoga. Asahara also culled from the teachings of Zen masters, Hindu holy men, and religious ascetics through the ages. But no concept would prove more important than that of impending doom.

Lord Shiva the Destroyer reigns above the Hindu pantheon of gods, standing with Brahma the Creator and Vishnu the Preserver as the faith's central deities. The four-armed Shiva lays waste to the world in a cosmic dance, only to recreate it in a violent cycle of death and rebirth. It was Shiva that Shoko Asahara chose to be the chief deity of his new religion.

The world's end held a great fascination for Asahara. His previous sect, Agonshu, had warned of an approaching apocalypse, which could be averted only by conversion to the group's holy cause. The doomsday talk worked well in recruiting young disciples. Asahara saw its immediate appeal and began building into Aum a theology of destruction. Eventually, this would consume all other thought and practice in Asahara's new faith.

To Shiva the destroyer, Asahara added the Judeo-Christian concept of Armageddon, which he drew from a cursory reading of Revelations. The idea of a biblical showdown between the forces of good and evil fit well into the budding guru's thoughts. There was a Buddhist equivalent, *mappo* – the time of chaos, when the world forgets the teachings of Buddha and descends into anarchy. But Asahara was more intrigued by the Bible's version, and he and his followers soon spoke at length about the coming of *Harumagedon*.

Along with Shiva and Armageddon, Asahara also drew heavily from the apocalyptic prophecies of Nostradamus, the sixteenth-century French astrologer. Translated into Japanese during the 1970s, Nostradamus's works had become best sellers, and Asahara was anxious to build on their popularity. Indeed, there was more at work here than mere doomsdaying. Like mystics since the beginning of time, Shoko Asahara was learning that profit and prophecy go together.

At an Aum seminar in May 1987, Asahara made his first major prediction based on "astral vision and intuitive wisdom." The news was not good. "Japan will rearm herself in 1992," he proclaimed. "Between 1999 and 2003, a nuclear war is sure to break out. I, Asahara, have mentioned the outbreak of nuclear war for the first time. We have only fifteen years before it."

Then came the hard sell. Nuclear holocaust could be averted – but only if every country had an Aum branch run by a "Buddha" or "awakened one." By this, of course, Asahara meant a disciple of his venerable self. "Spread the training system of Aum on a global scale and scatter Buddhas over the world," he declared. "Then we can avoid World War III for sure. I guarantee it."

In sermons and in books with titles like *Day of Annihilation*, Asahara's gloomy forecasts grew frighteningly precise. First, he said, trade friction with the U.S. will cause Japan's standard of living to plummet in 1990 and lead to a virtual police state. The year 1996 will witness "the sinking of Japan" – an evil land mass devoured in its entirety by the waves. Then, in 1999, the end of the world begins. Early next century, Russia, China, the U.S. and Europe will collapse. In the year 2003 – from October 30 to November 29, to be precise – Armageddon will enter its final phase with a nuclear war that lays waste to civilization.

From the rubble of this post-apocalyptic world will rise a race of "superhumans" – the followers of Shoko Asahara. All-out thermonuclear warfare, the guru explained, "is not a big problem for one who has attained enlightenment."

Asahara, of course, had one eye on catastrophe, the other on cash flow. He would use his apocalyptic preaching as a means to build whole communities and raise millions of dollars. If his religious credentials were questionable, one could at least give him credit for being a clever businessman. Aum Supreme Truth began to grow.

The Reverend Master of Aum Supreme Truth sat resplendent in purple robes on a raised platform, gazing down upon a sea of anxious young faces. A faint, benevolent smile played on Asahara's lips. His assembled devotees were about to undergo the Aum faith's ultimate experience: Blood Initiation.

One Aum follower in his mid-twenties had eagerly awaited this moment for months. Still grieving over the recent death of his mother, he had joined the cult after reading Asahara's *The Secret to Developing Supernatural Power*. He had saved up nearly $7,000 from part-time jobs to pay for the bizarre ritual about to begin.

"We sat down before the guru," he recalled. "I had heard that a doctor and a nurse had already drawn some of his blood. Soon a female follower brought in thirty small wine glasses. She gave one to each follower. Each glass contained about three or four spoonfuls of blood. There was also something else that kept blood from congealing. The female follower said, 'Please drink.' Slowly, I put the glass to my mouth."

The thick, warm liquid slid easily down the man's throat. Then he waited for something to happen. He had been led to believe that Asahara's blood had "magical properties." It had been scientifically proven, they said. Now he was crestfallen. "I expected to feel a surge in energy and to suddenly become superintelligent. But nothing happened. Not even after one month."

With the founding of Aum Supreme Truth, Shoko Asahara's

bloated ego had finally gone supernova. Drinking the guru's blood
was one of twenty so-called "initiations" the cult now offered. Holy
Hair Initiation was a bizarre variation on the traditional Japanese tea
ceremony, wherein snippets of Asahara's locks were brewed in boiling
water and then drunk. His beard clippings were also on sale ($375 per
half-inch). Just as he had once peddled tangerine peel in alcohol as
"Almighty Medicine," Asahara now repackaged his dirty bathwater
as "Miracle Pond" and sold it for nearly $800 per quart. Then there
was "Nectar Water" – tap water blessed by Asahara which
supposedly glowed in the dark. "Jesus changed water to wine," he
wrote in a later book, *Declaring Myself the Christ.* "I changed ordinary
water to the water that emits light."

One summer Asahara told followers he would demonstrate his
amazing power of "Underwater Samadhi," meditating for an hour in
a closed tank without oxygen. Unfortunately, the guru turned out to
be rather busy on the appointed day. Instead, the cult announced, his
disciple Gavanti had established the world record on the Master's
behalf. (Somehow the *Guinness Book of World Records* never got the
word; the register gives Gavanti's record to two-year-old Michelle
Funk of Salt Lake City, Utah, who made a full recovery after a
terrible accident left her submerged for an hour.)

Still the believers came. By the end of 1987, Aum had 1,500
members and branches in several major Japanese cities. In autumn
that year, a nonprofit firm called Aum USA was incorporated in the
state of New York, and an Aum office opened for business on
Manhattan's East 48th Street. But despite urging followers to "donate
to Aum and help cleanse yourself," Asahara needed more money.

The answer was the Japan Shambalization Plan. Shambala,
Asahara explained, was "a legendary world where the guru once
lived" in a former life. The plan's goal was straightforward: to open
Aum offices and training centers in every major Japanese city and
establish a "Lotus Village" or utopian community where Aum
members would survive Armageddon. "The Japan Shambalization
Plan is the first step to Shambalizing the world," Aum's leader
declared. "If you take part, you will achieve great virtue and rise to a
higher world."

Aum began a new recruitment drive, advertising in far-out
magazines like *Twilight Zone* and loading mailboxes with Aum leaflets.
Those who called Aum's number would be answered by a tender-
voiced young woman. She was trained to ask for the caller's name,
address and telephone number before giving out any information.

Then she would extend an invitation to a Truth Meeting at an Aum branch. There the caller would watch a video sermon by Asahara, then consult privately with an Aum recruiter.

One prospective member told a recruiter how she had once witnessed the shadow of her friend blur. Soon after, the friend had died. To her surprise and delight, the Aum recruiter believed her story – as he had been instructed to. "You were a trainee in a previous life," she was told. "You are innately at a higher level. If you train yourself hard in Aum, your superpower will increase." The woman signed up.

Once inside the cult, Asahara ensured there were many paths to enlightenment. Aum offered courses to suit everyone's schedule, salary and mystic tastes. One program promised to help followers enhance their supernatural powers. Another targeted "those who want to be reincarnated at a high level in the next life." Most new recruits were encouraged to sign up for the Yoga Tantra Course ("Achieve enlightenment and enjoy absolute freedom!"). This took two years to complete and cost over $2,000. The more time-pressed follower could take an Aum correspondence course, or attend intensive midnight-to-dawn seminars. Course fees could be paid in handy installments.

Aum's young adherents found a structure that must have seemed comfortably familiar. The entire faith was set up like a Japanese public school, with frequent exams (initiations), grades (levels of enlightenment) and an all-knowing teacher (the guru). At no point would they have to think for themselves.

The difference here was that Asahara was running a business, and a very profitable one at that. Every new recruit had to make a donation to the Shambalization Plan Fund. The minimum amount was set at some $700, but followers were pressured to give much more. Larger donations were rewarded with gifts, such as a personal photo session with the guru or private lessons from his leading disciples. Believers who donated over $2,000 received the best prize of all: two gallons of Shoko Asahara's dirty bathwater.

Asahara slipped easily into the role of guru. He now lectured in a mesmerizing monotone. As he spoke, his body remained nearly motionless in the cross-legged posture of a yogi; only the lips moved as he imparted wisdom to his followers. His immobile, near-blind eyes added an other-worldly quality to a face framed by a thick beard and long hair. His believers now doted on him, waiting on Asahara's every whim, treating their new-found teacher as a true holy man.

Asahara's epic journey from country bumpkin to modern messiah was almost complete. He was "a very brilliant person," noted a religious scholar at the time. "If he succeeds as a religious leader, he will become a great figure. On the other hand, if he becomes a crook, he will become a great crook." Shoko Asahara would be both.

3

BAD KARMA

When the end of the world arrives, there can be few more spectacular backdrops than Mount Fuji. The near-symmetrical flanks of this dormant volcano rise over 12,000 feet into the clouds. Japan's highest mountain is also its most revered: Mount Fuji is the nation's single most potent and unifying image.

In 1988, in the shadow of this great mountain, a shabby compound was built by an obscure religious cult. Beneath the mammoth slopes of Mount Fuji, Aum Supreme Truth opened its first community in the township of Fujinomiya. Windowless warehouses stood beside ramshackle wood shacks and prefab trailers. Ten-foot gates were thrown up, shielding the compound from curious neighbors. Those who stood near heard only the noise of constant construction, punctuated by the notes of Indian ragas and the preaching of a Japanese holy man.

Inside, Shoko Asahara was laying the cornerstone of an empire. Devotees flocked to the Mount Fuji center, where the cult charged over $2,000 for week-long meditation seminars. Expenses were negligible: participants slept on the floor and were served only one meal of boiled vegetables each day. Asahara's childhood talent for mathematics was paying enormous dividends. By the end of Aum Supreme Truth's first full year in business, the guru was seeking advice on stock investments from a Tokyo consulting firm.

The inauguration of the Mount Fuji complex marked a new rejection of the outside world. "When you are converted to our religion and live the life of Truth, you may cut your ties with your parents or children if they prevent you from doing so," Asahara preached. He had little time for those who clung to past lives. During one sermon, a believer asked the guru about the fate of his recently deceased wife, who had belonged to a different religion. "Your wife went to the hell of starvation," Asahara replied. There was little talk now of Aum helping the unenlightened masses avoid the coming nuclear holocaust. "Rather than helping human society, which has become like hell, I have started to think that my role is to help the new believers of high spirituality survive," he said.

Among these new believers were the "monks" and "nuns" who lived at the Mount Fuji headquarters. Those wishing to join Aum's priesthood had to declare everything they owned: cash savings, securities, real estate, jewelry, clothing, even telephone cards and postage stamps. They also had to disclose their bank-account number and PIN code. Then they swore an oath: "I entrust my spiritual and physical self and all assets to Aum Supreme Truth, and will cut off all involvement in this world." Once inside Aum, every yen they spent required authorization from the cult treasury. These donations proved a windfall to the group. As a handful of the wealthy joined, Aum's assets ballooned.

To hold their membership, Asahara used a battery of mind-control techniques familiar to cults worldwide. Devotees ate spartan diets and slept as little as three hours a day. This left them wide open to absorb Aum's teachings, which came in an unceasing barrage. The cutting of ties to family and friends also ensured that the cult slowly became the only life its disciples knew.

Minors – meaning, in Japan, anyone under twenty years old – could not join the priesthood without parental consent. Parents were asked to sign a document stating, "We waive any claims against the sect and Shoko Asahara in the event of anything happening to our child." But many kids joined without their parents' permission, a fact the cult made some effort to hide. During Aum's later battle with Tokyo City Hall to gain official religious status, five underage female members were sent to Japan's northernmost island to keep them out of sight.

Many worried parents phoned Aum's Mount Fuji HQ to talk to their children. They would be given a string of polite excuses: "He's training now" or "We've never heard of that name." Indeed, Aum's monks discarded not only their possessions, but also their identity. They were given "holy names" such as Manjushury or Ajitanatado-dorug, derived (often ungrammatically) from Sanskrit. Parents who turned up outside the Mount Fuji HQ were denied entry. Letters to children went unanswered. By 1990, an estimated 15 percent of Aum's monks and nuns were under the age of twenty.

Parents of Aum children could take some solace in the cult's avowed policy of nonviolence. "Here's a man who says, 'I will kill whatever is harmful to me!' and commits a lot of killing or is cruel to others," lectured Asahara in Tokyo. "How is his state of mind going to be? It's going to be brutal. Therefore, you should not kill; you should love all living beings." On another occasion he declared, "Non-violence means loving each and every living creature."

Inside the growing communes, though, Asahara or his disciples would beat followers for the smallest act of disobedience. This was termed "karma disposal," the dumping of spiritual baggage that holds one back in this life or the next. "I often pick on my disciples," Asahara freely admitted. "It's not because I am a sadist. It is because I have to rid them of negative karma." Asahara's theory of karma was simple: pleasure bad, pain good. Eating good food or daily bathing created bad karma and delayed enlightenment. So did "betraying the guru." Good karma was gained by enduring cold, hunger, and other discomforts, or by buying Asahara's books. Donating money to the cult was also good karma. Donating to schools or welfare groups was not.

Those considered "serious offenders" were, upon the guru's order, locked inside a tiny room. The room contained a television, a video of Asahara, and a portable toilet. The video was played for twenty-four hours a day, and the volume had just one setting: deafening. One ex-believer spent five days in this fashion.

> I barely slept, and when I did Asahara's voice went on in my dreams. I could only take a blanket and a bottle of water inside. I wasn't allowed a watch. Once a believer took tissue paper inside and filled his ears with it. After that they checked for that sort of thing thoroughly. Food was given once a day at 10 p.m. I couldn't bathe, wash my face, or brush my teeth. They emptied the toilet every two days but it smelled awful.

Children were not spared either. A ten-year-old boy, who had presumably joined the cult with his parents, was caught playing in a closet at the Mount Fuji HQ. He too was locked in a cell. "It was pitch dark inside and very humid," the boy said. "There were mushrooms growing from the *tatami* mats. When I pushed the mats, water leaked out. A meal was served once a day, but I was too hot to eat. Nobody helped me, even when I cried out."

Asahara fired off regular memos to all Aum branches dictating penalties for various transgressions. One memo ordered a week-long fast in a tiny cell for anyone who napped or chatted during training or had an accident in an Aum vehicle. Monks and nuns received the same punishment for leaving the Mount Fuji premises without permission. The school-yard bully had re-emerged in Asahara with a vengeance.

Aum Supreme Truth was earning a fortune for Shoko Asahara. But that fortune was taxed. So in the spring of 1989 Aum filed an application with Tokyo City Hall requesting religious status – and with it sizable tax breaks – under Japan's Religious Corporation Law.

Any group seeking religious status in Japan must meet three simple requirements. It must have its own religious facilities and a three-year history. It must also allow followers freely to join and leave the group. It was standard practice to reject applications from "antisocial" groups, and Aum had already been the target of complaints from parents who charged the cult had taken their children away. Facing a dilemma, officials at Tokyo City Hall fell back on a time-honored Japanese tactic: they stuck their heads in the sand and hoped the problem would go away.

It didn't. Asahara's devotees hounded officials, sent protest letters, and demonstrated in white robes outside City Hall. The cult filed a lawsuit against Tokyo's governor for unduly delaying an administrative decision. Eventually, in August 1989, City Hall caved in and registered the cult. Aum Supreme Truth was a religion at last – and that was official.

Aum's bullying had won the day. Flush with his latest victory, Asahara grew confident that his aggressive tactics were the key to success. His next target was a meddlesome editor and his muckraking weekly. Like all bullies, Asahara was extremely sensitive to criticism, as Taro Maki soon discovered. Maki, editor in chief of *Sunday Mainichi*, began running a series of critical articles on Aum's Blood Initiations and Asahara's criminal past. Maki's reporters also exposed the exorbitant donation system and interviewed parents who had lost underage children to the cult.

Asahara and a band of followers visited Maki's Tokyo office to ask him to stop the coverage. Maki refused. The following Sunday, every utility pole in the editor's neighborhood was posted with flyers reading, "Stop making up stories!" His family received late-night calls from people shouting, "You'll go to hell!" An Aum book called *The Insanity of the Sunday Mainichi: Taro Maki's Ambitions* hit Tokyo's bookstores. Security personnel arrived at the *Mainichi* office one morning to find that over a hundred more flyers had been secretly posted throughout the building. When Maki later suffered a severe stroke, Asahara called it "heaven's vengeance."

Journalists like Taro Maki could run all the exposés they wanted. No one in the Japanese police cared to investigate sensational press reports and be accused of religious persecution. After the ugly history of prewar oppression, authorities were prepared to give a wide berth to organized religion – and that now included Aum Supreme Truth. Asahara, meanwhile, responded directly to media allegations that Aum was practicing mind control. "Modern society is so polluted that people who are living in it already have had the first brainwashing," he told followers. In a document sent to cult members, he made his own position quite clear: "Aum's system of brainwashing is the best," he wrote. "Brainwash one new member after another."

Shielded behind official religious status, Aum Supreme Truth seemed unstoppable. The cult ran a series of magazine ads urging people to forsake their families for the cult, and welcomed more and more members into the faith. "Aum is the fastest-growing religious group in Japanese history," Asahara announced, and he may have been right. In a matter of years, he had built a religious empire that now boasted some $3 million in assets. Membership surged past the 4,000 mark as the cult began buying up chunks of land across Japan.

Shoko Asahara had every reason to be confident. In a television appearance, he told the interviewer that he did not consider himself "at the same level as Buddha." But he did claim to be a living god, a deity as holy as Lord Shiva himself. "I intend to become a spiritual dictator," he declared. "A dictator of the world."

4

PLANET TRANTOR

They came from college campuses, from dead-end jobs and fast-track careers. Thousands now flocked to Asahara's embrace, seeking Aum's promise of enlightenment, community and, most of all, supernatural power.

They were nearly all young, wide-eyed kids in their early and mid-twenties. Some dropped out of Japan's finest schools to join the cult, leaving behind families, friends, and bright futures. Others left the nation's top companies in steel, computers, insurance, and other fields.

Asahara had found the weak point in Japan's new generation and then pressed with every resource he had. In magazines, videos, and books, he took his message to the youth of his country, appealing to the lost and alienated. Aum members wrote stories and placed ads claiming they had gained powers of telepathy and levitation, offering to teach others these secret skills.

Their favored publications were part of a wave of popular culture that dealt in the far out and the fantastic. Young people immersed themselves in a world of fantasy – movies, cartoons, computer games, comics – in violent tales of half-human, half-computer cyborgs and explosive, galactic battles fought between superbeings. A whole generation grew up watching brilliantly animated cartoons like *Space Battleship Yamato* and *Naushika in the Valley of the Wind*. Many graduated to the *gekiga* – ultraviolent, book-length comics drawn with realistic pictures and dramatic narratives, filled with graphic depictions of rape, murder, and a decadent, retrograde future. All this created fertile ground for Asahara and his apocalyptic vision.

Of those seeking out Aum, many were students of the sciences or technical fields like engineering. More than a few were *otaku*, Japan's version of computer nerds – techno-freaks who spent their free time logged onto electronic networks and amassing data of every type.

They were invariably described as quiet kids, with little apparent interest in the outside world. They spent what free time they had absorbed in their comics and their computers.

If Japan's youth retreated into these far-out worlds, one could understand why. For many, there was nowhere else to go. They were pushed there by a culture that crushes individualism. And nowhere was this more true than in the schools.

Studies dominate the life of young Japanese. Students spend 240 days at school each year – a third longer than their American counterparts. Late afternoons are spent at cram schools, working to pass the examinations that begin in kindergarten. Nights are spent doing homework. The system has helped breed a generation of nerds, of technically literate, highly knowledgable young people who lack basic social skills and have little understanding of the world outside.

Young, talented people are ground through this educational mill, through a system that pounds originality out of its pupils. The emphasis is on fitting in, on following rules, and on rote memorization. Students are not encouraged to analyze or challenge; questions are not asked in Japanese classrooms. They are there only to swallow facts and spit out answers on exam after exam, like human computers uploaded with gigabytes of data. It is possible to go through high school in Japan without a single class on ethics, philosophy, or religion.

"Always there are rules here," said one educator. "You can go through your life easily just by following the rules. If someone comes along with a completely different world view, it might be easy to influence young people. The outlets for individualism are few."

If the schools don't drive you into your own mind, the environment does. In a land where urbanization knows few bounds, where homes and offices are torn down in endless succession, the only land most Japanese know is the growing sprawl of the megalopolis. Mile after mile the cities of Japan go on, a relentless, urban sea of power lines, roads, and uninspired buildings of steel and concrete. There are crowds seemingly everywhere, on the trains, the streets, the highways. Into the same area as California are crammed more than four times as many people.

One can understand why, then, the Japanese say they prefer to cultivate inner space – the inside of their homes, the inside of their minds. And Aum offered the ultimate inner space, one that would take its followers on a direct line to outer space. "Aum members lived in a purely imaginary world," observed Shoko Egawa, a journalist who followed the cult for years. "One that combined primeval fear with a computer-controlled cartoon version of reality." Another Aum-watcher said, "It was virtual reality made real."

So they came. Not just the curious and alienated, but the very bright and very talented. By 1989, remarkably, Asahara had gathered around him some of the finest young minds in all Japan – chemists, biologists, doctors, computer programmers. The hi-tech children of postindustrial Japan were fascinated by Aum's dramatic claims to supernatural power, its warnings of an apocalyptic future, its esoteric spiritualism.

There was Seiichi Endo, twenty-eight, who left Kyoto University, where he did experiments in genetic engineering at the medical school's Viral Research Center. Another, Masami Tsuchiya, twenty-four, a first-rate graduate student at Tsukuba University, abandoned cutting-edge work in organic chemistry to join the cult. Fumihiro Joyu, twenty-six, arrived with an advanced degree in telecommunications from Waseda University, where he studied artificial intelligence. Joyu had gone to work at the National Space Development Agency of Japan, but resigned after only two weeks. "The job," he told stunned officials, "is incompatible with my interests in yoga."

And then there was Hideo Murai, the astrophysicist. Brilliant, intense, and soft-spoken, Murai would become the chief scientist of Aum and engineer of the apocalypse.

At first glance, Murai looked more a provincial schoolteacher than a mad scientist. He had elfin features etched on a perfectly round face, with a fragile build that suggested he could do harm to no one. But a closer look revealed eyes that turned from benign to beady in a blink. His hair was short but disheveled, and he often looked lost in some unreachable thought.

Murai was a native of Osaka, Japan's second-largest city. A quiet kid who enjoyed bicycling and science, he won acceptance to prestigious Osaka University, where he earned an advanced degree in astrophysics from its highly competitive Graduate School of Science. There, he studied the X-ray emissions of celestial bodies and proved a whiz at computer programming. On graduation, he joined Kobe Steel, a $10-billion-a-year conglomerate with interests in metals, machinery, electronics, and biotech. Murai worked in the firm's R & D section, running experiments to make steel super-malleable, like hot caramel. Interesting work for the young physicist, but not fulfilling.

After two years of Kobe Steel, Murai's behavior began to

change. Browsing through a bookstore, he had picked up an Aum publication on yoga and ESP, and he was hooked. He spoke to colleagues at work about how levitation and telepathy might be possible, and lost interest in his career. For his wedding he took his wife not to Hawaii, as do many Japanese, but to Nepal. On his return, Murai announced he was quitting the company to devote himself fully to Aum and the spiritual life.

Murai's parents tried desperately to talk him out of it. But their son simply handed them a copy of *Jonathan Livingston Seagull*, the one-time best seller about a seagull's struggle to learn to fly. The novel, he told them, expressed his true feelings. ("I hate that book," his mother later said.)

Murai thrived inside Aum. He devoured Asahara's teachings and became a prize disciple. So ascetic was Murai's life that he moved permanently into a tiny cell used for meditation. "This room is very small and dark for those who want to escape," he once said. "But if one wants to meditate, it is as big as the universe."

At thirty, Murai was the senior scientist at the cult, and Asahara looked upon him with growing favor. Murai and the others had suggestions on how to push forward Asahara's ideas, using the tools and techniques of modern science. There were ways to analyze the unique qualities of their guru's blood and brain waves, Murai explained. And there were technologies the cult could use to protect itself from the coming dark age.

Murai and the other scientists lent chilling detail to Asahara's vision of an apocalyptic future. The guru was fascinated as his young brains trust talked of fantastic weapons that would hasten the world's end: of lasers and particle beams, chemical and biological agents, new generations of nuclear bombs. The land would be laid waste as never before, they assured their leader.

Hideo Murai had at last found a place in the world. What he heard from his master's voice fit perfectly with his own thoughts of the universe. Indeed, all this had been predicted before, he told the others. Far more important than *Jonathan Livingston Seagull* was another work by an American writer. And this man's books would serve as the master plan for the scientists of Aum.

"The Empire will vanish and all its good with it. Its accumulated knowledge will decay and the order it has imposed will vanish."

It could be Shoko Asahara talking. But it is Hari Seldon, a science-fiction figure 10,000 years in the future. Seldon is the key character in the *Foundation* series – Isaac Asimov's classic sci-fi epic – and he would give Murai and Aum their high-tech blueprint for the millennium and beyond.

Seldon is a brilliant mathematician who discovers "psychohistory," the science of true prediction, and warns that the galactic empire will fall into ruin for a thousand generations. "Interstellar wars will be endless," Seldon tells a skeptical but threatened government. "Interstellar trade will decay; population will decline; worlds will lose touch with the main body of the Galaxy."

The empire fails to heed his warnings, prompting Seldon to take matters into his own hands. Asimov's core trilogy, written in the 1940s, depicts his hero's efforts at saving humanity by forming a secret society that can rebuild civilization in a single millennium, instead of the 30,000 years they now face. Asimov's full story spans six books and is known to fans of science fiction and fantasy around the world.

At the center of Asimov's universe lies Trantor, the ruling planet of an empire that spans 25 million worlds across the galaxy. Trantor is a planet of 40 billion souls that, writes Asimov, holds "the densest and richest clot of humanity the race had ever seen." The surface of the planet comprises a single vast megalopolis, extending a mile deep into the ground in a mind-boggling labyrinth of humanity. Nature has long since disappeared, replaced by the sight of gray metal protruding skyward and then deep underground. All that remains of the natural world is the emperor's palace, an island of trees and flowers amid the sea of a planetary city.

It is not hard to see the parallels between Trantor and modern Japan, right down to the leafy grounds of the Emperor's palace that stand incongruously in central Tokyo. For years, in fact, Japanese engineers have worked at developing what they call "super-depth construction," with plans to build the world's first underground city by the year 2020.

The coincidences could not have escaped Hideo Murai as he read a Japanese translation of *Foundation*. But the similarities did not end there. In the *Foundation* story, Hari Seldon gathers the best minds of his time – scientists, historians, technologists – and, like monks in the Middle Ages, they set about preserving the knowledge of the universe. Seldon, however, has in mind no less than controlling the future.

Hari Seldon dies, but true to his predictions the empire falls into chaos. To survive, Seldon's secret society (the Foundation) transforms itself into – what else? – a religion. His followers create a hierarchy of scientist-priests whom the rest of the galaxy, having lost the command of science and technology, look upon as wizards and holy ones. "The religion we have is our all-important instrument," explained one follower. "It is the most potent device known with which to control men and worlds."

The similarities to Aum and its guru's quest were remarkable. Aum's central mission seemed a mirror image of the Foundation's struggle to save humanity. "If Aum tries hard, we can reduce the victims of Armageddon to a fourth of the world's population," Asahara had preached. "However, at present, my rescue plan is totally delayed. The rate of survivors is getting smaller and smaller."

In an interview, Murai would state matter-of-factly that Aum was using the *Foundation* series as the blueprint for the cult's long-term plans. He gave the impression of a "graduate student who had read too many science-fiction novels," remembered one reporter. But it was real enough to the cult. Shoko Asahara, the blind and bearded guru from Japan, had become Hari Seldon; and Aum Supreme Truth was the Foundation.

Surprise registered on the face of the young woman. She had been summoned by Asahara himself to assist in a special project. In her early twenties, like so many of Aum's membership, she was a loyal follower of the Master, and went immediately to the building in Tokyo where Asahara waited.

Inside she found Asahara surrounded by advisers. Murai was holding an elaborate device covered with electrodes and wires. "Aum's finest minds have created an instrument that will bring you closer to enlightenment," Murai explained. "It will send electronic impulses to your brain and synchronize your brain waves with those of the Master. By doing so, your mind will come to know the blissful, meditative state that the Master himself feels every second."

The device was now finished, Murai said, but they needed someone to test it on. While they could duplicate the frequency of Asahara's brain waves, Aum's scientists were unsure of how much voltage to use. Neurobiology was not yet part of Aum's expertise, so they needed a human guinea pig.

Murai carefully placed the cap on the woman's head. Tangled threads of brightly colored wire led to a series of electrodes embedded in cloth. Murai pulled the contraption tightly until the straps covered much of her scalp.

Murai went to a control panel and began sending shocks to the woman's brain. Steadily, he increased the voltage. Every few seconds the woman felt jolts across her head, as if needles were poking through her skull. As the voltage went up, she felt a burning sensation.

Murai turned to Asahara. "If I continue increasing, she will die," he said.

Asahara laughed, and turned to the woman. "Do you want to die?" he asked.

The woman gave an emphatic no, and the experiment stopped. But they had found what they wanted. Murai and the others settled on six volts for adults, three volts for children. The PSI – Perfect Salvation Initiation – had been invented. The electrode-laden shock caps would become a standard feature of Aum followers, and a phenomenal money-maker for the cult.

The origins of the PSI went back months earlier. Aum had somehow procured an electro-encephalograph, an EEG. Widely used in medicine and brain research, the device measures the electrical activity of the brain. Electrodes are taped to the head and, for a half-hour or so, they pick up changes in the charge of the brain's millions of nerve cells. Like a lie-detector machine, it has half a dozen needles which graph out the changes on a rolling sheet.

Murai had hooked up the EEG to a computer and then recorded Asahara's brain waves. The cult then proclaimed to the world that their guru's blissful brain, incredibly, registered almost nothing on the EEG. Asahara's mind operated at a frequency of below .05 hertz. He was, in other words, a flatliner – a dead man.

"Doctors say that it is an inconceivable phenomenon that I am alive and talking to you today," Asahara explained in a lecture. "They say I should be dead." But these people simply mistake an enlightened state for that of a vegetable, he said. "In other words, I am leading a regular life in a state deeper than what is normally considered deep sleep." It is, he went on, "a state in which there is no thought at all, a state in which deliberation and examination are completely stopped."

One Aum text tried to explain it simply to his followers: "Master Asahara's brain is usually brain dead."

Not only was this okay, it was desirable. All this would lead to enlightenment as well as powers of telepathy. Asahara wrote: "If the mind becomes clear, our brain waves become flat, we will be able to know at will what other people are thinking when we synchronize our mind with the mind of that particular person." Those in Aum who had achieved advanced stages of enlightenment, he declared, "all have the ability to read each other's minds."

How to achieve all this? Join Aum. Meditate and follow the Revered Master's teachings. And buy or rent a PSI, synchronizing your brain waves with those of the Master.

If the science was dubious, the marketing was brilliant. While PSIs were given free to full-time monks, they were offered to others at a monthly rate of about $7,000, or sold outright for ten times that amount. The electric caps would bring millions of dollars into the cult.

Other devices soon followed. Murai and the others produced the Astral Teleporter. This, wrote Asahara, "faithfully reproduces the vibration of my mantra through electric signals" and will "clean one's astral dimension." At Aum training centers, technicians installed the "teleporter" by wiring the cult's meditation mats, pulsing Asahara's off-key chants through the bodies of his followers. Cult scientists even wired electrodes to ordinary tap water, hooked it up to a microphone and had Asahara chant mantras. The resulting "holy water" was then sold to a gullible public.

Work was underway to found a cult research center – what Asahara was calling his Cosmic Science Institute. With the growing number of young physicians joining Aum, plans were also launched to set up a clinic, the Astral Hospital, "a movement to incorporate medicine from a higher dimension into modern health care."

Meanwhile, the cult's work at the fringes of science continued. Aum's scientists began research into locating the chakras, the bodily points of mystical energy long described by yoga and other disciplines. Experiments were made in applying magnetic fields to the chakras, in the hopes of awakening the powerful energy within.

Aum science had even discovered that the Master's DNA possessed magical properties, and offered it to their members – for a price. This was a new spin on Asahara's Blood Initiation. Those who now drank DNA drawn from the Master's blood, assured the cult, would gain supernatural powers and rise yet another rung on the ladder to enlightenment. Aum claimed that no less an authority than the Medical School of Kyoto University had studied the guru's blood and found its qualities extraordinary. The price for this magical potion: $7,000.

Old wine in new bottles, goes the Chinese expression. After all the pseudo-science was stripped away, it was the same old Asahara with the same old snake oil, but with a hi-tech twist. Electrode caps, astral teleporters, magic DNA – one could give Aum credit for enterprise, at least. Unfortunately, the cult's darker side would not be limited to scamming naive youths out of their hard-earned money.

While his scientists sent shock waves into the brains of disciples, Shoko Asahara felt another force rush through his system: a surge of power. As Aum increased in numbers and sophistication, Asahara now commanded his own world, full of eager followers, millions of dollars, and his own band of scientists. But not all was well in the land of Aum.

Beneath the veneer of Buddhist dogma and spiritual thought, a quiet rage simmered inside the guru's head. For years, as he built an empire, Asahara had struggled to hold back his childhood feelings of rejection and revenge. But the bully in him never remained far from the surface. He demanded absolute devotion from his followers, and was quick to punish those who fell short. Now those emotions, heightened by followers who believed he could do no wrong, would soon erupt into plain view. With a few words from his mouth, Shoko Asahara was about to open Aum's killing fields.

5

DEATH AND REBIRTH

Shuji Taguchi was like so many of those joining Aum. Only twenty-one, the enthusiastic youth from southern Japan had felt his life to be adrift until, one day, he came across the astounding claims of Aum Supreme Truth. Enchanted and seduced, he quit his job at an electronics factory, donated his savings, and moved to Mount Fuji.

That was in the spring of 1988. After months of life in Aum, though, Shuji began to have doubts. The promises of supernatural power never seemed to materialize. People within the cult appeared no more enlightened than those outside; indeed, a few seemed a good deal meaner. But what put Shuji over the edge was the death of another follower.

This disciple had been a nervous sort, but Shuji found him likable. The twenty-five-year-old had joined Aum about the same time and, like Shuji, he had grown weary of the cult's monastic and arbitrary rules. One day he told his teachers he was ready for a change; life in Aum was probably not for him.

The guru did not take well to anyone leaving the cult. Aum was meant to be a lifetime commitment, a profound dedication to one's teacher and the holy way. Those wishing to leave were not merely let go; their souls were deemed confused and in need of guidance. The guru himself had examined this particular disciple and found him mentally unstable. For this, Asahara had prescribed a sure-fire cure: repeated dunkings in near-freezing water, to "remove heat from the man's head." Apparently such warmth interfered with the man's mental acuity; the guru believed a bout of hypothermia was just the remedy. The man went into shock and died within the hour.

Shuji was horrified. He couldn't understand how Asahara could have been so heartless. Worse yet, the cult had covered up the man's death, cremating the body so as to leave no trace. Shuji cursed the guru and complained to others in the cult. He began to feel that Aum itself was evil, and even fantasized about killing Asahara. Mostly, though, he tried to summon the courage to leave and begin his life anew.

Criticizing the cult was not a wise move around Aum's close-knit compounds. Word soon got back to cult leaders about Shuji's doubts and dissatisfaction. In February 1989, he was ordered to undergo special rituals to "clear his mind." But these rites seemed too similar to what his late acquaintance had gone through. Shuji declined. At that point, he was confronted by a group of disciples, bound by rope, and imprisoned in a tiny meditation cell. Hour after hour, he was grilled by his former teachers. Scared and exhausted, he finally confessed his worries about the cult – his doubts about Aum teachings, the death of his friend, even his fantasy about killing the guru.

Asahara was enraged. Near midnight he called Murai and six other disciples to an emergency meeting at the cult's head office. There, his followers found him in a white robe, sitting in the room's only chair. The others sat down around him in a circle.

The guru described the serious problem at hand. If Shuji were set free, he might expose the follower's death the previous year and attract the attention of police. He would be causing trouble just as Aum was about to fulfill its destiny. Membership was doubling, money was pouring in, and there were plans to expand further overseas.

"We should do something about him," the guru said carefully. He then spoke of *poa* – the taking of one's soul to a higher plane. Everyone in the room understood the message.

"Go see Taguchi again," Asahara then ordered. "Ask him if he still intends to leave the cult. If he insists, then you know what you must do."

Immediately, Murai and four of the men walked to the cell holding Shuji. As one stood guard, the others entered and began to question him again. Did he intend to quit Aum? they asked.

Shuji was now more sure than ever. "I want to quit the cult," he told them.

Someone placed a blindfold across Shuji's head while another distracted him, saying they would now bring him before the guru. Then two others curled a rope around his neck and yanked it tight. Shuji put up a fierce struggle, pulling his arms free and thrashing about. A third follower jumped in, helping to restrain his body while the strangling went on. Finally, a fourth disciple slipped behind Shuji and sharply wrenched his neck. There was a loud snapping sound, and their victim crumpled to the ground, face down.

Asahara's killers wrapped the body in a vinyl sheet and drove him to a courtyard used for offerings of fire and incense. Shuji's corpse was stuffed in a metal drum, dowsed with gasoline, and set on fire. Murder was new to Aum, however, and the body continued to burn through the night. A nervous Asahara visited the site repeatedly. "Completely reduce the bones to ashes," he told them, "so that the remains can be scattered."

After ten hours the deed was done. Shuji's remains were unceremoniously dumped beneath a nearby bush.

Some days later, Shuji's parents called the Mount Fuji center, asking for their son, as they often did. They received the same reply as always. "We're sorry," a cultist said. "Just now he is deeply involved in training and cannot be disturbed."

The Taguchi family could not believe their son would simply cut off all contact. Then, later that year, they received an anonymous postcard. "Aum Supreme Truth is a very dangerous organization," it read. "Many of the members are more dangerous than gangsters." Worried sick over Shuji's fate, the family contacted local police and asked for help in tracking him down. The cops found nothing.

Six months had passed since the murder of Shuji Taguchi. The killing was a well-kept secret within the cult, known only by Asahara and his top aides. Meanwhile, Aum had continued to grow. Cult members preached doom, opened new training centers, and gathered more recruits.

But killing young Shuji had not solved Aum's problems; it had only made them worse. A crime far graver than consumer fraud or accidental death now needed covering up. The murder added an extra layer of paranoia to a cult leadership that already believed the world was ending. At the same time, Asahara began to see that Aum's greatest threats came not from inside the cult, but from beyond the walls of his Mount Fuji fortress. Parents were demanding their children back, neighbors complained about noise, and local police eyed cult members with suspicion.

Particularly nettlesome had become a Yokohama lawyer who represented a group of parents insisting that the cult return their kids. Tsutsumi Sakamoto was a gutsy thirty-three-year-old human-rights attorney who had launched a campaign against Aum. First, he had taken on the case of a family demanding their underage daughter back. Then a flood of parents had turned up at his door, many in tears, saying they had lost their children to the doomsday cult. By October 1989, no less than twenty-three families were asking the young attorney for help; their kids had joined Aum and then simply vanished from their lives. Although most of the youths were minors, the police and prosecutors seemed wholly uninterested. It was, the cops suggested, a matter between parent and child.

Sakamoto was very interested, however. The case was, in fact, just the kind of challenge he enjoyed. His law firm had fought against police brutality, filed suits for laid-off workers, and demanded rights for the disabled. He and his colleagues had taken on the Moonies, right-wing nuts, and now Aum – all targets most Japanese would never dream of confronting.

To deal with the cult, Sakamoto formed the Society of Aum Supreme Truth Victims and began negotiating on the parents' behalf. Those fleeing the cult also sought Sakamoto out. One former member had paid $7,000 for the Blood Initiation; to the man's dismay, he had received no magical power from the potion. The client now wanted his money back, and Sakamoto was preparing to sue.

Sakamoto did not hate Aum. He simply wanted the group to grow up and act like a respectable religious organization. Aum's heavy-handed treatment of minors, along with its absurd claims to magic powers and potions, needed to stop.

The idealistic, hard-working attorney had always fought for the underdog, and his friends and family loved him for it. He had the thick glasses and messy hair of a favorite professor, with an open face and a ready smile. He was a graduate of Tokyo University's law school, the cream of the elite in status-conscious Japan, yet he was at ease among working people and the disadvantaged. Helping to reunite broken families and saving a few lost souls was all in a day's work.

Becoming a public-spirited attorney had been Sakamoto's dream since junior high school. Japan's law schools admit few students, however, and fewer still pass the bar. Sakamoto almost didn't make it, failing his bar exam several times and telling friends that perhaps he wasn't, after all, cut out for the law. But in late 1984 he finally passed and soon was working at a Yokohama law firm known for its human-rights cases.

Sakamoto's wife also worked part-time at the law firm. The two had met at university, where she was studying sociology and campaigning for the rights of the disabled. The twenty-nine-year old

Satoko was known for having a big heart and, like her husband, an easy way with people.

The center of the Sakamotos' life was their much-anticipated first child, Tatsuhiko. A bright, happy kid, the boy was doted on by his parents and grandmother. He was now fourteen-months-old and seemed all that Satoko could talk about. She told friends how determined he was to walk, and that he seemed even to watch the TV news with interest. As the autumn of 1989 came to a close, the family had much to be grateful for.

Sakamoto knew it would not be an easy meeting. After he had criticized Aum on a radio show, cult members spread leaflets near his home denouncing him for religious persecution. The group had stonewalled his efforts at dialogue, insisting he stop his meddling immediately.

Still, Sakamoto persisted in the hope of reaching an agreement with Aum. He had invited its chief attorney to his office, to see whether there was a way to settle the various complaints against the cult. Surely, he thought, Aum's counsel would listen to reason.

It was a Tuesday evening, on October 31, 1989. The tension began from the moment Aum's delegation walked through the door. Instead of coming alone, as agreed, the cult attorney brought along two other senior members of the group. Sakamoto insisted the others wait in the front office while the attorneys conferred.

Aum's top lawyer was Yoshinobu Aoyama, twenty-nine, the son of a leading businessman. He had longish hair, a robotlike delivery, and darting, nervous eyes that made it easy to underestimate him. Aoyama boasted a quick legal mind. He was a graduate of Kyoto University and, unlike Sakamoto, he had been first in his class to pass the Japanese bar.

Sakamoto brought up the Blood Initiation first. Aoyama already knew he had checked the cult's claim of Asahara's DNA being studied by a leading medical school. Of course they hadn't researched Asahara's blood, the school said. Now, in their meeting, Sakamoto insisted on proof that the blood was special. If not, those paying for the Blood Initiation should be compensated.

Aoyama said there had been misunderstanding. The study in question had actually been done by a graduate of the medical school, at an Aum facility. But Aoyama declined to provide the study. Sakamoto warned of what seemed a pattern of fraud by the cult.

Sakamoto then spoke of the families he represented. Legally, he said, their children inside the cult were his clients, and he stressed the importance of meeting with them. Aoyama flatly refused, and from there the tone deteriorated quickly. Sakamoto asserted that Aum should return its minors to the custody of their parents. They can enter the priesthood when they reach twenty, he said. If Aum does not comply, the families are prepared to go forward with lawsuits.

Aoyama grew angry and the men began to argue. Aoyama bitterly criticized the association of parents Sakamoto had helped form, calling it an attack on religious freedom. He waved legal papers across the table, saying they were powers of attorney given Aum by the children. "If you take us to court," Aoyama warned, "Aum followers will sue their own parents."

By now their voices were loud. A frustrated Sakamoto suggested an end to the meeting.

As Aoyama joined his fellow Aum members, one turned to Sakamoto. "What about freedom of religion?" he barked at him. Sakamoto ushered them out of the door. "Freedom that makes other people unhappy should not be allowed," he shot back.

The entire office heard the men arguing. After they left, Sakamoto told his co-workers Aoyama had been "unreasonable" and the meeting "meaningless." Frustrated, he left with two colleagues and promptly got drunk.

The meeting had left Sakamoto with a sense of unease. Soon after, he called representatives of the parents' group and warned them to be on guard. There was no telling what Aum might do. He told an acquaintance he might have an extra lock installed on his front door. In the meantime, he promised his wife he would try to relax. There was a holiday weekend coming, and then in a few days a long-awaited family vacation. By then, he hoped, Aum's leaders would come to their senses.

Two days had passed since the meeting in Sakamoto's office. The guru summoned a handful of key disciples to a meeting. Sitting in a circle, for thirty minutes they discussed how to stop the attorney.

In menacing tones, Asahara blamed Sakamoto for fostering "a hysterical atmosphere to wreck Aum." This man could destroy everything we have built, he warned. The Reverend Master then made his own wishes unmistakably clear: "We must send counselor Sakamoto's soul away by any means."

As his disciples listened wide-eyed, Asahara then grew much more specific. Apparently the guru had given the matter careful thought. "Get Sakamoto into a car and inject him," he instructed. "Nakagawa has a good drug that can kill a man in five minutes."

Nakagawa was a cult physician eager to do the guru's bidding. With the doctor's help, there seemed no reason to wait, the group decided. They would deal with Sakamoto the next day.

With that, Shoko Asahara raised his beefy hand into the air and snapped his fingers. The meeting was over.

The clock at the Sakamoto home showed 3 a.m. It was the end of an exhausting week for the family, and the Sakamotos had long since gone to bed. Next to Tsutsumi slept Satoko; exhausted, she had fallen asleep in her clothes. Next to her stirred their little son. They could not have known that, at that moment, six Aum members were creeping into their home.

The team had left the Mount Fuji complex earlier that day. Among them were some of Asahara's top aides: Murai, the chief scientist; Satoru Hashimoto, twenty-eight, the cult's martial-arts expert, with a black belt in karate; and Dr. Tomomasa Nakagawa, a twenty-nine-year-old physician. Nakagawa had joned the priesthood only two months ago. Now he was about to commit murder for Shoko Asahara. A year before he had graduated from a respected medical school and started work at a hospital. But Aum had given his life meaning and direction, and finally he took the ultimate step, renouncing the world and donating his assets to the cult.

Now, as he climbed the stairs that led to Sakamoto's darkened apartment, Nakagawa felt proud and elated that his master had chosen him for such a sensitive mission. He understood that his role was key, that he was to be the final instrument of death. Inside a small pouch Nakagawa carried seven syringes full of potassium chloride. Used in small doses during surgery, the chemical saves people's lives; used in large doses, it induces massive cardiac arrest. The other weapons present were more crude: ropes, hammers, a club.

The group had hoped to nab Sakamoto on his way home from work, but their plans hadn't worked out. Secluded within Aum, they had forgotten today was a national holiday; Sakamoto stayed home the entire day, nursing a cold. They had called Asahara and asked what to do. There was no other choice, the guru commanded: they would have to deal with the entire family.

Inside the small apartment, the cultists moved silently across the living room to where the Sakamotos slept. But as they crept into the bedroom, their movements woke the Sakamotos' son, who began to cry. One of the killers slapped a hand across the toddler's mouth and began to suffocate him, while Dr. Nakagawa shot a fatal dose into the child's small body. Two of the men then lunged at Sakamoto, one of them trying to thrust a syringe into his body. Sakamoto's wife by now had woken, only to be struck on the skull and strangled.

Sakamoto fought back wildly, making it impossible to inject the hypo. Two of the men then held him down while another smashed the hammer repeatedly into his head, until he struggled no more. His wife at first also battled fiercely, biting into Murai's hand and drawing blood. But soon she too lay still.

Again the syringes appeared. Dr. Nakagawa yanked down Sakamoto's pants and plunged the potassium chloride into the man's buttocks. Still the stubborn attorney refused to die. The doctor then moved aside while his comrades put their hands around Sakamoto's neck, squeezing until at last there was no more pulse.

Aum's team of killers then bundled the Sakamotos in blankets and futons, threw them in the back of their cars, and hustled back to Mount Fuji. There, they reported to a waiting Asahara that the deed was done. The guru offered his gratitude and sent them away with new instructions. Dispose of the family, he told them, where they will never be found.

The bodies were dumped in metal drums and placed in the back of two vehicles, one of them a four-wheel drive. For the next three days, the group drove across central Japan, looking for remote burial sites, stopping to buy food and tools for digging. The first to go was the son. They dumped the little boy's body in the wetlands outside a town in the Japan Alps. Next went the attorney, whom they buried on a forested mountainside a full prefecture away. Then the wife, tossed into a makeshift grave near an alpine stream in another prefecture. Before burying the adults, the group yanked their teeth out with pliers and smashed them to powder with a pick-axe, making it impossible to identify the bodies through dental records. The family's pajamas and bedding were then burned, and the drums and shovels tossed into the Sea of Japan.

On their return, Asahara assured his killers that they had done holy work. "The child ended up not being raised by Sakamoto, who tried to repeat bad deeds" from a previous life, and there was no need to feel guilt, the guru explained. The child would be "born again in a higher world."

Some days later, Asahara summoned the killers to his private room in the Aum headquarters. As the guru looked on, a top aide read aloud the Penal Code penalties for murder, which in Japan carries the death penalty. Sakamoto's name was never mentioned, but the point was clear: if any one person dared to betray the group, all would face death together.

6

SHOKO, SHOKO

Sakamoto's colleagues were alarmed when the attorney failed to show up for work the next week. The family had not been heard from since a phone call by his wife the previous Friday evening, thanking a friend for a box of apples. Sakamoto's parents came by the apartment and found a strange scene. There were teacups still on the table, dirty dishes in the sink, and the rice cooker left on. Despite the cold October night, the family's coats were still there. Hanging by the door was Sakamoto's jacket, with his diary, train pass, and keys. Both their wallets had been left behind, with nearly $1,000 in cash. All that was missing were three futons, some blankets, and the Sakamotos themselves.

There was no blood and no sign of a struggle. But one item caught the parents' attention. On the floor beside the closet where the futons were kept, Sakamoto's mother found a cream-colored badge. Inscribed upon it was the Sanskrit insignia of Aum Supreme Truth.

Dropped by Dr. Nakagawa during the struggle, the badge should have sent a clear message to police. But the local cops, strangely, were uninterested. Investigators seemed to do their best to look at every angle except Aum. They suggested the family might have fled for personal reasons. It was well known that people in Japan sometimes go *johatsu* or, literally, evaporate. Occasionally, too, there are family suicides. These things happen, police said.

But such events invariably happen to Japanese deeply in debt or shamed by some unforgivable act. And neither description fit the Sakamotos. The truth was that the cops were wary of going after a religious organization. Furthermore, Sakamoto's law firm was seen as a bunch of leftist troublemakers. They'd handled cases against the police, a fact that hadn't endeared them to local investigators. "They thought we'd organized the incident ourselves to discredit Aum," one of Sakamoto's colleagues told the press.

Others were more skeptical and, as word of the Sakamoto case reached the news media, Aum's name inevitably became linked to the disappearance. Pushed by the publicity and demands from Sakamoto's colleagues, police finally requested an interview with Asahara. By now, sixteen days had passed since the murder. Asahara's response: he was busy. The guru, said an Aum spokesman, was in a training session and could not be disturbed. Two days later, Asahara left for Germany with an entourage that included Murai and at least two other killers.

History was being made on the other side of the world. Just a week before Asahara's arrival, the German people had begun to tear down the Berlin Wall. The prospects for unification looked strong, as forty-five years of communist rule crumbled along with the hated wall.

Aum had established a small office in Bonn which was to serve as its European beachhead. From the German capital, Aum hoped to expand across the continent. Moreover, there was strong interest among the Germans in yoga and Eastern philosophy; other cults, like Scientology, had prospered there. Still, Aum's early recruiting had gone slowly among the Germans, and Asahara wanted to push things along. He held a series of training sessions in the city and somehow wangled meetings with German officials. Among them were sit-downs with Hinrich Enderlein, whom Aum described as chief scientist of the government's Science Ministry (actually he was a mid-level bureaucrat), and with Hans Büchler, then a Social Democrat member of parliament. Aum publications boasted of the status accorded their guru by German officials, who spoke to their holy guest about education, the future of communism, and German unification.

While Asahara pushed Aum's presence in Europe, back home the Japanese media continued their coverage of the Sakamotos. The guru's rapid departure from Japan only fueled speculation about Aum's involvement. But the police remained unconvinced, while liberal scholars rushed to defend the cult. Japan's crime rate was simply too low, and the history of persecution too recent, to believe a Buddhist sect would resort to kidnapping or even murder.

At least one newsweekly wasn't buying it, and sent a reporter to Europe to demand a response from the guru. *Sunday Mainichi* knew from its prior coverage of Aum how aggressive the cult could be, and figured murder was not beyond Asahara's capabilities. When the magazine's reporter landed in Bonn, he found Asahara at a training session. Immediately the journalist was surrounded by ten white-robed followers. As he was being pushed out the door, he yelled at the guru, "Isn't Aum responsible?"

"I have nothing to do with the incident," Asahara shouted back. "If I was going to kill someone, I would kill Mr. Maki," he said, referring to the reporter's editor. The magazine staff did not find the joke funny.

Soon after, Asahara called a press conference in Bonn, denying that the cult had played any role in the Sakamoto case. He admitted Aum was having trouble with the attorney, but that was hardly reason to abduct him and his family, he said. It all sounded incredible. Regarding the Aum badge found at the house, he added that there were more than 40,000 in existence; anyone could get them.

In fact, the badges had been tightly held even within the cult. Only 100 or so had initially been produced, leaving police an obvious trail to follow. But Yokohama's slow-footed cops didn't bite, allowing Aum plenty of time to cover its tracks. On learning of the loss, Asahara had ordered the badges to be mass-produced, distributed to the membership, and offered through the mail. Now, 5,000 miles away in Europe, the guru could calmly assure the press that the badge in question was one of many. Someone probably planted the piece, he said, in a bid to frame his peaceful group.

About the time Asahara spoke, his team of killers was sitting in a German kitchen not far away, watching a set of pots and pans heat to boiling. One by one, they placed their fingertips firmly on the scorching metal, burning away their fingerprints. Then the knives came out, and slowly they cut away the remaining skin.

Voters in Tokyo had never seen anything quite like it. On stage, attired in a shiny white suit with matching shoes, was the rotund, bearded leader of the new Supreme Truth Party. Flanking the man were campaign workers wearing large elephants masks. A soft New Age tune hung in the air, with people singing "Shoko, Shoko." Asahara was running for office.

It was February 1990. Three months had passed since the Sakamoto family's disappearance, and police seemed clueless about how to proceed. The media's interest, meanwhile, had faded. Some critical stories had reported on the cult's confinement of followers and bizarre rituals, but Aum's leadership could feel secure they had gotten away with not one murder but three. Asahara took this as a sign that he could keep pushing, keep bullying his way into power.

Winning souls was not enough; Asahara wanted votes. There

was a national election for the Japanese parliament, and the guru had decided to take Aum's case directly to the people. Aum was contesting no fewer than twenty-five seats in the Lower House. The cult was serious about the move and poured millions of dollars into campaigning. Years ago one Buddhist sect, Soka Gakkai, had backed its own candidates and now controlled the third-largest political party in Japan.

Officials from Soka Gakkai, however, dressed in conservative business suits and campaigned against corruption. Aum's candidates were a little harder to figure out. The cult's platform comprised a blend of apocalyptic preaching, calls to end a new consumption tax, and an appeal to utopian socialism ("Freedom, equality, and benevolence for every being," demanded party leader Asahara, "especially for the Japanese"). The cult paid dearly for hundreds of oversized, papier-mâché masks that bore a striking resemblance to Asahara, complete with long hair and beard, fat cheeks, and thick eyebrows. It was like a freaky dream – dozens of Asaharas of every shape and size, marching through Tokyo streets with placards about taxes and health care.

Aum took the same approach to politics as it did to religion: anything goes. Cult members approached voters at home, campaigned past allowable times, and ripped down the posters of rival candidates – all violations of Japanese election law. One ex-member later claimed the cult even tapped the phone of an opponent, a technique they would use increasingly.

The election proved a disaster. Japanese voters wanted nothing to do with elephant-masked cultists and doomsdayers. All twenty-five Aum candidates went down to miserable defeats, including Asahara. The all-knowing guru had predicted he would sweep to the largest of victories, but ended with a mere 1,783 votes out of half a million cast. Yet his own followers numbered over 1,800 in his district.

"It was a complete loss," conceded the guru. He charged officials with vote fraud, but the damage had been done. Aum had spent $7 million on the race and had nothing to show. One member even stole nearly $1.5 million and fled. He was not the only one to leave. Dozens of cultists, brought back to the real world as campaign workers, left the communes and returned to their former lives. Aum's meteoric growth suddenly slowed to a crawl.

Only weeks earlier Asahara had bragged, "We will eventually swallow up the whole of Japan." But now the cult fell into crisis. On top of defections and bleeding coffers, opposition to the cult was growing. Residents outside Mount Fuji and other communities had organized, demanding the cult scale back its constant building. At Aum's community near Mount Aso in southern Japan, relations deteriorated so badly that a near-riot ensued with local townspeople. The town now refused to let cult members register as residents or use public facilities, prompting a lawsuit by Aum. Parents continued their campaign against the cult, trying to get their teenage children back. Support committees of relatives and colleagues kept alive the Sakamoto case, prodding police to investigate the group. And a handful of reporters took on the cult, tearing away fragments of Aum's wall of secrecy.

Professor Hiromi Shimada, an authority on new religions, offered a bleak warning about Aum in a Japanese weekly. "Aum's growth has been blunted and the number of followers has declined, and it is experiencing an economic crisis that may result in its adopting extremist measures," she wrote in a story entitled "Aum Supreme Truth as Disneyland." "In line with the group's predictions of an end to humanity, if increasingly severe social crises do not continue to occur, they will face a dilemma."

The loss at the polls signaled a radical break for Asahara and Aum. Their failure, Asahara proclaimed, only confirmed how decrepit society had become and showed the need for more extreme solutions. From here on, he would abandon trying to work within the system; he was now intent on destroying it.

Following the election defeat, Asahara's preaching dwelled more and more on the disasters awaiting humanity. The dates for Armageddon varied, according to the Master's mood. Sometimes oblivion was scheduled for 2001, sometimes for 1999. But Aum believers could rest assured it was coming, and it was coming soon. Moreover, the guru no longer told his followers to save the world's souls; those who did not believe in Aum would perish in the coming holocaust.

Typical was "Heading for Catastrophe," an Asahara sermon in the spring of 1990.

> We are heading for Armageddon. It becomes very clear if you analyze the situation in the Middle East. Also the coming of Haley's comet, the frequent appearances of UFOs, the Soviet Union's democratization and its introduction of the presidential system, the unification of Europe, and so forth – what are all these incidents telling us? They are telling us that the world is getting ready for Armageddon. And what will happen after Armageddon? After Armageddon the beings will be

divided into two extreme types: the ones who will go to the Heaven of Light and Sound, and the ones who go to Hell.

Masami Tsuchiya, who left his doctoral work in organic chemistry to join Aum, scribbled across seven pages his own vision of the apocalypse. "Shoko Asahara will be imprisoned in the 1990s," he wrote, "but his trial will prove the existence of supernatural power and all 100 million Japanese will become followers of Aum." By 1995, he believed, the cult would grow more powerful than the Japanese state; by 1998 it would be Japanese bureaucrats living in small colonies and Aum disciples at the wheels of government. Aum would then advance into Jerusalem in 1998–99, where its followers would be captured and tortured as heretics. By then, however, Asahara's great movement would control its own military, which they would dispatch to the Holy Land and stage a brilliant rescue.

The apocalypse would soon follow. Master Asahara would die a martyr's death, sparking the final world war. Mount Fuji would explode and the Japanese islands sink into the sea. As for Tsuchiya himself? In his vision, the young scientist would survive to the age of ninety-two and complete the foundation for a thousand-year Kingdom of Aum.

The constant talk of Armageddon was having a dramatic effect on the cult. Combined with the loss at the polls and other setbacks, it enforced a kind of siege mentality at Aum's Mount Fuji center. Asahara himself was the biggest contributor. He had taken the defeats personally and swore revenge on those who dared to stand in Aum's way. "Those who say they have been victimized by Aum Supreme Truth will go to hell," Asahara proclaimed that spring. "So will the media."

A favorite target was *Sunday Mainichi*. In a meeting of the Aum leadership, Asahara put his latest idea simply. "Can we place some dynamite in a truck, drive it into the *Mainichi* building and explode it?" he asked. His followers somehow talked their enlightened guru out of the plan.

Around this time, Asahara also hit on the idea of raising an army. As a first step, he directed his top staff to create a "shadow corps," a paramilitary unit that would strike against the cult's enemies and train members in the martial arts. But his full plans went well beyond this. "How about having female members bear my children and make the children into a special attack corps?" he suggested.

"The children will be seen as juveniles so they won't get heavy sentences when they kill."

Asahara had even developed a theological rationalization for the coming carnage. In public, the guru preached about the sacredness of life. "Killing insects means accumulating the bad karma of killing," he once said, explaining the abundance of cockroaches at Aum's Mount Fuji center. But secretly, he instructed top disciples that killing by the enlightened few was justified because it helped send their victims to a higher plane. "It is good to eliminate people who continue to do bad things and are certain to go to hell," he told his closest followers. And by so doing, he assured them, they themselves would rise yet another level toward nirvana.

It was the ultimate corruption of all that was good in Buddhism. Central to the religion's teaching was the role of the Bodhisattva – enlightened beings who reach the doors of nirvana, yet instead of entering stay in the mortal world to help others gain enlightenment. Aum had somehow taken a great religion's concept of compassion and turned it into a justification for murder.

Even more disturbing were the disciples who took Asahara at his word. Aum's volatile leader had assembled a youthful corps of scientific and technical talent around him, followers eager to do their master's bidding. Their guru had listened intently as they described fantastic weapons of the future – and the present. Asahara began to talk of secret plans, of hi-tech warfare and Aum's critical role in the coming wars. Some of the plans were hard to believe, even for his most loyal followers.

7

BIOLAB 1

In April 1990, one of Aum's young scientists was summoned by Asahara to the Mount Fuji center. He was led to a small prefab building where he found the guru and his wife, sitting silently on floor mats. The master appeared in a state of meditation; beside him stood a top aide.

Asahara opened his eyes and asked, "Are you willing to risk your life?"

"Yes," the scientist replied. Asahara then directed his aide to take the man away.

He was escorted to a larger building next door. At the entrance he found a row of full-body protection suits, the kind used to shield people from biochemical hazard. They looked like space suits, with thick windows at the face and heavy-duty plastic skin the color of faded orange.

"Suit up," the aide said. Once inside the next room, the man immediately recognized his surroundings: he was in a biolab. Around him were microscopes, chemicals, row upon row of test tubes, and a large stainless-steel tank. Four other men and women, all in protective suits, moved intently about the lab. Inside the steel tank was a pool of water, partitioned into three or four parts. Outside it, a liquid-nitrogen device monitored the temperature. A humidifier hummed in the background, controlling moisture in the lab.

The young scientist would work here for weeks, never quite sure what the cult was up to. He and the others were ordered to vacuum-pump a brown, sticky ooze from the steel tank and pour it through a filter into a cylindrical plastic tank. The man recognized the liquid as a nutrient medium used to grow bacteria. After transferring it to the plastic tank, he poured the substance onto large metal trays and, still in a vacuum, applied heat until it dried into solid cakes. He then painstakingly grated the cakes into a fine powder. The ugly liquid sometimes leaked or spilled onto the floor. Quickly, the workers poured on calcined soda to neutralize any danger.

One supervisor hinted that the final product was a drug, but the man had his doubts. From talk at the lab, he knew they were cultivating some form of anaerobic bacteria – microscopic organisms that thrive in the absence of oxygen. Whatever it was, he knew it was very toxic.

In fact, it was as deadly a substance as exists on Earth. Aum Supreme Truth was culturing *Clostridium botulinum*, the bacterium that causes botulism.

Armageddon was coming, Asahara had assured them. And to fight the coming battles, Aum required the greatest weapons possible. Crude techniques like those used to murder the Sakamotos would never do; millions were to perish in the coming dark age, and Aum needed instruments of mass destruction. Murai and the other scientists had completed a survey of available literature and apparently picked botulinus as their first weapon of choice. They had built secret labs not only at Mount Fuji but also at Mount Aso in central Kyushu, and ordered equipment through various front companies the cult now controlled. The entire project was then placed under the direction of Seiichi Endo, the molecular biologist who had left Kyoto University's Viral Research Center to join Aum.

Botulinus toxin seemed an ideal killer for the cult. It is relatively cheap to produce and appeared well within the abilities of Aum's young biochemists. The bacteria that cause botulism produce seven highly toxic strains, of which Type A is the most deadly. The toxin is best known for its effects in severe food poisoning, but its potential as a biological weapon has long been recognized by the world's militaries.

Botulinus toxin A has been called the most poisonous substance in the natural world. It is 16 million times more toxic than strychnine, 10,000 times more toxic than cobra venom. Only radioactive isotopes, like plutonium, are more toxic. A lethal dose for a human being is less than one microgram – one-millionth of a gram. To give an idea of scale, a single grain of sugar weighs about 500 micrograms.

Like nerve gas or cobra venom, botulinus is a neurotoxin. The poison attacks the body's nervous system, an intricate network of millions of nerve cells that carry messages to and from the brain. These messages are transmitted by a chemical known as acetylcholine. After doing its job, the acetylcholine is destroyed by enzymes, making way for new transmissions. But neurotoxins like those in botulism interfere with the enzymes' work. The acetylcholine soon builds up at the nerve endings, overloading the system and shutting it down. Your body's involuntary nervous system, in effect, no longer functions; the throat is no longer told to swallow, the lungs to breathe, the heart to beat.

All this does not happen quickly. The symptoms usually begin within eighteen to thirty-six hours. The victim starts to feel nauseous; vomiting and diarrhea follow, with abdominal cramps and sometimes dizziness. The eyelids swell and the mouth and throat go dry. A partial paralysis then begins in the face, growing stronger and working its way through the rest of the body. As the victim's heart and lungs fall into paralysis, breathing and blood circulation inevitably stop. Death either of suffocation or heart failure follows.

With such a deadly agent, Aum's scientists also began work on an antitoxin, using horse serum. These efforts were centered at a second biolab at the cult's Mount Aso facility. To accommodate the research, Asahara ordered the group to build a stable and buy horses, from which the scientists drew blood.

By the end of spring, the botulinus was ready for testing. Along with the horses, the cult had procured a number of laboratory rats. Endo, the microbiologist, ordered the powder mixed in their food and waited. And waited.

Nothing happened.

Surprised by their lack of success, Endo now had his technicians sprinkle the stuff over the animals. Again, nothing. Finally, they mixed the toxin with a solution and injected it directly into the stubbornly alive rats. Still no effect. "They won't die," complained one supervisor. "This is a failure."

This "failure" undoubtedly spared the life of several Aum members. Given the toxicity of botulinus, the cult's scientists were remarkably careless. While they were grating the toxin into a powder, bits and pieces flaked into the air. Although protected by their space suits, when finished the technicians simply threw them off with no decontamination. "If the powder had worked, we would be dead," said one grateful worker.

Endo believed he knew the problem. Because the botulism bacterium is anaerobic, it dies when exposed to oxygen. The cult laboratories simply needed better equipment.

Asahara was disappointed. He had grown excited at the thought of possessing such a powerful weapon, and had already planned the cult's first attack. Endo and Murai assured the guru of their eventual success. There were many toxins available, they told him, including other biological killers, as well as chemical agents such as nerve gas and cyanide. Indeed, the cult's scientists would try again – and they would succeed.

In 1347, the Mongols laid siege to a Genoese trading fortress on the Crimean peninsula. As their own troops fell to the Black Death – bubonic plague – they grew increasingly desperate. Finally, they took to catapulting the corpses of plague victims over the walls. The tactic worked: soon the Genoese were in the midst of an epidemic. They fled to their ships, carrying the bacteria with them to the port cities of the Mediterranean. By 1349, the disease had wiped out at least 20 percent of Europe's entire population.

In 1763, during the French and Indian War, the commander of the British forces in North America suggested that smallpox be spread among enemy Indian tribes. Two contaminated blankets and a handkerchief, given to a pair of Indian chiefs, were enough to cause an epidemic.

In the 1930s and 1940s, the Japanese Imperial Army in China conducted heinous experiments and attacks with biological weapons. The notorious Unit 731 unleashed epidemics in Manchuria and outside Shanghai by releasing thousands of fleas infected with plague and cholera. At least 2,000 Asians and Russians were used as human guinea pigs, murdered in gruesome tests using tuberculosis, salmonella, typhoid, cholera, and anthrax. Their dehumanized victims were simply called *maruta*, Japanese for "logs."

For centuries, warring peoples have sought to wreak havoc on each other by use of biological weapons. Poisoned wells, tainted food, and toxic arrows have all been used through the years. But only in the last half-century have the world's militaries explored the full potential of biological agents. Secret arsenals of infectious microorganisms and vaccines, toxins and antitoxins now sit in the laboratories of nearly a dozen countries, and the number is growing. Worse, the explosion in biotechnology since the 1970s has helped spread the techniques and training involved worldwide.

There are few more frightening forms of warfare. Biological agents conjure up images of invisible killers, unstoppable epidemics, entire populations decimated. There is an apocalyptic air about them shared perhaps only by nuclear weapons. Students of the subject are fond of bringing up the great influenza epidemic of 1918–19, a natural disaster that suggests the power of a single pathogen. Brought home by returning troops after World War I, the unforgiving virus circled the globe repeatedly. Before the epidemic ended, at least 20 million people were dead, more than twice the number who died in the war.

Biological warfare is often called bacterial or germ warfare, but the substances available are much broader than that. Aum sent its scientists to the top libraries in Japan – and later the United States – where they studied the full range of biological agents: bacteria, viruses, fungi, rickettsia, and various toxins. Among them are Agent C (a fungus), Q fever and flea-borne typhus (both caused by rickettsia, a bacteria-like organism), anthrax and bubonic plague (bacteria), and Venezuelan equine encephalitis (a virus). Most of these pathogens have one thing in common: they are very, very deadly. Also, many are extremely contagious; once ingested by human beings, they multiply and can spark an epidemic which is difficult to contain.

The toxins, like botulinus, stand in a class by themselves. They are not contagious diseases but simple killers, drawn from the poisonous by-products of living organisms. Because of this, they are closer in some ways to chemical agents like nerve gas. In the depths of the Cold War, military scientists made worldwide searches for the deadliest substances on Earth. The Pentagon sent repeated expeditions to the South American rainforest to search out hundreds of plant and animal species for their toxic effects – snake and spider venom, blowfish toxin, poisonous mushrooms.

One example is saxitoxin, known for causing paralytic shellfish poisoning. The effects of saxitoxin begin with a tingling around the face and loss of feeling in the extremities; they end quickly with death by paralysis. Or consider batrachotoxin, nearly five times as deadly as eating the wrong shellfish. Drawn from the skin of a South American frog, batrachotoxin has long been used by Indians of the Colombian rainforest for their blow-gun darts. There is also ricin, derived from the lowly castor-bean plant, which throws its victims into bouts of nausea, vomiting and fatigue, followed by kidney failure and death.

Along with chemical weapons, biological agents have been called the "poor man's atomic bomb," and for good reason. The relative ease with which these killers can be made may herald a new age of terrorism and indiscriminate murder. A U.S. Congressional study in 1993 found that the number of countries believed to have chemical and biological weapons had more than tripled since 1972. Among those keen on biowarfare are such global citizens as Iraq and Iran, North Korea, Libya and Syria, as well as China and Taiwan. By the start of the 1991 Gulf War, Iraq had armed at least 200 bombs and Scud missiles with anthrax, botulinus and aflatoxin. Information on their make-up is widely available in public libraries as well as through the Internet. And unlike nuclear and chemical weapons, biological ones are subject to virtually no international controls. For years, experts have warned that long before terrorists gain control of a nuclear bomb, they will be launching attacks with biological weapons.

It doesn't take a great deal to set up your own biolab. The production of biological warfare agents is, in fact, largely similar to work in any public-health or medical lab. The difference is one of intent. The basic requirements are the same: some specialized chambers and sampling gear, standard lab equipment, test animals, a knowledgable microbiologist, and a pathogen − the organism you're trying to culture and process.

How did Aum get its botulinus? Like many industrial nations, Japan has no system to register or inspect pathogen facilities. Despite calls for closer regulation, the nation's Ministry of Health has preferred a hands-off approach. This means that because legitimate researchers use bacteria like anthrax and botulinus in their work, they are routinely made available to the scientific and medical communities. Ads in professional trade journals even offer these organisms through the mail, freeze-dried and lab-ready. One needs only a letterhead and a legitimate-sounding purpose.

Aum's journey into toxic terrorism was not the first. In 1972 U.S. authorities stopped a homegrown fascist group, the Order of the Rising Sun, from causing a public-health disaster. The neo-Nazis reportedly were caught with 80 pounds of typhoid bacteria cultures, and had plans to poison the water supplies of large Midwestern cities.

Then in Paris, in 1980, police raided a German Red Army Faction safe house and found, along with forged documents and bomb instructions, publications on bacterial infection. In the margin were the notes of a suspect who worked by day as a medical assistant, by night as a terrorist. And in the bathroom was a home-made lab, the tub loaded with flasks full of *Clostridium botulinum*, the same culture Aum would later use. Earlier the terrorist group had threatened to poison water supplies in twenty German towns if radical lawyers were not permitted to defend an imprisoned comrade.

Another incident occurred in 1984, when mysteriously 715 people came down with salmonella poisoning in Antelope, Oregon. The small town was home to a free-love commune headed by Bhagwan Shree Rajneesh, an Indian guru. Like Aum, Rajneesh followers didn't get along with their neighbors. Behind the sickness were top officials of the cult, who poisoned local salad bars in a move to influence a town election. Two months later, a pair of Canadians were seized after nearly obtaining botulism and tetanus cultures from a U.S. medical supply house. They claimed to represent a research company that did not exist.

There are more cases, but the point seems clear enough. Today, ordinary people can produce biological weapons of alarming reach. All you need is a modest investment of money and equipment, some training in microbiology, and a complete disregard for human life.

By April 1990, Seiichi Endo believed he now understood how to hold the toxicity of botulinus. Moreover, Aum's microbiologist and his team had rigged up a spraying device that could distribute the poison over a wide area.

Asahara was elated at the news. The weapon arrived just in time, for Aum had continued losing members and cash. With his top aides, the guru formulated a plan. They began spreading rumors that a terrible vision had seized Asahara. No one seemed quite sure what it was – a comet passing near Earth would strike Japan; the dormant volcano within Mount Fuji would explode, killing thousands; Japan would sink into the sea.

The rumors were aimed at luring Japanese to a retreat on Ishigaki Island, a subtropical speck of land at the southern tip of the Okinawan chain. Aum members did the hard sell of a "comet-watching tour with the guru," suggesting the distant island might be the only safe place in Japan that particular week. To prove their point, they intended to blanket the Diet – the Japanese parliament – with neurotoxin.

8

DIVINE SERVICE

For twenty years, unbeknown to most Americans, their government waged war against them with "simulated" biological weapons. Between 1949 and 1969, the U.S. Army conducted at least 239 tests using bacteria and other agents deemed "relatively" harmless by the Pentagon. The agents were released from a ship off San Francisco, spread through the New York subways, and blown through the streets of Minneapolis and St. Louis. Mock attacks were staged on the White House and Pentagon command centers. The tests showed a startling vulnerability to a biological-weapons assault. Army commandos found they could contaminate the entire Pentagon by inserting two pints of bio-agent into a single air duct.

The CIA tried an equally alarming technique. In the early 1950s, agents drove around New York in a car with a modified exhaust pipe, spraying vast tracts of the city with bacteria. Their results apparently were just as impressive.

Aum opted for the CIA's approach. In April 1990, cult technicians outfitted a vehicle with a special spraying device and painstakingly filled it with a solution of botulinus toxin. They then drove through the area surrounding the Diet, emitting a colorless vapor filled with the neurotoxin.

As Aum's hit team drove through the streets of Tokyo, Shoko Asahara was holding court on a distant Okinawan island, warning followers of the world's end. The plan must have seemed brilliant to the guru and his aides. Before a day would pass, hundreds, perhaps thousands of government officials would be keeling over with nausea and creeping paralysis. The Diet would cease to function, leaving the world's second largest economy in crisis – and Shoko Asahara's prophetic power clear to all.

Yet while Asahara preached of Armageddon, life in Tokyo went on as usual. Aum's top scientists searched in vain for reports of an epidemic, a medical disaster, a government shutdown. But there was none. Events seemed tediously normal around the Japanese parliament. The enterprising Mr. Endo sadly returned to Aum's laboratory, wondering if it was time to try another pathogen.

Fortunately for Endo, the guru could overlook his latest failure. Despite the absence of disaster, Aum's island retreat had proved a grand success, boosting morale, gaining new members, and cashing in. About a thousand people answered Asahara's call, each paying over $2,000. Yet the cost to Aum was almost nothing: participants took public transport and stayed in tents at free camping sites (while Asahara and staff stayed in a nearby hotel). Add in fees the cult took in from Blood Initiations, electrode-cap rentals and the like, and Aum raked in an easy $2 million.

Another windfall came with Aum's recruitment of new monks and nuns – a special target of the retreat. Cult leaders "kept telling us that the world was going to end and we would be saved only if we believed in Asahara," recalled one ex-follower. Over the next month, 125 people joined the monkhood, donating their life savings and putting Aum Supreme Truth back on the fast track.

The cult made a fortune from its true believers. To join one of Aum's communities as a monk or nun, one needed to donate not only every possession, but also fork out more than $8,000 as an initiation fee. Millions of dollars more poured in.

Adding to Aum's renewed attraction was the collapse of Japan's much-vaunted economic miracle. During the late 1980s, the Japanese economy blew a speculative bubble that pushed land and stock prices sky-high. The "bubble economy" brought to Japan a remarkable share of the world's wealth, with Tokyo bumping aside New York as the world's richest stock market; the value of land in Tokyo, at least on paper, exceeded that of the entire United States. At the same time, the yen's value against world currencies began to rise dramatically, giving the Japanese unprecedented buying power overseas.

By 1991, it was clear that the bubble had popped. Real-estate and stock prices plunged to half their peak value, pushing Japan's economy into its worst recession in decades. Aum's real-estate values also plummeted, but that mattered little to the cult; Asahara was interested in acquiring land, not selling it, and he could afford to be patient. Moreover, for many Japanese the bubble's end also finished their worship of money; the god of cash and easy credit was dead, and people began looking for something more meaningful. In his lectures, Asahara spoke of "this filthy world of desires" and called on fellow Japanese to join his spiritual quest.

Join they did. By 1991, Aum had grown to some 7,000 believers, including a handful of devotees in America and Germany. Flush with donations, Aum began buying real estate in the nation's depressed property market. New Aum centers opened in smaller cities, old centers expanded, and the cult opened a nine-bed hospital in Tokyo. With the apocalypse just years away, work on the Mount Fuji headquarters proceeded day and night. The place was now a bustling settlement, with more than a dozen buildings large and small. Fulfilling Asahara's dream of a self-contained community, there were homes, workshops, offices, a clinic, a school, and places for religious training.

All this activity led to yet more followers and more funding. The pressure on believers to give was relentless. Their souls depended on it. "Do you think that a person who thinks nothing of failing to pay alms will ever be able to attain salvation?" the guru asked his followers.

People were willing to pay a lot for enlightenment. Yet those who dedicated their lives to the cult – giving up their life savings, their families, even signing over their wills – often got only misery in return.

Many of the 1,500 devotees who lived inside Aum's communities fervently believed they were building a new Utopia, a glorious Kingdom of Aum. In reality, they were little more than cogs in what would become a massive killing machine.

Aum's soulless compounds now littered the northwest foothills of Mount Fuji. In Kamikuishiki, a remote farming hamlet less frequented by tourists, residents watched as Aum built a series of facilities near their homes. Each one looked like a cross between a canning factory and a concentration camp – jerry-built monoliths with a sprinkling of barbed wire and raised sentry boxes at each corner. The windswept lanes linking each isolated facility were busy with grimy Nissans and Toyota pick-ups loaded with heavy equipment. At the compounds, cranes swung housing material high over the roofs, which were lined with bulging garbage bags. The racket of twenty-four-hour construction and mantras droning from loudspeakers shattered the rural peace. Figures moved with mute, robotic purpose among bags of concrete and rusting machine parts. All followers wore thin, grubby robes and, on their heads, what resembled an unraveled bandage – the PSI brain-wave hat, delivering regular shocks to the scalp.

Aum's scientists constituted the cult's elite, but the Mount Fuji community needed a variety of lesser workers. The compounds themselves were designed by cult engineers and thrown up by manual laborers. There was an editorial department to publish Asahara's lectures and cult magazines such as *Vajrayana Sacca* (meaning, in Sanskrit, "Unbreakable Truth"). The design section immortalized the guru in *manga* (comic strips). A clothes shop produced robes and ritual costumes. Followers toiled hard, convinced their good work would bring spiritual rewards and propel them up the cult's strict hierarchy. In stark contrast to the lives of the rank and file, Aum's leaders had their own rooms, and came and went as they pleased.

An Aum follower's day began at around 7 a.m. In one cleansing ritual adapted from yoga, a cultist flushed his nose with warm water and threaded string through his nostrils and mouth. Another purifying rite – drinking ten pints of water, then vomiting it up – doubled as a punishment. Followers subsisted on a miserable twice-daily helping of unprocessed rice, seaweed, fermented bean curd, and a tasteless vegetable stew known as "Aum food." Those undergoing religious training ate the once-daily offerings in a ritual called Holy Fire Service. This could be anything – two whole cabbages one day, dozens of tangerines the next – and believers were forced to eat it all, even if they threw up afterwards.

Another staple food was a kind of bitter cookie. Disturbingly, these were not made by the cult's bakery, but by its scientists – the same ones then experimenting with botulism. More substantial meals like curry were served on the birthdays of Asahara and Buddha. Treats were rare and subject to the guru's whims. "Once the Master said, 'The gods love high-calorie food,' so we were given *mochi* [sweet bean cakes] for a month," said one ex-follower. Another believer was treated to a delicious breakfast of fresh fruit – but only for the benefit of a visiting television crew. Meanwhile, Aum's high-ranking members ate handsomely. The owner of a nearby sushi shop counted them among his regular customers. On one occasion he prepared a $1,000 take-out order.

Believers drank only "holy water," the tap water supposedly "blessed" by the guru. This was stored in metal drums outside. "Moss grew inside the drums and sometimes mosquito larvae too," recalled one believer. She, like her brethren, was expected to swallow the polluted liquid regardless. Drinking tea, coffee, alcohol, or "unblessed" tap water was forbidden.

Sleeping times varied. Cultists regarded as more enlightened were expected to sleep for three hours a day. New recruits slept an average of five hours. Long working hours, little sleep, and poor nutrition left many followers permanently exhausted – and easy to control. "These days, my head feels really dizzy. I just can't stay awake," wrote one cultist in his diary. Aum's drones slept in bunk beds in vast plywood honeycombs of tiny boxes. Others curled up in sleeping bags on the workplace floor.

What passed for recreation was dominated by the cult. The only television or reading material available was Aum-produced. Believers needed permission to leave the compounds and had no access to family and friends. Many found it tough adjusting to this spartan existence, but were reluctant to turn back. Everything they owned now belonged to the cult.

Every aspect of their lives now twitched to the vibrations of one colossal ego. Asahara issued regular "decrees" ordering beatings and demotions for disobedient followers. "Disobedience" included theft and fraud ("acts of the ego," the guru called them), criticizing the cult or its leaders, and leaking information to the outside world. Followers who slept too much received "extra divine service" – that is, even more work – and anyone who bought delicacies had their meager allowance stopped for a month.

Even so, adult believers, for the most part, freely chose this deprived existence. The hundred or so kids raised in Aum's Children's Annex did not, but they lived lives of similar desperation. Children who arrived at Mount Fuji were separated from their families and given new Sanskrit names. Many forgot their original names and saw their parents rarely, if at all. Babies were born in unsanitary conditions and named after the alphabet – "Child A," "Little B," and so on. Followers who tried to register one infant with the municipal authorities were told by cult leaders not to bother. The world was going to end anyway.

Children wandered barefoot around the cult's work areas. They ate with their hands, bathed once every three days, and changed their clothes only when they looked dirty. They were taught that people who undergo religious training need not wash so often. Most had to wear smaller, three-volt versions of the PSI headgear, and were punished if they removed it. A nine-year-old girl was given injections by cult nurses, even though she told them she felt fine. Children later rescued from the cult suffered from malnutrition, pneumonia, and psychiatric problems. When one little girl was handed a pair of socks by social workers, she asked, "What are these?"

Formal education was virtually nonexistent. Up to a quarter of

GIVEN NEW SANSKRIT NAMES

Aum's children had never attended proper schools. Kids as young as five were taught to admire Adolf Hitler, and told that he was still alive. The rest of their curriculum consisted of Asahara's teachings, cult rituals, breathing exercises, and chanting. Children had cleaning duties at 6.30 a.m. and spent their evenings on such "spiritual" training as working in the cult's food factory. "Leisure" time meant watching Aum videos or reading Aum comics. Children who attended one workshop on Asahara's home island of Kyushu were simply detained in a room for one week. Slow students had cult doctrine beaten into them with sticks.

The intensely competitive hierarchy among the cult's adults was mirrored in the world of their children. A nine-year-old who had been a follower for two years would consider herself superior to a twelve-year-old who had only recently joined. But the undisputed leader of the juvenile pack was Shoko Asahara's third daughter, Reiko, the most adored of his six children. She was known by the "holy name" of Aajadi. Now in her early teens, she lived in her father's well-guarded family compound, where she was privately tutored by a Tokyo University science graduate. She was considered Asahara's successor as cult leader.

Aajadi grew up in a brutal atmosphere dominated by her tyrannical father. Asahara encouraged her to hit other children with poles, supposedly to remove their bad karma. Once she dipped a boy's fingers into three different kinds of acid. "It was just an experiment," said the guru's daughter, and nobody argued with her.

ASAHARA'S DAUGHTER AAJADI

9

HUMAN SOUP

From the outside, the Japanese police force appears a model of efficiency. Dedicated officers man their *koban,* or police boxes, giving directions, checking bike registrations, and watching for suspicious activity. Career bureaucrats are drawn from Japan's finest schools and dispatched to local police departments across the nation.

Rates of murder and mayhem are low compared to those in most of the world. Japan – a nation of 125 million – typically posts the same number of murders each year as New York City. Women can walk the streets at night without fear of rape or robbery. Postwar Japan has become an orderly, secure society, where crooks turn themselves in and prosecutors boast a 99 percent conviction rate.

Yet in the case of Aum, the system broke down entirely. By the fall of 1990, the cultists of Aum Supreme Truth had committed massive fraud, held minors against their parents' will, killed one person with a crackpot cure, slain four others, including a one-year-old boy, cultured the world's deadliest bacteria and attempted to use it to commit mass murder. Incredibly, they were just beginning.

Where were the police? In part, Japanese law enforcement simply did not want to interfere with a religious group, but other reasons were at work. The impressive crime statistics hid a system in crisis. The high conviction rates are based almost entirely on confessions. Painstaking detective work and forensic science take a back seat to interrogation methods that are criticized by human-rights groups worldwide. Fear of police overstepping their bounds has also kept them from gaining investigative tools that most Western law enforcement agencies take for granted, such as undercover work and electronic eavesdropping. As gangsters and other crooks have grown in sophistication, police in Japan have stayed much the same for fifty years. The result was that, when faced with a cohesive, disciplined enemy like Aum, Japanese cops were nearly helpless.

By now, Aum had gained a nasty reputation for its bogus claims and quack cures. Parents of missing children had filed numerous complaints. The family and friends of the missing Sakamotos continued to keep the case alive. They passed out thousands of flyers, opened a hotline, and offered a reward of nearly $400,000. They even pleaded for help on a blimp high above Tokyo. In the end, most of the leads pointed back to Aum. But as the months passed after their murders, investigators remained unsure how to proceed. Yokohama police had received an anonymous letter telling them to look for the lawyer's son in the swampy grounds near a certain mountainside. "Little Tatsuhiko is sleeping . . . Hurry! Help him!" read the note, with a map attached. The cops dispatched a small team, but they suspected the letter was a hoax and gave up after a few days.

Finally, in the fall of 1990, a year after the family's murder, police got around to raiding Aum's facilities. Scores of local cops pushed their way into Aum's communities and training centers. The official reason: land fraud. Aum, it seemed, had lied to the county about the source of land for its Mount Aso retreat, pocketing some fast money in a tax dodge. But the raids were also meant to put the aggressive cult on notice – to let Aum know the authorities were watching. To make their point, Asahara was questioned and several of his top staff arrested.

Police raids in Japan are often announced in advance, carefully stage-managed, and crowded with enough cops to fill a police academy. The cops, in turn, are outnumbered by representatives of the news media, who dutifully report the occasion as high drama to a willing public. Favorite targets of these hard-hitting attacks are crime-syndicate offices, high-rolling tax-evaders, and the occasional corrupt politician.

Predictably, the raids on Aum didn't turn up much. No minors were reunited with their families. The secret biolabs completely escaped notice. And if the cops were looking for evidence of murder, they were a little late. While police questioned cultists on the Sakamotos, nobody talked and the cops came away empty-handed.

Moreover, if the raids were meant to pressure Aum, they only made the cult more militant. Asahara fired back, publicly charging the state with a campaign of persecution. "This investigation is Aum-bashing," he told the press. "The reason for Aum-bashing is that Aum Supreme Truth is a dangerous religion" which speaks of the life beyond, he said. "Therefore, we can't avoid conflict with ordinary society." At least that prediction would ring true. Aum also responded with a lawsuit against local officials. The cult demanded $1 million in compensation for the raid, claiming police had damaged its good name and caused members both spiritual and physical pain.

True to form, Asahara told the world he had predicted the police raids. "I've known about this investigation since the middle of September," he said to a reporter. "Because I meditate, I know the future . . . I will be arrested too. Within a year there will be some sign."

The reporter wondered about Asahara and the Sakamotos. If it were true that the cult was not guilty, he said, perhaps the guru's psychic ability could help police in breaking the case. "In your meditation, can you see where Mr. Sakamoto is?" he asked.

"Yes," the guru replied. "I am in a position where I can. But as I have said before, if I say something about the case, people will think Asahara has something to do with it. If I say nothing, then they will think me a liar. Please forgive me."

"But you can see him, can't you?" the reporter asked.

"Yes, of course."

Seeing the Sakomotos and the world's end were not the only mystical feats performed by Shoko Asahara. In recent months, UFOs had been on the guru's mind. At a 1990 lecture, Asahara explained how extraterrestrials fit into the universal plan.

"UFOs often appear on Earth these days," he began. "It will become one of the main factors of Armageddon whether we can benefit from UFOs or not." The guru then told of how these strange beings come from levels of consciousness higher than that of mortal man or woman. "They may be from the Heaven of Degenerated Consciousness or the Heaven of Playful Degeneration. Anyhow, they are superior to human beings without doubt." But that doesn't mean they can be trusted.

"I hear that these aliens eat human soup," Asahara confided. "It is just like humans eating beef. In the final analysis, my view is that human beings will not benefit from the aliens."

What should be done about these alien visits? "Since aliens surpass man in technology," he said, "we will have to protect ourselves not by technology on the earthly scale, but by more excellent technology than aliens, and at the same time we have to advance our practice too. This is the principle."

Those who didn't follow the Master's logic could no doubt pay for training sessions and have it explained in greater detail. Perhaps they could even question the guru himself, who now seemed to have all the answers. Asahara's egomania had continued to grow, fueled by his adoring young followers. "The Buddha in our times is Master Shoko Asahara," proclaimed his disciples in a 1991 book. The guru himself was even more expansive. "I hearby declare myself to be the Christ," he wrote after reading through the Bible for the first time. His similarities to Jesus in the New Testament were simply too close to be otherwise, he explained, before warning of false prophets: "I am the last messiah in this century."

As if being Buddha and Jesus were not enough of a load, in April that year Asahara shocked followers by announcing his imminent death. He had been diagnosed with fatal cancer of the liver, he told them, and his eyesight too was failing completely. He was dying, soon to take his place in Maha Nirvana. But like Armageddon, the date of Asahara's own demise proved flexible. By the year's end he claimed to have made a miraculous recovery, curing the cancer through "extreme practices." As for his eyesight, "I have left it uncured," he explained. (Like so much in Asahara's life, his blindness is open to question; one ex-member claimed to have seen the guru playing catch.)

Fading eyes or not, Asahara found time to travel the globe and plot Aum's expansion overseas. The cult was now flush with cash, and those yen bills held enormous buying power abroad. Between 1984, when Asahara began building his empire, and 1991, the yen's value against the dollar rose by nearly 60 percent. Asahara saw his opportunity. Already the cult fielded offices in New York and Bonn. These would serve as gateways to expansion across North America and Europe. But the guru had plans further afield.

Asahara felt it important to establish a base in south Asia, birthplace of Hinduism, Buddhism, and yoga. In May and June of 1991, he and a band of followers traveled to India and Tibet, making a pilgrimage to sacred sites tied to the Buddha. At a temple in Bihar, India, Asahara climbed on top of the sacred seat where Buddha is said to have found enlightenment. A shocked priest ordered him off, but Asahara refused. "I am Buddha," he explained.

The priest thought otherwise, despite Asahara's name-dropping of the Dalai Lama and other high priests, who he bragged were his friends. When a policeman finally yanked the Japanese off the holy mount, Asahara was stunned. "Why is everybody angry? Don't they know I'm Buddha?" he asked. The dethroned guru then joined the scores of Aum faithful nearby, who greeted their leader with trumpet blasts and beating drums.

The Indians, apparently, had seen their share of holy men, prompting Asahara to look elsewhere for a south Asian retreat. He found one in Sri Lanka. This time the cult's approach was strictly business, waving money and big plans in front of local officials. Their talk of opening factories won audiences with Prime Minister D. B. Vigetunga and his top ministers.

Other ventures abroad were more mysterious. Also in 1991, cult leaders paid a visit to Laos, a nation better known for its opium traffic than for Buddhist scholarship. Asahara arrived "as a guest of state" according to an Aum publication, and held meetings with top officials and the head of the Lao Buddhist Union.

Far more intriguing is the case of North Korea. Cult members visited the reclusive regime several times, according to police sources. Rumors run wild about Aum intentions there, but precious little evidence exists. Some accounts suggest the cult hoped to build its own community near the border with China and Russia, in an area destined to become a free economic zone. Other reports, however, suggest a more sinister purpose. At the time, the North Koreans were hard at work on a nuclear bomb and had built impressive stores of both biological and chemical weapons. Some speculate that the dictatorship offered the cult weapons training and cash in exchange for access to hi-tech goods, such as computers and lasers. With its growing international network, Aum was well placed to act as a purchasing agent for Pyongyang. Unfortunately, the proof is lacking. "We keep hearing the rumors, but we just haven't seen any evidence," said an intelligence official at a Western embassy in Tokyo.

For a cult hoping to arm itself with weapons of mass destruction, North Korea could have been one-stop shopping. But even if such a connection did exist, it was overshadowed by a far richer, more chaotic country next door. For by 1992, Aum had discovered Russia.

10

RUSSIAN SALVATION

Shoko Asahara stood in the shadow of the Kremlin's mighty walls, gazing across the expanse of Red Square. It was March 1992, and the guru was dressed for Moscow's endless winter in a purple quilted jacket with matching fur hat bearing Aum's Sanskrit insignia. First Asahara "blessed" Red Square, stirring the icy air with one finger waved above his head. Then he posed for photos with 300 followers before the candy-colored, onion-domes of St. Basil's Cathedral. As the shutter clicked, Asahara smiled and flashed a "V for Victory" sign.

Aum Supreme Truth's "Russian Salvation Tour" had begun.

The guru's spiraling ambitions had already led the cult around the world. But nothing could prepare him for the staggering success of Aum's first Russian adventure. Within months, the cult's influence would reach to the highest levels of Russian politics and education, and, in the smoldering rubble of the Soviet empire, its membership would explode.

Asahara and his disciples had arrived in Moscow on a specially chartered Aeroflot aircraft. The guru was ushered into a limousine bearing Russian government plates and whisked off to a plush hotel in downtown Moscow. Asahara drove into a blitz of publicity. Lampposts and Metro stations across the capital were plastered with full-color posters announcing the Russian Salvation Tour – a packed ten-day program of concerts, rallies, and photo opportunities, all of it blessed by the most powerful figures in the land.

Asahara's pilgrimage to Red Square was deeply symbolic. Ivan the Terrible's enemies were executed on its ancient cobbles, as was Peter the Great's palace guard. Vladimir Ilyich Lenin was entombed there, and a string of Soviet leaders – Stalin, Khrushchev, Brezhnev – later stood somberly on top of his mausoleum as tanks, troops and ICBMs poured past in displays of Cold War might. Asahara clearly ranked himself among these historic leaders, and shared their dreams of world conquest.

The guru was reportedly scheduled to meet Russia's newest leader, Boris Yeltsin, but the President was too busy. In his place, Vice President Aleksandr Rutskoi performed the obligatory meet and greet. The guru also met the parliamentarian Ruslan Khasbulatov, and told him of the cult's humanitarian dream for Russia. Aum would establish an AIDS prevention fund, build a hospital offering free treatment, employ the jobless in two new food-processing firms, and restore priceless Russian art works. As a promise of things to come, the sect donated several thousand dollars' worth of medical supplies to two Russian hospitals.

Next stop: Lenin Hills on the capital's outskirts, site of elite Moscow State University (known by its Russian acronym MGU). Built by convict labor, MGU's Stalinist-era building is a thirty-six story heap of soaring spires and statuary topped with a red star. MGU's staff welcomed Shoko Asahara with open arms, a warmth in part generated by Aum's donation of $80,000-worth of computers. Sitting cross-legged on a king-size white armchair, Asahara delivered a sermon entitled "Making the World Happy with the Truth" to a packed auditorium of students and staff. He was introduced as "Japan's representative Buddhist leader."

The cult spared no expense on the tour's well-rehearsed extravaganzas. Inside the Kremlin's forbidding walls, the cult rented the Palace of Congresses, the site of the Soviet Union's last Communist Party plenums. Where Mikhail Gorbachev had once passionately expounded *perestroika* and *glasnost,* Aum performers now pranced in tinsel-covered leotards through clouds of dry ice in a bizarre musical called *Death and Rebirth,* composed by the guru himself.

Asahara saved his greatest performance for Moscow's Olympiski Stadium, the largest covered arena in Russia. The guru sat on the same white chair in center field, gazing out at a sea of some 19,000 Russian faces. A giant video screen flashed up images of Asahara as Christ crucified, while charts purported to show that limited oxygen consumption during meditation allowed Aum followers to go for hours without breathing. Asahara spoke of "awakening the power of kundalini," of the mysteries of Eastern spirituality, of the healing power of yoga, of Truth. At one point, the stadium's lights were dimmed for a vast meditation session. One academic described the meeting as "an awe-inspiring, overwhelming experience in the state of mass hypnosis."

By the time the Olympiski rally was over, Shoko Asahara's message was clear: Aum Supreme Truth was determined to save thousands of Russian souls – whether they wanted to be saved or not.

Promises of miracle cures and supernatural powers struck a deep chord in many Russians. More by accident than design, Aum had tapped into a rich history of mysticism stretching back for centuries. Healers and "holy fools" have often appeared in Russian history at times of crisis or rapid change. In the last years of Romanov rule, for example, an illiterate Siberian peasant called Rasputin convinced Tsar Nicholas II that his magical powers could cure the hemophilia of the tsar's son Alexey.

In 1917, the Bolsheviks did away with religion (and, for that matter, the Romanovs). Churches were systematically destroyed or turned into "museums of atheism." Believers were murdered or branded "enemies of the state." Only in the late 1980s, when cracks began to appear in the Soviet monolith, could spiritually starved Russians turn once again to the heady pre-1917 blend of folk healing, fortune-telling and witchcraft.

The Russian Orthodox Church – widely distrusted as a tool of the former KGB – watched in horror as new groups and gurus sprang up every month. In the Ukraine, 144,000 followers of the White Brotherhood vowed to commit mass suicide before the world ended on November 14, 1993. (Four days before "Judgment Day," forty followers battled with police in Kiev's St. Sofia Cathedral, which the sect regarded as "the closest point to the cosmos.") A faith healer called Anatoly Kashpirovsky drew television audiences of 300 million in Russia and Eastern Europe by persuading a woman to undergo major surgery with only his "healing powers" as an anesthetic. (She underwent the operation in agony.) And Mikhail Gorbachev welcomed the Unification Church leader Sun Myung Moon to the Kremlin with a full Russian kiss on the lips, and allowed Moonies to perform a ritual in a Kremlin cathedral. (The Russian Orthodox Church countered with another ritual there – namely, an exorcism.)

Shoko Asahara's plan to conquer Russia was hatched as early as 1990. But cult overtures to high communist officials came to nothing; perhaps Gorbachev had no room for another Asian guru in his life. Then, in late 1991, something happened that not even Asahara had predicted: the Union of Soviet Socialist Republics spectacularly collapsed. An abortive coup by communist hardliners led to

Gorbachev's downfall, and Boris Yeltsin was swept into office on a wave of popular support.

Within months, Aum had found an influential Russian backer among Yeltsin's circle called Oleg Ivanovich Lobov. As chairman of Russia's powerful Security Council, Lobov was one of the nation's top ten politicians, a heavily jowled man with dead eyes and the build of a retired prizefighter. He hailed from the Ural Mountains city of Sverdlovsk, where Yeltsin had first made his mark as local Communist Party chief.

Oleg Lobov's pet project was the Russia-Japan University. Established by presidential decree in 1991 with Lobov as its chief, the university acquired a grand columned building on Moscow's Petrovka Street, a stone's throw from the Bolshoi Theater. Whatever Lobov wanted for his university – a summer camp outside Moscow, a fleet of cars – Lobov got, and in double-quick time. But there seemed to be no immediate plan to hire teaching staff or admit any students. The university wanted to attract millions of investment dollars from big Japanese companies, but had its share of financial difficulties. A Moscow press acount alleged that one bluechip Japanese firm had already backed out of plans to refurbish the aging Petrovka building. The university needed money. Fortunately, a rich Japanese cult had plenty to spare.

Oleg Lobov's first meeting with a top Aum official took place in December 1991, according to a Japanese police report. Also present was Vladimir Muravyov, an ex-bureaucrat and vice-president of the Russia-Japan University. Then, in February 1992, during an official Russian delegation to Japan to seek investors, Lobov left an entire evening free from his tight schedule to meet Shoko Asahara at a Tokyo hotel. The details of the meeting are unknown, but a 1995 *Izvestia* report alleged that Lobov returned to Moscow with a guarantee to fund the university. Soon after, it was reported, Japanese investors would abandon their interest in Lobov's scheme. Rumors of the sect's involvement were the equivalent of professional leprosy.

In the following weeks, cult leaders shuttled back and forth between Mount Fuji and Moscow. Then, one month after the Lobov-Asahara summit, the invasion of Moscow began.

In 1812, Napoleon failed to capture Moscow with 700,000 troops. Shoko Asahara's Russian campaign 180 years later was rather more successful. And all it took was $14 million in cash.

Hundreds of thousands of dollars went into "some very

influential pockets who gave the sect the green light over the vast expanses of Russia," *Izvestia* reported. Aum spent huge amounts on hiring Olympiski Stadium and the Palace of Congresses. Then there was the cost of taking 300 people, including a guru with a taste for luxury, on a ten-day round-trip from Japan; chartering the Aeroflot flight alone cost nearly $250,000. The cult's first Moscow branch was established at the Russia-Japan University's upmarket Petrovka address, prompting media speculation that Aum might have poured as much as $5 million into the university's coffers.

Aum also threw money into a huge media campaign. In April, the state-run Radio Moscow began two daily broadcasts of *The Absolute Truth of the Holy Heaven*, a half-hour program later relayed to Japan via a transmitter in Vladivostok. The program featured Aum's curious mix of faith and physics, with Asahara explaining how cult beliefs accorded with Einstein's theory of relativity and Newton's laws of motion. There was also a section called "Song of the Week," composed and sung by Asahara – a sort of karaoke corner for gurus. By summer, the whole world could tune into Radio Aum Shinrikyo's short-wave broadcasts. Or, as the show's slogan urged, "Tune into the Truth."

For this service, Aum paid Radio Moscow over $700,000 a year, allowing the station to upgrade its equipment for the first time since the 1980 Olympic games. Thousands more dollars poured into Moscow's independent television network, 2x2, for a weekly half-hour prime-time slot for Aum's show, *Learning the Truth*.

The Russian Salvation Tour, as the name suggested, was billed by Aum as a spiritual mission. In fact, saving Russian souls mattered little to the cult's leaders. Far more important was forging contacts with Russian scientists. In Russia, as in Japan, Aum's core following was sought in the science and engineering classes of top universities.

Aum's timing was perfect. During Soviet times, scientists had been a pampered elite. They were the high priests of "scientific materialism," their achievements glorious examples of Soviet superiority over the West. Then communism died, and Russian science fell into decline. Many scientists fled low-paid jobs at cash-strapped institutions for lucrative posts in the West. Three researchers who remained dramatized their plight by locking themselves in an orang-utan cage at Moscow Zoo. A sign outside read: "*Homo sapiens* sub-species: scientific workers."

Morale in the student body was equally low. The year before Asahara's arrival in Moscow, the chemistry department at MGU could not find enough qualified students to fill its classes, and over 10 percent of its graduates left to study in the United States. Others found inventive ways to supplement their measly stipends. Eleven former honors students from three Russian universities had been arrested for synthesizing trimethylfentanyl, a narcotic more powerful than heroin.

Aum's welcome at MGU was repeated at the Moscow Institute of Engineering and Physics (MIFI), known worldwide for its advanced studies of nuclear physics. Asahara gave MIFI another generous donation and another lengthy sermon. The guru also sipped tea with MIFI's most famous son, Nikolai Basov, who shared the 1964 Nobel Prize for Physics with American scientists for his work on lasers. The two men reportedly discussed physics for thirty minutes, although Basov's secretary described the meeting as "sort of ceremonious." A photo of Asahara with the eminent physicist was later printed in the cult's Russian-language publicity material.

Shoko Asahara, once spurned by Tokyo University, was apparently now the toast of Russia's scientific community. "A religious person of a new category," gushed Alexander Caplan, MGU's head of neuro-physiology research, in a back-cover testimonial for Asahara's *The Bodhisattva Sutra.* In a cult leaflet, an MGU physicist writes of "collaborating in various scientific areas" with Aum, while a chief researcher at MIFI looked forward to "new scientific breakthroughs at the border of science and religion." In their preface to a Russian translation of another Aum book, two MGU professors explained how only Asahara's "kindness and mercy" could avert an environmental catastrophe early next century that would leave "barely a quarter of the current population alive on a polluted planet." Then the professors present "scientific proof" of past lives and reincarnation.

With several teachers already in their pocket, it was easy for the cult to attract students. Recruiters set up tables of colorful literature around Metro stations near MGU and MIFI, with strict orders to target the bright and the young. The vice president of MIFI refused a request to set up an "Aum club" on campus, but cult missionaries roamed freely through the institute's grounds, handing out pamphlets. Anyone interested in Aum classes completed a form asking which of twenty-four fields they wished to pursue in the future. The cult's priorities were clear: at the top of the list were physics, chemistry, and biology. Curiously, students were also asked which Metro line they used regularly, and which station they changed at.

Hundreds, then thousands thronged to the cult's classes on yoga and meditation. The cult opened another branch in northern Moscow near the soaring Ostankino TV Tower. Within a year, the membership in Russia outstripped Aum's 10,000-strong following in Japan. For cult leaders, here was proof of the universal appeal of their guru's teachings. Aum's classes were bustling, not with recruits called Kenji or Michiko, but with wide-eyed kids named Sergei, Yuri and Natasha.

With the cult able to show its guru meeting top politicians and scientists, parents were helpless to dissuade their children from joining a group they instinctively distrusted. "So many respectable people seemed to support the sect," said Zinaida Zakharova, the mother of an Aum monk. "What could we say to our children?"

Shoko Asahara left Moscow with a bulging photo album and a big smile. One man, however, stayed behind. His name was Kiyohide Hayakawa.

Many Aum members believed Hayakawa was the power behind the throne. In some ways his authority outstripped even that of the cult's scientists. By trade, he was a designer and civil engineer. By nature, he was an ambitious back-room operator who by the 1990s had earned Asahara's complete trust.

Hayakawa stood out among Aum's predominantly young flock. He was of an older generation, born in 1949 in Osaka. A leftist in his college days, he became active in the sixties student movement. After earning a master's degree in agricultural engineering, Hayakawa spent much of his early adult life developing golf courses and other sites for an engineering firm. An abiding fascination for science fiction led him to join Aum in 1986. Asahara took an immediate interest in the man, putting him in charge of Aum's operations in Japan's Kansai region. Hayakawa later proved his loyalty by helping strangle Taguchi and the Sakamotos to death.

A somber figure with graying temples, Hayakawa spoke in rapid Osaka dialect and hid an explosive temper behind keen negotiation skills. Within years, he was overseeing all the cult's land holdings and facilities. Asahara gave him the holy name "Tiropa" and declared, "Without Master Tiropa's efforts there would be no Aum Supreme Truth." The guru called Hayakawa "a Bodhisattva in his past life." Hayakawa's staff simply called him "Boss."

Hayakawa was never fanatical about Aum's spiritual message. But backed up by the cult's awesome buying power, he was dangerous in another way, as perhaps the most powerful leader next to the guru himself. One critic described Hayakawa's 1992 book *Principles of a Citizen's Utopia* as a "declaration of war" against Japan's constitution. Hayakawa was well aware of the guru's growing interest in weapons of mass destruction. Asahara had charged him with investigating their availability in Russia. With Armageddon coming, Aum needed every resource available.

Hayakawa was looking in the right place. Two months before Aum's triumphant arrival in Moscow, then CIA director Robert Gates had given disturbing testimony to a U.S. Senate committee which Hayakawa might well have read. Gates spoke of the proliferation of chemical and biological weapons, with special concern about the "brain drain" from former Soviet republics. "A modern pharmaceutical industry could produce biological warfare agents as easily as vaccines and antibiotics," he said. "The most worrisome problem is probably those individuals whose skills have no civilian counterpart, such as ... engineers specializing in weaponizing CW and BW agents."

To Kiyohide Hayakawa, Russia was much more than a recruitment ground. It was a former superpower which had researched some of the world's most advanced weapons systems. Now in post-Soviet chaos, Russia and its former dominions were a giant shopping center for scientific talent and military hardware. Aum was well placed to recruit Russian experts in weapons of mass destruction. It now had at least one follower at the I. V. Kurchatov Institute of Atomic Energy, Russia's oldest nuclear-weapons laboratory, and several more at the Mendeleyev Chemical Institute, where every chemistry graduate had the know-how and materials to synthesize World War II nerve gases.

Over the next three years, Hayakawa would make repeated trips to Moscow. The cult's operation there eventually boasted over 350 monks and nuns, the majority of them students from elite institutions – a Russian scientific monkhood dancing to the tune of a Japanese techno-shaman. And behind them would be Kiyohide Hayakawa, quietly criss-crossing the volatile former republics of the Soviet Union, the dark priest behind the guru's burgeoning dreams of world domination.

11

THE GOOD DOCTOR

The opening of the Aum Supreme Truth Hospital was a proud day for Shoko Asahara. The new health center, he announced, offered a "unique combination of Oriental and Western medicine, as well as knowledge brought back from higher dimensions." Here was a chance for Aum's growing medical staff to provide the public "ideal treatment" for the New Age. On call were nearly ten doctors, among them a gynecologist and a psychiatrist.

While Aum built an empire in Russia, its world back home continued to expand. This latest addition sat on a busy shopping street in northeast Tokyo. It would have been easy to miss the place – a second-floor clinic in a modest four-story building. But what went on behind its doors would shock Japan's medical community.

Like Aum itself, the hospital would become a chamber of horrors, a place not of enlightenment and life but of darkness and death. And the angel of death was the hospital's energetic director, Dr. Ikuo Hayashi.

Before joining Aum, Dr. Hayashi was a man both liked and respected by his many patients and colleagues. For years he had served as head of cardiopulmonary medicine at a government hospital just outside Tokyo, treating people with heart conditions and circulatory problems. Handsome and youthful-looking, the 44-year-old Hayashi sported an impressive pedigree in status-conscious Japan. He was the son of a Ministry of Health official, a graduate of Keio University's top-ranked medical school, and had studied at Mount Sinai Hospital in America.

Dr. Hayashi's odd behavior began with his accident, say colleagues. It was back in April 1988 when the doctor, exhausted, fell asleep at the wheel. His station wagon smashed into the car ahead, sending a mother and her nine-year-old daughter to the hospital for weeks. Horrified, Hayashi paid daily visits to the family, bringing the girl gifts.

At work, the nursing staff noted that Dr. Hayashi became frequently despondent. Soon after, he joined Aum. And that, they say, was when his treatment of patients grew increasingly bizarre. He told those under his care that their illnesses would never be cured through conventional means. Instead, he prescribed a range of treatments that included drinking quarts of hot water, swallowing string, and jumping.

As complaints piled up, the hospital's chief doctor called Hayashi to a meeting. Such treatments "were unthinkable by common sense," the director told him. Hayashi replied his techniques were widely used by Aum and their benefits were a proven fact.

"Don't bring religious belief into a national hospital," the director warned. "If you do, then you must leave."

Hayashi resigned. He later returned briefly to the hospital, but only to bring books on Aum to the staff. He followed up with phone calls, assuring the doctors and nurses that their children's grades would improve if they came to Aum training centers. Then, with his wife and two children, Hayashi moved into an Aum compound.

Shoko Asahara recognized what a prize he had in Dr. Hayashi and his wife Rira, an anesthesiologist. Both seemed true believers and were eager to put their skills at the service of the cult. They brought with them a knowledge of surgery, drugs, and disease. There was much that Aum could do with such talent.

There are many stories of what went on in Dr. Hayashi's hospital. Not everyone lived to tell them. While Aum claimed phenomenal success at curing people with terminal diseases, the cult's hospital became best known for its extraordinary death rate. According to the logs of a Tokyo ambulance service, the company hauled away nine bodies from the small clinic during an eighteen-month period starting September 1993. Four calls came during a two-month period alone. "We got several calls from regular-size hospitals with around 200 beds," said a spokesman for the ambulance service. "But for a place with only nine beds, the number is shocking."

The cult responded that the high death rate was due to the number of terminally ill patients the clinic cared for. But even Dr. Hayashi seemed usure. "We heaped caution upon caution to care for the entire system," he wrote in an Aum publication. "Nonetheless, so many people just kept dying ... We must recognize that some mysterious force was at work." That mysterious force apparently not only killed people, but first confined them, extorted huge sums, and then transferred their estates to Aum. Consider the case of Mr. Sato.

Mr. Sato (a pseudonym), sixty-three, was a small shopkeeper and resident of Tokyo. Sixteen years earlier a stroke had rendered him speechless, leaving him to communicate only by paper and pen. By December 1991, he was frail and needed full-time medical care. The family admitted him to a local hospital, but a month later the man's daughter received an unexpected call from Aum.

Sato's daughter was not an Aum believer, but she had met cult members while pursuing religious studies at Tokyo University. Somehow they had learned of her father's fate.

"Your father will be killed by an overdose of drugs if he stays at that hospital," an Aum follower pleaded with her. "Do you want him to die?" The person urged her to move her father to Aum's new hospital, where the quality of care would be infinitely better.

The daughter agreed at least to visit the clinic. There she met Dr. Hayashi, who spoke impressively of the wonders offered by Aum health care. The monthly fee, moreover, would be only $1,600. And there was no need for them to be Aum members.

After the visit, the hospital staff were strangely persistent. Different people would call, urging the family to bring Sato to the Aum clinic. Then, on January 14, Dr. Hayashi and several staff arrived unannounced at the Sato house, where the father was now resting. "We'll help you move your father to the Aum clinic," he said.

The family was surprised but, impressed by Hayashi's sincerity, they eventually agreed. As Hayashi and the others drove away with their father, the family hoped for the best.

Once inside the clinic, Sato was led to a narrow room packed with eight beds, overseen by a large portrait of Asahara smiling benignly. Aum's "astral music" echoed loudly through the place. In the hallway were piles of medicinal herbs. Woeful-looking patients filled the beds, their heads shaved. Around their necks hung amulets – lucky charms. Doctors and nurses strode through the hallways with Aum's electrode caps on their heads.

The clinic's interior looked shabby. Sato's wife was disgusted to see cockroaches scurry along the floors. When she mentioned this to Dr. Hayashi, he replied airily, "Deeply religious people like ourselves aren't allowed to kill any creatures." After a few days of this, Hayashi himself no longer inspired much confidence. His doctor's coat was filthy, covered with black stains. The nurses were even worse. They wore casual clothes and displayed a surprising ignorance of basic hygiene. The contents of bedpans were poured down the same sinks where patients washed their hands and faces.

The next surprise for the family was the demand to join Aum. Hayashi must have made a mistake, they were told: only believers were allowed to become patients. Sato was forced to join the cult. When the family came to visit, a doctor would keep them first for a thirty-minute lecture on Aum. The staff then discouraged them from visiting at all. "Long visits reduce the patient's energy," the doctors said. The meetings were soon reduced to five minutes, and videotaped by hospital staff.

In May 1992, Sato's "rehabilitation program" began. Doctors prescribed that their patient drink "honeydew water," a beverage no doubt unique to Aum medical science. The price: $80 per cup. They also strongly advised "thermotherapy," which meant submerging the already weakened Sato in a bath of 117 degrees Fahrenheit. This was to "extract toxic elements" from the body. The price this time: $8,000. When Sato refused, citing the cost, hospital staff insisted he sell his store and repeatedly phoned the family asking for money.

Reluctantly, the family agreed to pay for the treatment in installments. On their next visit, they were shocked to find their father covered with burns: Aum's "thermotherapy" had scalded much of his upper body.

Not surprisingly, Sato's health did not improve. Meanwhile, the staff exerted steady pressure on him to make donations to Aum. One day a nurse asked him – casually, it seemed – if he owned any real estate. Yes, he replied, the family owned a Tokyo apartment worth $800,000. Soon, the staff began telling Sato he would get better only if he donated the apartment to the cult. It was all part of Aum's teachings, they explained. To be healthy, one needed to shed bad karma, and the way to do that was by donating to the only organization that preached supreme truth.

By this time, Sato's family had grown alarmed and asked that the father be discharged. But Aum's medical staff were insistent. "The treatment is starting to work," argued one Aum doctor. "What is more important to you – your father or money? Why not sell the apartment and spend it on his treatment?"

Sato was no longer allowed to leave the hospital, and his family were rarely let in to visit. Isolated, constantly pressured to donate, and scared of more hot-water treatments, he finally offered the cult half his real estate. That wasn't good enough, he was told. If you want a complete cure, you must give it all.

Soon after this exchange, a patient in an adjoining room died. For a full day his body remained on the bed. Strangely, the staff let it lie there for another day. Then another. For five days the dead man stayed where he had died. As the stench of the corpse filtered into Sato's room, he began to fear for his life. At the end of August 1992, the embattled Sato finally gave in and donated his property to the cult.

A few weeks later, Sato was told to practice using his *hanko* – the round seals that Japanese use as signatures – in what doctors called yet another act of "rehabilitation." Aum apparently used the imprints to make a copy, and took the opportunity also to make a few changes in Sato's life. First, they moved his official residence to the hospital's address. Next, they stamped his signature on papers signing over his apartment to Aum. That same month, Aum filed divorce papers for Sato and his wife at Tokyo District Court, an attempt, the family believes, to cut them out of his will. When the family discovered that Aum now owned their one piece of real estate, that at last was enough. In early March, Sato's son arrived at the hospital with several well-built friends and forcibly removed the father. It had been a fourteen-month ordeal.

The family would later sue Aum. The cult not only denied the allegations of forced donations, confinement, and limited visits; they countersued the family for libel. As so often when Aum was involved, somehow the Japanese authorities never got around to investigating the incident.

So pleased was Asahara with the money flowing in from patients that Hayashi soon became part of the guru's inner circle. The doctor was placed in charge of more than a dozen physicians and nurses, as well as pharmacists and health aides. Aside from raising funds and making the occasional diagnosis, Aum's medical corps offered another, increasingly popular service to the cult.

By 1993, perhaps earlier, Aum had begun to experiment with mind-altering drugs. The cult's medical staff opened their pharmacies to Asahara, who directed they be used to enhance the growing number of initiation rites. Among the drugs of choice were tranquilizers and anesthetics.

The favorite from the Aum pharmacy appears to have been sodium thiopental, a barbiturate perhaps better known as truth serum. At 100 milligrams the drug acts as a sedative; double the dose, and the effect is hypnotic. In surgery, the fast-acting drug is used to induce sleep as part of general anesthesia. Used in hypnosis, it causes the patient to pass through a short period of unconsciousness and then lapse into a trancelike state. The heart rate and breathing slow, and for about twenty minutes the subconscious is accessible. The effect can be prolonged with larger doses.

With the help of thiopental, Aum created new rituals, including an initiation for those unsure about joining the cult. Before going through the rite, they now had to sign a release, stating, "I will commit myself to any treatment by Guru Asahara if I go into a coma for reasons such as an accident."

Then initiates were told to strip and given a diaper to wear. Some received the drug by injection, others in a glass they were to drink while chanting Buddhist sutras. The guru then placed his hands on those present to "fill them with religious energy." As they fell into a stupor, Aum's priests would preach to them, uttering phrases like "join the priesthood" or "convert your spouse." Others were reportedly made to sign documents turning over their wealth to the cult.

Another rite which made use of thiopental was the Christ Initiation. One woman, a young nurse, described her experience:

> I was told to undress and was handed an unusual robe and a diaper to wear . . . Master Asahara handed me a drink with a faint color, and I was moved to a tiny room . . . I felt very sick and lost sense of time. Everything around me was spinning. I felt as if I could not remember who I was. A door happened to be open and there was nobody watching me, so I went through it. However much I walked, I felt as if I were flying and felt very comfortable. Then I ran to a mountain . .
>
> On regaining consciousness, my legs and arms were bound with rope and I was in a dark room. Gradually, a vision like hell came to me. I began to see scenes of hungry demons. I thought that the guru's teachings must be right and true. Then I began to hear the guru's mantra, then two sets of the mantra at once. I felt I must do better in Aum.

Then came the hot-water treatment. Like Mr. Sato, the nurse was lowered into a scorching tub. Afterward, she was made to drink six pints of lemon juice and given a vitamin pill and drugs to make her release urine and bile.

The nurse later helped with other initiations. "Some believers were given I/Vs afterwards, to stop dehydration," she said. "The drugs have an aftereffect – they sometimes caused fever. Many suffered from this. When their temperature reached over 100 degrees Farenheit we poured ethanol on them and used a fan to cleanse the body."

The psychoactive drugs opened new vistas for the cult, boosting recruitment along with the number of "mystical" encounters by members. Asahara wanted more, and his chemists were eager to please. They had come across a remarkable book from America which offered a road map into this new world: *Recreational Drugs* by "Professor Buzz." It was an underground cookbook that detailed how to manufacture everything from hallucinogens to methamphetamine and PCP. Aum was about to rediscover the Sixties, and put its chemical firepower in the service of Shoko Asahara.

12

CLEAR STREAM TEMPLE

While Aum's doctors plunged their patients into scalding water and cult chemists studied how to make LSD, Shoko Asahara's mind wandered into uncharted lands. Armageddon, once a fantasy with the guru, had now become an obsession.

Early in 1993, Asahara had been gripped by another terrible vision. For months, the day of apocalypse had grown closer and closer – 2002, 2000, 1999. Now Asahara's tortured mind brought the world's end as near as 1996. That, he promised, was when civilization would begin its descent into apocalyptic fire. The guru warned followers of a terrible genocide, unleashed upon Japan by an unexpected enemy: the United States. Asahara predicted the Americans would attack the Japanese, sinking the islands into the sea and igniting a world war:

> From now until the year 2000, a series of violent phenomena filled with fears that are too difficult to describe will occur [Asahara predicted]. Japan will turn into wasteland as a result of a nuclear-weapons attack. This will occur from 1996 through January 1998. An alliance centering on the United States will attack Japan. In large cities in Japan, only one-tenth of the population will be able to survive. Nine out of ten people will die.

Knowing that Aum's spiritual power posed a threat to their plans, the Americans had already begun attacking Aum directly, the guru warned. Every day, their aircraft now flew over the Mount Fuji compound, spraying Aum with biochemical weapons. Not just jets, but cleverly disguised prop planes and helicopters. The Japanese military was behind the attacks as well. The constant flights explained the large number of illnesses at Aum centers, the guru added, and his medical staff readily agreed.

By spring of that year, Asahara had ordered sweeping changes within the cult. Aum was woefully unprepared, he proclaimed, for the great disasters at hand. His disciples must arm themselves for the coming darkness. "We need a lot of weapons to prevent Armageddon," Asahara told those around him. "And we must prepare them quickly."

The warnings of imminent war sharpened an already keen sense of paranoia and isolation within the cult. Over one thousand members now lived on Aum compounds, cut off from their families and the outside world. Police raids, a critical press, angry neighbors and parents all contributed to the feelings of persecution and alarm. Aum's teachings, meanwhile, had grown more dogmatic, more absolute, drilling into its subjects the idea of impending doom. To followers who toiled long days on little sleep and meager diets, it must indeed have seemed as if civilization might stop.

Like Isaac Asimov's scientists in *Foundation*, Asahara preached that the only way to survive was to create an alternative society, a secret order of beings armed with superior intellect, state-of-the-art technology and knowledge of the future. He then called his closest advisers together: Murai, the astrophysicist; Hayakawa, his chief engineer; Nakagawa, the physician; Endo, the biologist; Tsuchiya, the chemist. It was time, he told them, to prepare for the worst. We must transform Aum into a military colossus.

Until now, Aum's approach to Armageddon had been mostly haphazard. Its scientists had tried to unleash a biological toxin with no success, and talked loosely of mass destruction. But now all that was to change. Asahara ordered a secret, far-reaching plan for militarization, putting into play the now formidable resources of his cult. Aum's young researchers held passionate discussions about what weapons to pursue. Biological agents and nerve gases were the favorite of some; others argued for lasers, particle beams, and nuclear bombs. Some stressed the need for conventional firearms and explosives.

Aum would pursue them all.

Asahara tapped Murai, his chief scientist, to oversee the effort. Hayakawa was made responsible for building an infrastructure: the factories, the laboratories, the weapons that would support Aum's army. Endo, still at work in his biolab, assured the guru that technicians were already culturing new agents that would prove extremely effective. Tsuchiya, with his background in organic chemistry, was given his own lab to develop chemical weapons. He had earlier suggested that a Nazi nerve gas called sarin might prove worthwhile. It was relatively easy to produce, he'd read, and could kill vast numbers.

Asahara liked what he heard. Murai's scientists drew up a production plan for the gas and designed a plant for mass production. Hayakawa's engineers were to build it right there at the Mount Fuji complex. Meanwhile, research into other chemical agents would continue.

Hayakawa was also to help in procuring conventional weapons: firearms, explosives, even tanks and planes. Murai himself would handle development of nuclear, laser, and microwave technology. At the same time, plans were made to raise an army. Aum members were to receive military training, led by army veterans who had joined the cult. A special commando unit was also formed, responsible for security and intelligence. And recruitment was accelerated, with a focus on grabbing scientists, hi-tech workers, and members of the Self-Defense Force – Japan's military.

Although it seemed far-fetched, the talents of Aum's scientists and engineers were not to be underestimated. Nor could their motivation. As the world well knows, Japanese tend to work extremely hard. Japan is, perhaps, the only country that officially recognizes a disease called *karoshi*, or death by overwork. This was the last place the world wanted a hundred young, highly motivated, out-of-control scientists arming for the end of the world.

"The Third World War will absolutely happen," Asahara assured his disciples. "I bet my religious life on it."

Okamura Ironworks had reached the end. Wracked by recession and mired in debt, the precision machinery company limped along, hoping for a friendly takeover. Its president, distraught at the company's course, had sought comfort in a new religion called Aum Supreme Truth.

The crafty recruiters at Aum saw their chance. The president was persuaded to sell the company to Aum for less than $2 million – a bargain, considering the firm's large assets. In return, the cult received a vast plant of computer-operated machining tools, one hundred workers, and a debt of some $16 million. A beaming Asahara announced that Aum would rebuild the company by producing small incinerators.

Of course Asahara had no such intention. Like a takeover by the Mob, Aum would loot the company and then leave town. But the cult wanted much more than fast profits out of the deal. With the machinery at Okamura, they could fashion the tools of Armageddon.

As Aum's management team moved in, workers at the plant noticed something was wrong almost immediately. Photos of the overweight guru went up around the factory. Aum's "astral music" played incessantly over the loudspeakers. A subsidiary's name was changed from Okamura High-Machinery Parts to Bajira Anutara Hita Abiviti Precision Machinery Company. Employees were encouraged to meditate and join Aum Supreme Truth.

As workers began to quit, they were replaced by young Aum believers wearing electrode caps. Within weeks, 90 percent of the original workforce was gone. Soon the company's banks were deserting it too, alarmed by nearly $4 million of new debt – money the firm apparently had given Aum as "donations."

One month after becoming president, Asahara abruptly resigned and Okamura Ironworks went bankrupt. Before other creditors even heard the news, Aum had hauled off almost a hundred of the firm's best machining tools, worth nearly $1 million. They were trucked across Japan to a vast warehouse about 20 miles from Aum's Mount Fuji headquarters. There, the cult set up its most ambitious project yet: Clear Stream Temple, headquarters for the new Supreme Truth Research Institute of Science and Technology – or, as the cultists simply called it, Supreme Science.

The building was massive, a sprawling crescent-shaped structure of high walls wedged into a mountainside along a dry riverbed. Two basement levels and a ground floor combined to give the cult some 47,000 square feet of space, enough room for, say, an arms factory. With the metal-working machines from Okamura, dozens of pneumatic lathes and borers now stood on the floor, computer-controlled and ready for mass production. Small furnaces filled another part of the plant, as did offices and research labs. The plant brought Aum's capability to an entirely new level. With the equipment in hand, the cult could now do its own metallurgy, machinery design, and manufacture.

As far as the prefectural government knew, Aum was operating an electrical assembly plant, putting together air cleaners, electrode caps, and other gadgets. While the cult did in fact produce these, they were not the primary focus of the factory. The Supreme Science Institute became headquarters for Aum's scientific brains trust, its research center and fabrication plant. When the factory started operation in the spring of 1993, it began turning out parts for the various laboratories, for the giant nerve-gas plant being built, and for various experiments in weapons technology. But the center of attention at the plant was Hayakawa and Murai's scheme to mass produce the AK-74.

The AK-74 is the standard-issue automatic rifle for the Russian Army: gas-operated, 30-round magazine, rate of fire 600 rounds per minute, successor to the AK-47, the favored assault rifle of armies and guerrilla groups around the world. This was the weapon with which Aum's leadership would arm its soldiers. Asahara had dispatched high-ranking cult members to Russia to obtain blueprints of the gun and smuggle them back to Japan.

The plan was remarkably ambitious: by 1995, Aum hoped to produce 1,000 rifles and 1 million bullets – enough to arm every man, woman and child living in a cult compound. Even more striking, this was to take place in a land that prides itself on 350 years of strict gun control. The nation's few underground gunsmiths, working for the Japanese Mob, produce no more than a few pistols per month. Yet Aum meant to build 1,000 assault rifles just a morning's drive from Tokyo.

There was much to do. The cult's computer hands worked on programming the equipment for mass production. Orders went out for steel, lubricating oil, and high-pressure gas. Aum engineers soon realized that the Okamura machine tools, while helpful, were not enough. Over the next year, the cult spent nearly a million dollars on some thirty different machines – large, sophisticated contraptions that changed tools automatically and could handle a true production line.

As the Clear Stream factory filled with equipment, work began on producing smaller parts, like triggers, and on building a prototype rifle. Aum technicians also turned out hundreds of knives with 4.5 inch blades. Within a year, the plant's workforce would reach nearly a hundred, and two support factories were set up at the Mount Fuji complex. The cost soon topped $2 million, then $5 million; eventually it reached nearly $10 million. Shoko Asahara was determined to build an arsenal for the apocalypse.

How to finance Armageddon? The sum needed to militarize Aum was enormous. The $10 million for the AK-74s was but one weapons program. As much as half a million dollars had already been spent equipping Endo's biolabs. And millions more were needed to produce nerve gas, not to mention the vast sums required for nuclear and laser research.

While hardly the Pentagon, Aum's resources were considerable. The careful marketing, the myriad scams, the life savings of over 1,000 monks and nuns – all this had filled Aum coffers and pushed annual income into tens of millions of dollars. By 1993, the money and employees under Asahara's control were large enough to list it on the Tokyo Stock Exchange. Aum Supreme Truth had become a great money-making machine.

There was no great secret to the cult's success. Aum businesses held two obvious advantages over other companies. First, as a religious organization, the cult received generous tax breaks on its earnings and assets. Unlike most Japanese religions, which kept their businesses tied closely to religion, such as schools and publications, Aum was intent on building a corporate empire. Second, most of its employees worked almost for free, a remarkable edge in high-salary Japan. Aum boasted hundreds of on-site employees – its monks and nuns – who toiled for only room and board plus some $150 per month. More than a thousand others worked for cult companies at meager wages, generously tithing much of their income back to Aum. And the companies themselves made huge donations to Aum, ensuring their own books stayed in the red.

Flush with cash, Aum borrowed a basic strategy from Japan, Inc. The cult organized itself as a *keiretsu*, or corporate family. An investigation by the Japanese edition of *Forbes* magazine found that by 1995, Aum had amassed a network of at least thirty-seven companies. Three firms comprised the core group of Asahara's empire: Aum, Inc., Mahaposya, and the Aum Hospital. A second group was made up of front companies – dummy corporations secretly controlled by the cult. The magazine tracked down twenty-one of these outfits in Japan, but there were many more overseas. A third group in the Aum family consisted of "associate" companies; these typically were firms owned independently by followers, who helped with cult business from time to time. The reporters at *Forbes* came away impressed. "There are two forces supporting Aum," the magazine concluded. "Madness and business."

Of the core companies, it was Mahaposya (Sanskrit for Great Prosperity) that ranked as the cult's largest corporate profit center. It was founded in January 1992, and the company's incorporation papers offered a revealing look at Aum's priorities. Mahaposya's purpose, the papers say, was to import, export and sell the following: metals and machinery; computers; chemicals; fertilizer and feed; drugs and medical equipment; agricultural products, salt, cigarettes and alcohol; textiles and fabrics; rubber, leather, pulp, and paper; construction materials; coal, oil, and other fuel products; animals and plants; jewelry and gems.

In addition, Mahaposya was registered to handle twenty other kinds of business: storage, insurance, transportation, sale of used goods, fishing, farming, ranching, lumbering, hotel management and travel, real estate, leasing, architecture, construction, labor consulting, management consulting, machinery design, stock-brokering, advertising, and restaurant operation.

In short, Mahaposya was prepared to manage every facet of Aum, and begin the task of building an alternative society.

In keeping with Aum's hi-tech bent, the company opened a chain of cut-rate computer shops in 1993. Young salesmen in gaudy satin jackets shouted at the top of their lungs at passers-by, touting IBM-compatible PCs with the latest features. By the end of that year, the company had 300 employees, opened a restaurant chain and a supermarket, and claimed annual sales of nearly $23 million.

Mahaposya expanded on-line as well. Two computer networks opened, Aum Supreme Truth Net and Mahaposya Net, which lured young techies into the world of Aum. Also, on NiftyServe, Japan's largest on-line service, Aum targeted a discussion group called the Spiritual Corner. Members posted transcripts of cult programs from Moscow Radio and thinly disguised pitches to join the group. Mahaposya even produced computer games based on cult teachings, targeted at high-school students. One program claimed that users would "master high-school level math in just one-and-a-half months." The software employs a story format, pulling the user through various math questions while fighting off enemies. The final sequence, dubbed "the last battle," ends with a scene of the world after Armageddon, followed by Buddhist imagery and a pitch to join Aum.

As Aum businesses continued to grow, the cult diversified further. New ventures were launched into construction and contracting, beauty salons and fitness clubs, as well as coffee shops, fortune-telling, and a telephone dating club.

Aum was not your average business, as a Tokyo advertising company learned in 1992 when scheduled for a visit by Asahara. The ad execs watched in amazement as the guru's followers hauled an oversized chair into their ninth-floor office. Asahara arrived in flowing robes, sat down, and assumed the lotus position. So tall was the chair that he stared down at the others with his half-blind eyes. "There is no better company than ours," he told them, and then proceeded to order $120,000 worth of ads.

Virtually all cult businesses doubled as recruiting fronts. Mahaposya's computer staff made home visits for instruction, but spent most of their time convincing buyers to join Aum. Those unable to pay off their financing were offered jobs at the company, only to find they were working for Shoko Asahara.

The recruiting was fundamental to Aum's success, for no source was more lucrative than the cult's own membership. Rich patrons donated vast tracts of property worth millions of dollars. One respected weekly estimated the cult gained $140 million from the life savings of its core members, and brought in $10 million per year.

With so much money at stake, it was no surprise that the guru flew into a rage when recruitment stalled. To ensure a growing membership, the cult created ever more seductive techniques to attract new recruits. An Aum guidebook directed followers to check for young singles in their apartment buildings and learn about their work, lifestyle, and income, even if it meant following them around. Prime targets were nerds, dropouts, the lonely, and the financially troubled. Special attention went to students, who brought energy and sometimes their entire families into the cult. In 1992, Aum paid nearly $10,000 for a computer database with the names, addresses, and universities of some 30,000 students scheduled to graduate the following spring. At the same time, the cult sponsored a lecture series on campuses across Japan, and set up companies designed to attract promising recruits. There was a counseling center in which bright students were "hired" to work with problem kids. Then there were translation centers offering part-time jobs to language students to translate Buddhist texts from English to Japanese. Another was a baby-sitting company. "We want cheerful, eager people who like kids," said the flyers tacked up at local colleges.

Land prices had plunged to half their value of two years before, prompting Aum to plow more money into real estate. New retreats and training centers opened, while the Mount Fuji headquarters added more land and more buildings. Aum became the owner of property at some 280 sites across Japan, with more overseas. Also under the cult's control were two yachts and a fleet of vehicles that included the guru's Mercedes and Rolls-Royce. Remarkably, the cult seems to have managed this without ever borrowing. All these assets were either donated or paid for with cash.

Shoko Asahara had traveled far since his days peddling quack cures in Tokyo hotels. By the mid-1990s, his cult was well on its way to holdings worth some $200 million – and possibly much more. Like many privately held companies, Aum officials guarded their financial data jealously. But in 1995, one of them put a figure on the organization's total assets. Aum, he boasted, was now a billion-dollar enterprise.

Supported by its sprawling financial empire, Aum's push into militarization moved at frightening speed. But while the money and the weapons were invaluable, what the cult ultimately needed was people – a spiritual army that would rally to the guru. If Aum were to be the savior of humanity, millions needed to flock to Asahara's embrace. Yet the number of Aum believers remained relatively small. "With the world ending, we felt it imperative to expand the cult's influence," said one senior member. The way to do that, ironically, was to start killing people.

Asahara and his top lieutenants still hoped to stage a public calamity that would prove the guru's prophecy of doom. Three years had passed since the failed botulism attack on the Diet. Since then, Aum had spent vast sums on new equipment and recruited scores of young scientists. Asahara felt confident at last that he now held the means to wake the people violently from their dreary sleep. And as the summer of 1993 approached, the guru saw the perfect opportunity to strike: the royal wedding of Japan's crown prince.

13

ANTHRAX

It was Japan's marriage of the decade, an imperial wedding of the crown prince and his beautiful bride. For years Prince Naruhito had searched for the right woman. Now, at thirty-three, he had found her at last in Masako Owada, the daughter of a diplomat. With an economics degree from Harvard and a law degree from Tokyo University, Masako was a bright young star at the Foreign Ministry.

Preparations for the wedding had all of Japan abuzz. The media speculated on whether Masako the career woman could adapt to the orthodox traditions of the imperial family. Foreign diplomats and VIPs vied for invitations to the great event, set to take place on June 9, 1993.

Shoko Asahara was not on the invitation list. However, the guru had decided that Aum should make its presence felt.

The cult's own plans for the imperial wedding had begun months earlier. Determined to stage a calamitous event, Asahara had first proposed an assault on Japan's most famous family. "Let's develop a laser weapon and attack the Imperial Palace," he suggested to his staff. If the attack were timed to a public event, he said, Aum could vaporize the Emperor and all the corrupt politicians that rule over Japan.

Asahara's advisers had come to expect outrageous comments from the guru, but this one surprised even his closest followers. Everyone, that is, except for Murai, his chief scientist. Murai calmly told the guru that development of a high-powered laser would take many months, but the cult had made great progress on much simpler, more deadly technologies. Endo, for example, had seen promising results in his labs, and was now sure he had not one biological killer, but two.

The cult began to plan. As imaginations spun out of control, Asahara dreamed of staging a coup d'état. While the rest of Japan focused on the royal wedding, Aum commandos would seize control of the military and launch simultaneous attacks on the Imperial Palace, the Diet and the Prime Minister's residence. The plan got so far that cultists looked at renting office space near the palace and central government.

Yet Aum was not ready for such an ambitious assault. The cult lacked the weapons, the personnel, and equipment – though that would change, Asahara promised. For now, the guru scaled back the battle plans to something much easier: a second attempt to spray botulinus toxin through central Tokyo. Following the attack, Asahara was prepared to hold a press conference, pinning the blame on the U.S. military.

Again cult engineers rigged up a vehicle with a special spraying device. Again a solution of neurotoxin was painstakingly loaded into the car. This time the guru himself went along for the ride. It must have been a bizarre scene. As Japan geared up for its royal wedding, the members of a Japanese doomsday cult sprayed their way across Tokyo, hoping to paralyze the city with an epidemic of botulism.

Halfway through the operation, Asahara panicked. Worried that toxin was seeping into the car, the guru ordered the driver to halt and jumped out. Dumbfounded and worried, the other cultists continued on their way. Fortunately for them, Endo still had not figured out how to kill with biological agents. Again the mission failed. The Crown Prince and his bride were married, and life in Tokyo went on as usual.

Endo was beside himself. He assured Asahara that his next attempt would not fail. In fact, he invited the guru to a personal tour of Aum's latest biolab. He would demonstrate the cult's other biological weapon in person.

A biohazard mask hugged the stocky head of Shoko Asahara, bunching the guru's bristly beard into a ball. Asahara's dim eyes focused on rows of test tubes, flasks, and beakers. Microscopes stood on the counters, flanked by incubators and refrigerator units. Piled in the back were cans of peptone, a protein used for culturing bacteria.

It was late June 1993. Three weeks had passed since the imperial wedding. Aum's highest-ranking officers had gathered on the top floor of an eight-story building the cult owned in eastern Tokyo, touring their latest biolab. Along with Asahara were Murai, Endo, Hayakawa, and others.

The facility had taken months to build, and Asahara must have been impressed. The laboratory emptied into a hermetically sealed

BOTULIWUS TOXIN

preparation room, which in turn opened to the roof. There, on the rooftop, stood what looked to be a large cooling tower. In reality it was an industrial sprayer, fitted with a powerful fan.

Endo had failed to solve the riddle of how to spread botulism. But the enterprising biochemist now had something new to offer: anthrax.

Bacillus anthracis, the scientists call it. The Bible calls it the Fifth Plague, the curse of blight which fell upon the hapless Egyptians in the Book of Exodus. It is a highly infectious, persistent disease that can rapidly wipe out entire herds of sheep and cattle. Although not contagious among people, the bacteria can spread from animals to humans, making it a favorite of biological arsenals around the world.

The consequences of anthrax infection are horrible. Three to five days after inhaling the spores, the victim feels the onset of what seems a mild cold. That, however, quickly gives way to a powerful flu with vomiting, chills, and high fever. The body then erupts with massive, excruciating blisters, turning the skin black and leathery.

As the infection builds, fever continues to rise and the lungs fill with fluid. Breathing becomes labored, then almost impossible. Brain tissue swells and bleeds, as parts of the body turn blue from lack of oxygen. The victim goes into shock and coma, and then, mercifully, finds death.

A 1979 explosion at a Soviet biological warfare facility in Sverdlovsk, a city of 1.2 million, released a cloud of anthrax, spreading the disease to at least 96 people; of those, 64 died, a kill rate of 67 percent. The Office of Technology Assessment, an arm of the U.S. Congress, estimated that a single warhead of anthrax spores released in Washington D.C., could kill 30,000 to 100,000 people. A small, private plane, loaded with 220 pounds of the stuff, could fly over the city and leave an invisible mist that might kill a million.

Back in the early 1940s, the British, anxious for a new weapon against the Nazis, released anthrax spores on Gruinard Island, a scenic spot off the northwest coast of Scotland. The local sheep died quickly enough, but the anthrax never went away – and that appears to be the main problem with using the disease as a weapon. Anthrax spores are remarkably durable. They can stay alive in the soil for decades until the right conditions for incubation present themselves.

Gruinard remained uninhabitable for fully forty-five years, until the British government stripped the land with defoliants and sprayed formaldehyde and seawater to destroy the spores. Just how Aum's scientists thought they might decontaminate Tokyo is unknown.

ANTHRAX   *

For four days, toxic steam poured from the tower on top of Aum's building in Tokyo. Cult scientists in chemical suits had revved up a steam generator and poured in their solution of anthrax spores. Next they turned on the sprayer and fan, and waited.

About this time, residents began complaining of a foul smell descending on the neighborhood. Small birds died, plants wilted, and pets grew sick. Neighbors lost their appetite. When the steam settled on pedestrians or cars, it left stains and a powerful stench. "When we smelled the horrible odor, some people who had survived World War II said it was the smell of burning flesh," one neighbor told the press.

Residents complained bitterly to the local ward office, and inspectors came by the Aum building to ask questions, but got few answers. Cult members refused even to let them inside. Shoko Asahara later told residents the smell was from a mixture of soybean oil and perfume (Chanel No.5) the cult had burned to purify the building. Officials declined to press matters, and the incident was soon forgotten. Aum, yet again, had been let off the hook. Fortunately, Tokyo had been spared as well.

Despite complaints locally of sickness, no reported cases of anthrax hit the city that summer. Tokyo doctors might well have misdiagnosed the less deadly, skin-borne version of the disease. It seems unlikely, though, that they would have missed the swelling and high death rate that accompanies its more severe pulmonary form. On discovering Aum's handiwork, Japanese officials would later do little follow-up work to gauge possible effects. Most disturbing, perhaps, is that Aum may not have properly incubated the spores prior to release. That means they could still be out there, waiting for the right conditions to become active.

For Seiichi Endo, however, it was the third time his team had failed to create a medical emergency. He promised the guru they would redouble their efforts. Already there were other biological agents in the lab, he said, some quite promising. He had obtained the spores of a poisonous mushroom, for example. He also now had cultures of highly contagious Q fever. And then there was the Ebola virus.

Ebola. The word struck fear into the hearts of doctors and nurses across central Africa. An incurable hemorrhagic fever, the virus burns through human beings with alarming speed, driving blood and guts from every orifice of its victims' ravaged bodies. Medical experts first isolated the disease in 1980 after watching it kill nine out of ten infected villagers in Zaire. The most deadly of the strains were

EBOLA VIRUS-dubbed Ebola, after the Ebola River which flowed alongside villages where it struck. Some specialists worry that the virus, like AIDS, is part of a new assault by Mother Nature on an overpopulated planet.

The scientists at Aum had thought of Ebola even before Asahara's call to arms. In 1992, the disease had made headlines in Japan. An alarmed Tokyo press reported that a Japanese traveler to Zaire might have contracted the virus. Suffering from a high fever and bleeding, he had died shortly after his return. Four months later, Shoko Asahara and more than forty Aum missionaries were on a plane, bound for Zaire on an "African Salvation Tour."

The young Japanese arrived with doctors, nurses, and wallets full of cash. "Our purpose was much more immediate than the trips to Sri Lanka or Russia," said an article in *Enjoy Happiness*, a cult magazine. "We were trying to save African lives from sickness and hunger." Aum's medical staff, however, appeared interested in more than a simple relief mission. Asahara and company visited six hospitals, three of which had reportedly dealt with Ebola patients in the past – and might still have had cultures of the virus.

Little is known of what transpired during the visit. What is known, however, is that Aum Supreme Truth cared little for humanitarian missions. What they did care for – a great deal – were agents of death and destruction. And in Ebola existed a weapon of unparalleled force.

Did Aum obtain the Ebola virus? That remains unclear. One sensational Japanese weekly claimed it was true. "We were cultivating Ebola, but it needed to be studied more," the magazine quoted an Aum member as saying. "It can't be used practically yet."

Endo's research into biological agents required a major investment in microorganisms, protective gear, and lab equipment. But his project was relatively cheap compared to the other work at hand. To synthesize nerve gases, Aum scientists required dozens of different chemicals and state-of-the-art equipment. The explosives research, too, required a major effort at procurement, as did the science staff's growing appetite for pharmaceuticals.

For this, Aum created an array of front companies, outfits with names like Shimomura Chemical, Bell Epoch, and Refined Optical Equipment. Posing as legitimate chemical and medical supply firms, these companies went on a buying spree that brought to the cult an extraordinary range of chemicals and hi-tech equipment. As director of at least two of these dummy companies, Aum installed twenty-four-year-old Shigeyuki Hasegawa, who seems to have switched names as often as he did letterhead. While gaining his degree in pharmacology, Hasegawa became skilled at synthesizing chemicals. When certain compounds were unavailable, he would simply break them down into their components and order the chemicals separately.

Aum's unlicensed warehouses soon filled with twenty-two-pound sacks of sodium fluoride, steel drums of phosphorus trichloride, and hundreds of gallons of isopropyl alcohol – all key ingredients for manufacturing the nerve gas sarin. For those intent on drug production, there was ergotamine for LSD and phenylacetonitrile for stimulants. Zinc, xylene, and paraxylene also came to the cult, as did potassium cyanide, ammonium chloride, and nitromethane. Then there were the acids: hydrochloric, sulfuric, nitric. The amounts purchased were extraordinary. In just over five months, Bell Epoch alone bought 180 tons of phosphorus trichloride, 90 tons of methanol, 50 tons of diethylaniline, and 2,100 pounds of phosphorus penta-chloride. All of it would go into Aum's chemical-weapons program.

The dual use of so many of these chemicals suggests the difficulty in stopping a determined organization like Aum. Over the next two years, the cult bought at least three tons of nitric acid and nearly 10,000 gallons of glycerin through its bogus medical-supply compa-nies. Combine the two chemicals and one gets nitroglycerin, used to relieve angina sufferers, make cosmetics – or fabricate dynamite. Another chemical, thiodiglycol, is used to make ink for ballpoint pens; it is also very helpful in making mustard gas. Dimethylamine goes into both laundry detergent and nerve gas. Even if they were keen to monitor where their products end up, large chemical wholesalers typically handle thousands of chemicals and hundreds of clients. Moreover, Aum seemed a legitimate customer. The cult operated industrial plants, medical clinics, and research centers – and they were willing to pay cash. By the spring of 1994, front companies had shopped at more than two hundred firms across Japan and purchased well over one hundred chemicals for Aum's weapons programs.

The cult was undoubtedly helped by being based in Japan. As the world's second largest economy, the nation offered an extraordi-nary range of chemicals, electronics, and industrial goods. But not everything was available close to home, the scientists found. For certain sensitive items, the cult would have to venture overseas. They would find the doors wide open.

14

AUM INTERNATIONAL

Zygo Corporation received the call in summer 1993. A Miss Hiraoka of Manhattan was on the line, and she was extremely interested in buying a Mark IV interferometer. "Aum USA Company Ltd.," the woman repeated over the phone. That was the name of the business, she said.

Zygo was not your typical stop for religious shoppers. The company was a relatively small, hi-tech concern in Connecticut, just across the state line from New York. Zygo had gained an international reputation for its interferometers – laser-based optical measuring devices used by the electronics industry and military.

Her business, Hiraoka explained, was in Manhattan, but the parent company was based in Japan. Aum worked in electronics manufacture and needed a Mark IV for research. Her company, she stressed, was willing to pay cash.

Around the "company," Hiraoka was better known as Subha, her Sanskrit holy name. Asahara had sent the former English teacher to New York that year to preside over the cult's growing network in America. From Aum's center in midtown Manhattan, the middle-aged manager worked long hours on directives coming from headquarters 7,000 miles away. She was, above all, a true believer in Aum and Asahara. "I am a disciple of the Master," she told a visitor. My ego has disappeared. I am detached from worldly things."

Not so detached as to ignore orders from the boss for high-tech items from across America. But her dealings with Zygo would end in trouble. Just before paying $103,000 for an interferometer, Hiraoka was told she could not ship it overseas without a special export license. Her company ran semi-conductor plants in Japan, she tried to explain, and needed the interferometer as soon as possible. The woman's story was a good one – the semiconductor industry does indeed use interferometers for key measurements. But the unit is what the U.S. government calls "dual-use," with both civilian- and military-

SANSCRIT HOLY NAME

applications. The Pentagon uses the device to design and test guided missiles and explosive detonators – including those used in nuclear bombs. By using light, interferometers can make extremely sensitive measurements, such as the velocity of high explosives and the spherical surface of plutonium triggers. Among its users are the U.S. Energy Department's nuclear-weapons labs and the Air Force Weapons Laboratory's High Energy Plasma Division.

It must have been a bit puzzling for the folks at Zygo. They referred Ms. Hiraoka to the proper government office, but for some reason the deal didn't work out. The woman never contacted them again.

Back at Mount Fuji, one can only guess what purpose Murai and the others had in mind for the interferometer. The Mark IV, though, was but one item on a multimillion-dollar shopping list. And much of what Aum needed from America would be far easier to obtain.

In the tumult that is New York City, the guru's poster could easily have been missed. Indian mystics, Haitian voodoo priests, New Age ascetics – New York had seen it all. Since the 1960s Americans had witnessed a steady procession of gurus from the East, peddling yoga, Buddhism, Sikhism, Hinduism, Zen, drugs, doomsday, and free sex. Aum's presence was just another voice in the din.

But there he was, nonetheless, one block from Rockefeller Center, next to a tailor shop on East 48th Street: a large color poster of a bearded Japanese fellow in meditative pose. "His Holiness, the Master, Shoko Asahara," the poster announced. "Self-realization and Enlightenment . . . profound mystical states." Passers-by were invited upstairs for a closer look at the world of Aum.

The rooms were on the second floor of a thin and grimy six-story building. Past a dim foyer with exhausted houseplants, one ventured upstairs to find a spare apartment office. From every room, posters of His Holiness, the Master, looked down at you: Asahara with the Dalai Lama, Asahara blessing a devotee, Asahara in purple robes in the wind.

On a table near the front, Aum offered Americans the words and music of enlightenment, for a small fee. There were English-language books for sale, Aum classics like *Teachings of the Truth* and *Declaring Myself the Christ*. Also available were tapes of its much-prized "astral music," including hits like "Hymns to the Holy Heavens." A brochure, featuring more pictures of Asahara, boasted how Aum science had freed followers from mental and physical disease, and given them entry to "other realms or godly worlds."

Further on, a worn beige carpet lined the floor of a meditation room, where followers listened silently to taped chanting. They knelt before an altar draped in purple cloth, watched over by yet more photos of Shoko Asahara. Sandals were placed neatly on a rack by the door, not far from a TV and VCR.

Aum USA was founded officially on October 28, 1987. Visiting cult officials registered the group as a nonprofit corporation in New York State, to "further the development of spiritual well-being." Shortly after its founding, Aum USA changed its name to the inexplicable Grebhtor Smoo, and then reincorporated as a separate entity. (The words "Grebhtor Smoo" have no meaning in English, Japanese, or Sanskrit, although backwards they spell Ooms Rothberg. Cult members were unable to shed light on this particular mystery.)

The going was slow in America. New Yorkers, apparently, were tougher to convince than Japanese or Russians. But after years of work, the cult had introduced hundreds of Americans to Aum. Attracted by free yoga and meditation classes, about two dozen committed members filled Aum's offices, among them New Age enthusiasts, students, and Japanese expatriates.

A handful of young Americans drew close enough to make the "ultimate donation," giving Aum their assets and becoming full devotees. One follower, named "David," sounded strikingly like his counterparts in Japan, when interviewed in 1995 by Nippon Television. Asked about the end of the world, the nineteen-year-old religious-studies major at Columbia University had this to say: "I believe in Armageddon, in the sense that there will be a catastrophic war between the U.S. and Japan, that the U.S. will attack Japan, and the world will go into chaos." The coming apocalypse, he added, was "purification of the karma."

How did he feel about Shoko Asahara? the reporter asked.

"He's the person I respect most."

"Which part of him?"

"His desire to end the suffering of all beings in the universe, to sacrifice his own happiness, his own peace of mind, and give that peace to other individuals."

While Aum followers revered the Master's "gift of peace" to the world, his top officials pondered how best to commit mass murder. The cult medical director, Dr. Hayashi, had been chosen with his wife

Rira for a special mission to America. They were to comb the nation's
finest libraries, searching for data on chemical-weapons manufacture
and defense. "We were attacked with poison gas," Asahara explained
to Rira. "We have to research how to immunize ourselves."

The search for knowledge extended to biological agents as well.
Aum computer experts, working through the Internet, downloaded
the entire Protein Data Bank from the Brookhaven National
Laboratory in New York. The database is a unique repository of
information on more than 3,000 proteins, nucleic acids, and other
organic molecules. A number of entries were no doubt of interest to
Seiichi Endo and company. Among them were the chemical
breakdowns of various toxins, such as the venom of the deadly green
mamba snake.

Lasers were also high on Aum's shopping list. The cult spent
$400,000 for an Amoco green-light laser in 1994. A company
spokesman later told the press the device had only "medical
applications," but Aum clearly had other ideas. A hint was provided
by another advanced tool, a $500,000 lens grinder, which the cult
bought that year from a second U.S. firm, Moore Special Tools. The
machine, say experts, can fashion mirrors used to aim and enhance a
laser, sharpening the beam's ability to daze or blind people.

The New York office scoured the country trying to satisfy Aum's
appetite for hi-tech goods and weaponry. To help, the cult enlisted
the services of a Silicon Valley shipping agent, which handled millions
of dollars in purchasing for the cult, much of it in semiconductors,
disk drives, and other computer equipment. Tens of thousands of
dollars more went for gas masks, rolls of air-filtration paper (the kind
used in laboratory "clean rooms"), camping gear, even tires for
Asahara's Rolls-Royce. At one point Subha was ordered to approach
steel companies to buy tons of the metal for making military knives.
Other requests apparently went to an obscure underground U.S.
publisher for books on paramilitary operations and espionage: a CIA
guide to making explosives using over-the-counter medicines; manuals on wiretapping, kidnapping VIPs, and assassination; and
handbooks to the AK-47 assault rifle, Uzi machine gun, and 9-mm
Beretta handgun.

"The U.S. is a big supermarket – for the whole world,"
bemoaned a retired CIA agent who had worked for years on nuclear
proliferation. "This kind of thing is difficult to track, and almost
impossible to stop."

Not everything Aum needed was in America. Millions of dollars flowed elsewhere overseas, to newly incorporated front companies, hi-tech firms, and real-estate deals. In Switzerland, Aum scientists found the chemical reactor they had been searching for – a $200,000 system that brought them a giant step closer to waging chemical war. And to Taiwan, Mahaposya wired a whopping $40 million, which it claimed was for purchase of computer equipment. But while Taiwan was indeed the source of Mahaposya PCs, police later found billing for only a fraction of the deals. Mahaposya could have been buying anything. One purchase reportedly went for a rugged fabric called Kevlar, used for making bulletproof vests.

The purchases were but one part of a growing global empire. Like a virulent strain of some bacterial agent, the cult had begun to spread around the world. An FBI investigation later showed heavy telephone traffic between Aum's New York office and at least eleven countries. Calls went out across the U.S. and Canada, to Germany, Israel, Russia, and the UK; across the Pacific to Australia, Taiwan, Japan, and Sri Lanka; even to Ghana and Nigeria. Fortunately, at least some of the hosts rejected the infection.

The sign on the glass door read, "A. Wakatake – *Buddhismus und Yoga Center* – Aum." Few found their way to the cult's European headquarters, tucked away in a former banking complex in Bonn, the German capital. Begun in 1991, the group had attracted "fewer than ten" true followers over the years, its leader admitted, despite offering cheap classes on the road to enlightenment.

To manage the German office, Aum had sent 36-year-old Akiro Wakatake. A lackluster electronic engineer, Wakatake had given up a well-paid job for life in the cult. On his arrival, he had studied German at the Goethe Institute and done his best to attract followers, but had little to show for his efforts. The failure was even more glaring given the success of other cults in the country, among them the Church of Scientology and the Rajneesh free-love sect. Recruiting was the key source of Aum's money and manpower, and Wakatake's performance did not escape notice back home. His budget was kept to a mere $140 per month, limiting him to one meal per day. Even worse, he complained, headquarters would not even send him an electrode cap. Unable to synchronize his brain waves with the Master's, with only a few followers in Bonn, it must have been a lonely existence.

Sri Lanka was another story. The tropical island nation in the Indian Ocean was known for its tea, spices, and stubborn civil war.

Somehow, Asahara and company had wangled an introduction to the president in 1991. Within a year, they had purchased a tea plantation near a resort area and begun transforming it into a "Lotus Village" – an Aum community. There were plans for offices, living quarters, and, ominously, a large factory said to be for "emergency foodstuffs."

To build Aum's center in Sri Lanka, the cult hired some fifty laborers and paid them twice the going wage. There was, of course, a catch: the workers had to become members of Aum and attend meditation classes each evening. Those who refused were fired. Asahara made several trips to the area, accompanied by scores of followers. On at least two occasions he flew by helicopter; another time, he arrived at the head of a large procession dominated by an adorned elephant, like a Rajah of Japan inspecting his domain. "The world will end in 1997," he told his assembled workers. "But we're going to survive."

Armed with the powerful yen, Asahara and his followers grew increasingly cocky. Their arrogance finally spilled out of control aboard an Air Lanka jet in May 1992. According to *Sunday Island*, a Sri Lankan newspaper, Asahara was returning to Japan with 150 or so of his disciples. They had received red carpet treatment by President Premadasa and were to fly home in first class on a chartered plane.

All was well until Asahara noticed that two off-duty flight attendants were sharing first class with Aum, a common practice on chartered flights. But the guru took great offense, accusing the airline of taking on additional passengers. He ordered his followers off the aircraft, and the group sat on the tarmac until the attendants moved to economy.

Asahara and company then reboarded, but apparently they were not appeased. About an hour after takeoff, Aum members began hurling abuse at the two flight attendants; alarmed at the commotion, the chief pilot came into the passenger cabin, only to be assaulted by the angry cultists. The copilot radioed Colombo's international airport to report "hijack" problems on board and asked permission to abort the flight and return. On landing, the runway was swamped with police, soldiers, and firefighters. Asahara and his followers suddenly grew "quiet as mice," the paper reported.

President Premadasa allegedly intervened on behalf of Aum, ordering all concerned to keep the incident quiet. With a new crew and no off-duty flight attendants, the plane again took off with the guru from hell.

Asahara's aggressive ways caused sparks elsewhere. The guru visited Taiwan twice in 1993, inspecting Aum's facilities and hoping to spread his apocalyptic gospel. By his third visit, however, Taiwan authorities had learned that their guest was proselytizing without the proper visa and declared him an undesirable. Asahara was never allowed past Immigration.

Undaunted, Aum's leader turned his attention to the other China, the People's Republic. One could give Asahara credit for ambition, at least. The guru had set his sights on the world's most populous country, hoping to win hearts and minds among 1.2 billion Chinese. In February 1994 Asahara and his entourage visited Shanghai at the invitation of the China International Friendship Group. Their host was something more than a "friendship group," however; the organization was tied closely to the military and its vice-chairman was the third daughter of Deng Xiaoping, China's paramount leader. But despite reports of money changing hands, Aum found their reception cool in China.

Elsewhere, Aum's world travels had paid off. By 1993, the cult had found an extraordinary place where they could do almost anything they wanted: buy weapons, buy access, win souls, even train an army. For Aum Supreme Truth, the key to the future lay increasingly in the ruins of the Soviet empire.

15

ARMS FOR ARMAGEDDON

In the winter of 1993, a Russian man contacted the Defense Ministry in Moscow. He introduced himself as an employee of Mahaposya, but didn't mention that Mahaposya was the corporate right arm of a Japanese doomsday cult. He had a request. Would it be possible for Mahaposya to charter the world's largest helicopter?

The question must have raised eyebrows. The Russian wanted to hire a MIL Mi-26 chopper, a twenty-seven-ton monster with eight rotor blades, a cruising speed of 183 m.p.h., and room inside for two infantry vehicles and eighty combat-equipped troops. What on earth did Mahaposya want a Mi-26 for? The employee said he wanted to fly from Vladivostok in the Russian Far East to Taiwan, via four Japanese locations. In Taiwan, he said, he would "make a deal." The Russian was refused permission, and Aum's mysterious bid to hire the world's largest helicopter failed.

It was one setback in an otherwise wildly successful year. Aum's Moscow operation was booming, with the cult opening more branches to accommodate ever-growing ranks of followers. Moscow's Japanese business community buzzed with rumors that Asahara, during one of his now regular Russian jaunts, brought a box full of $100 bills. One respected Moscow newspaper reported that Aum's total spending in Russia – on recruiting, property, media campaigns, and bribes – amounted to some $50 million.

And there were plans to spend even more. Aum was eyeing a 163-acre plot of land in Klin, a town near Moscow famous as the home of the composer Tchaikovsky. There the sect hoped to build a Lotus Village, a self-sustaining community of schools, hospitals, dormitories, and factories, all modeled on its original Mount Fuji complex. Other money-spinning schemes were floated – a Chinese noodle factory, a donut chain, a computer shop, a casino. Meanwhile, cult missionaries fanned out across the former Soviet Union: to St.

Petersburg; to the Belarus capital of Minsk; to Kiev in the Ukraine; to Vorkuta in the Ural Mountains; to Tyumen on the Siberian border.

Significantly, the year 1993 also saw a surge in visits by Aum's top scientific minds. They kept a low profile in Russia, but one can make educated guesses about their mission there. Take Seiichi Endo, the cult's microbiology chief. After spending years in a biolab dabbling with botulism and other killers, Endo had picked the perfect place to further his education in germ warfare.

The Soviet Union's bioweapons program was mammoth. It included development of tularemia, plague, Q fever, cholera, and various deadly toxins, according to a 1993 U.S. congressional report. By the 1970s, Soviet scientists were believed to be using biotechnology to create genetically engineered killer bugs. One program attempted to splice toxin-producing genes into the DNA of a common flu virus. U.S. intelligence identified more than twenty facilities for bioweapons development and production. At an ostensibly civilian pharmaceutical and medical complex in St. Petersburg, some 400 scientists worked in a secret lab developing anaerobic bacteria for antidote-resistant bioweapons. The bacteria were dried and ground into powder for packing into munitions shells.

By the time Endo arrived in Russia, the secret Soviet biowarfare program had ended. But a dangerous inheritance remained. Across the former Soviet domain, Russia now struggled to keep the lid on a Pandora's box of deadly bacteria and other biohazards. In 1992, the Interfax news service reported that units from the tiny republic of Abkhazia allegedly shelled Georgian troops with biological weapons from the Russian army. Another report from the Georgian Defense Ministry said that Georgian guardsmen had raided a Russian military biolab near the Abkhazian capital a month before, and stolen viral cultures and lab animals with deadly diseases.

Seiichi Endo no doubt found all this profoundly interesting. Russia also held many fascinations for Masami Tsuchiya, the cult's chief chemist – not least of which was the world's largest stockpile of chemical agents and munitions. Russia is committed to destroying this arsenal of about 40,000 tons of mostly nerve agents stored at seven declared sites, a task which will cost an estimated $10 billion.

The security at Russia's chemical storage facilities is also poor. While American chemical bases have intruder alarms and electronic sensors, Russian facilities depend on mesh grills and padlocks. To break into these facilities, all one needs is "a bribe, a dark night, some dark clothing, a little bit of muscle, and a crowbar," said Amy

Smithson, a chemical-weapons expert at the Henry L. Stimson Center, a Washington, D.C.–based think-tank.

Guarding chemical stockpiles is hard enough; keeping track of now jobless experts in chemical warfare is almost impossible. One factory in Volgograd suspended production of sarin in 1987, putting thousands out of work, including 100 with manufacturing know-how.

Tsuchiya spent at least three weeks in Russia. With Aum's high-level contacts in Russia's science community, both he and Endo would have had easy access to experts in biochemical weapons. A leading Russian member of the cult claimed that Aum's Moscow membership included former chemical-warfare troops: Tsuchiya might have consulted them too. One thing is certain. When Tsuchiya returned to his Mount Fuji lab, he began experimenting with sarin. This nerve agent can be produced by several different methods. Tsuchiya would use a Russian recipe.

After the 1992 Salvation Tour, the cult's construction chief Kiyohide Hayakawa visited Russia over twenty times. He used a multiple visa issued with a Russian government invitation, and traveled restlessly around the former Soviet republics. Only the privileged few in the Moscow HQ knew his exact itinerary, but fortunately Hayakawa left a trail of sorts. It took the form of a small notebook.

"February 20," he wrote. "Went to see submachine gun. AK-47 – $1,000, $1,100, $500. Golf bag – brought back barrels. Rifles – minimum five people, maximum 15 people." Then: "7.6, same as AK-47 is fine. Is 5.54 available?" That 7.6 refers to the 7.62-mm caliber AK-47, or Kalashnikov. The notes continued with Hayakawa practicing how to write the same Russian phrase over and over again:

Did you buy an AK-47?
Did you buy an AK-47?
Did you buy an AK-47?
Did you buy an AK-47?
Did you buy an AK-47?

He didn't. But the cult did buy an AK-74, another 7.62-mm Kalashnikov. In February 1994, Hayakawa, chief scientist Hideo Murai, and three other followers visited Russia to acquire the rifle. The mission was tense, since Murai and Hayakawa were long-time rivals for the cult's number-two position. Hayakawa despised Murai's blind devotion. "The monks are slaves to the leader's ego," he once wrote in his diary. His globetrotting left little time for religious practice, and this irritated the devout Murai, who once grumbled, "Hayakawa's too busy chasing Russian women."

The Russian trip saw a power struggle between the two men. On the guru's orders, Hayakawa was suddenly recalled to Mount Fuji, accused of spending cult money on a Russian woman, and stripped of his high rank. Now the cult's undisputed number-two, Murai acquired an AK-74 – and took all the credit.

There were conflicting versions of how the rifle then reached Japan. One report suggested it was taken apart and smuggled in an X-ray-proof bag. Another version holds that only the gun barrels – the trickiest part of the AK-74 to copy – were smuggled through customs in a bag of golf clubs, a version Hayakawa's notes seem to confirm. Whatever the AK-74's route, its arrival at Clear Stream Temple, the cult's Mount Fuji firearms factory, had an immediate effect. Aum's scheme to mass-produce automatic assault rifles – its machine guns for Armageddon – kicked into high gear.

Where in Russia could Aum acquire an AK-74? Just about anywhere. In the capital, the ready availability of firearms went hand in hand with a surge in violent crime, as the streets were carved up by the Moscow *mafiya* and their rival mobs from the Caucasus mountain republics of Georgia, Armenia, Azerbaijan, and Chechnya. There were some 300,000 registered firearms in the city; only a few hundred yards from Aum's Petrovka branch was a legal gun shop called Defense, guarded by two Kalashnikov-toting sentries. Such legitimate businesses were mirrored by a furious black-market trade in assault rifles, as well as Tokarev, Makarov, and Stechkin pistols.

Moscow's arms bazaar was only one of Aum's options. In early 1993, the cult set up a branch in Vladikavkaz in the republic of North Ossetia in the Caucasus. Of all the cities in Russia's vast federation, Vladikavkaz was a curious place to look for converts to a Japanese Buddhist sect. It was, however, an excellent place to buy weapons.

Vladikavkaz is very close to Grozny, the capital of Chechnya, which was later battered by Russian shells in an attempt to crush the republic's breakaway movement. But long before Chechnya hit world headlines, the whole Caucasus region had been famed for simmering civil and ethnic conflicts. Such conditions fueled a free-wheeling atmosphere for arms trading.

"With contacts in Chechnya, you can buy almost anything," said a seasoned Russian journalist. "Not just Kalashnikovs, but also grenade launchers, anti-tank and anti-aircraft weapons." Corruption in the Russian military also helped; stories abound of Russian soldiers selling firearms to the Chechens for extra cash, then finding themselves being shot at with them the next day.

Whatever the source of the AK-74, Aum now faced another problem. With the prospect of Clear Stream Temple mass-producing assault rifles, who would be skilled enough to use them? Guns are scarce in Japan, unlike trigger-happy America, and most Japanese would be hard-pushed to find the safety catch. But Hayakawa had thought of that, too.

For self-proclaimed Buddhist saints, Shoko Asahara and his band had already displayed an unseemly fascination with Russian military matters. In 1993, Murai and Hayakawa were among several cultists who visited a university weapons-research center to study missiles and bazookas. Later that year, Shoko Asahara and other cultists took part in shooting drills on a Russian military installation, according to Russian investigative sources. Asahara also visited an elite tank division outside Moscow, where he posed for photos from a gun turret.

Hayakawa was less interested in those Kodak moments:

Training – planned for 6,7, and 8 April. Controlled program – $2,800 to army. Day one: We can get inside tanks, armored vehicles. Day two: Various guns, rockets, machine guns. Day three: Rifles, machine guns. Day four: Day off.

These notes almost certainly refer to a spring 1994 program in Russia attended by forty-five Aum members, including three former Japanese soldiers and one of Asahara's bodyguard. According to *Izvestia*, it was run by veterans of the former KGB's Alpha Group, an elite unit trained in sabotage, assassination, kidnapping, and intelligence gathering. Alpha Group had a notorious reputation. Its troops murdered the Afghan dictator Amin, thus providing the Soviet Union with its shaky pretext for invading Afghanistan in 1979.

Among Alpha Group's trainees that spring were two young Japanese who would become Aum's most ruthless killers. Yoshihiro Inoue and Tomomitsu Niimi no doubt learned some useful tips on kidnapping, firearms, wiretapping, and murder, all skills they would later put to use. For Niimi and Inoue – both men in their twenties who hailed from sheltered backgrounds – training with Alpha Group must have been exhilarating.

KGB veterans may have provided other services, too. Aum was "intimately linked" with the Russian intelligence community, said Vitaly Savitsky, who investigated the cult as chairman of the State

Duma subcommittee on religious sects. A "very exclusive club" was how Savitsky described the circle of KGB veterans. "They all know each other and support each other," he said. "They are very well trained and a lot of weapons circulate among them. They buy and sell from each other, and also sell weapons beyond their circle."

Did Aum buy weapons from former KGB agents? It is difficult to prove, but the trade route was clearly established. Media reports in Russia and Japan identified one allegedly good friend of Aum: a former high-ranking bureaucrat at the Economics Ministry and an ex-KGB colonel. In March 1994, this man visited Aum's Mount Fuji HQ at Asahara's personal invitation, after which he helped the cult acquire a suitcase-sized detector used by the Russian military to test for nerve gases.

Aum's cozy links with the intelligence community might also explain why the cult could carry out its Russian activities with almost no official interference. In 1992, Russia's Federal Counterintelligence Agency reportedly began scrutinizing Aum after it started its television broadcasts. However, the cult was later dropped from a list of "organizations to be watched," perhaps owing to intervention by Russian friends in high places. Said former KGB agent and journalist Konstantine Preobrazhensky, "Russian intelligence covered its eyes and let Aum do whatever it wanted."

Kiyohide Hayakawa wanted weapons – and not just AK-74s. He was also interested in the kind of Russian military hardware that doesn't fit into a golf bag.

"Tank, T-72," Hayakawa's notebook read. "Second-hand, $200,000 to $300,000. Several million dollars if eight years old. License issued by Russian govt." The T-72 tank is a 40-ton Russian stalwart whose 125-mm gun has a range of nearly six miles. Hayakawa planned to buy four T-72s, according to Russian investigators quoted in Japan's *Aera* magazine. The notes of Tetsuya Kibe, another key cultist involved in Aum's weapons program, suggest an even grander scheme. "Aum to broker 300 T-72 tanks from Russia. Plan to sell to China," Kibe wrote in his notes. Japanese investigators believe Aum planned to act as an intermediary for Russian arms sales to China, in preparation for procuring arms for itself in the future.

Hayakawa's mother of all shopping lists continues with the entry "F29s." This referred to the MiG-29 fighter jet. The Russian aircraft has a top speed of Mach 2.3 (1,520 m.p.h.) and bristles with a 6,600-

pound armory of bombs, rockets, napalm tanks, and radar-guided
missiles. Kibe's notes included the entry, "New, $20 million. Used,
$12–14 million" – a fairly accurate pricing of the MiG-29.

There was one item on Hayakawa's list with even more power
than a MiG-29: the Russian-made Proton launcher. The rockets on
the 195-foot SL-13 Proton produce 2 million pounds of takeoff thrust
to propel satellites into geostationary orbit. Hayakawa records such
vital statistics, and stresses the need to build a Proton launch site in
Japan. It was a vastly ambitious plan. The only launch base equipped
to fire the Proton is the Baikonur Cosmodrome in Kazakhstan. The
cost of building a new base has been estimated at $750 million.

But few schemes were beyond Hayakawa's feverish imagination,
as his diary revealed. He recorded important outings – "Listened to
lecture by chief of Mendeleyev Chemical Institute" – and drew crude
illustrations of trench mortar systems. He noted down gifts for Aum's
influential friends: "To Lobov and others, Polaroid camera, Cross
ballpen, and Walkman." He made a list of Russian cities, with their
distances from Moscow, then a reminder: "Get a room and put bars
on window. Use for weapons storage." (Interestingly, the windows of
Aum's large northern Moscow branch were covered with a thick iron
grill, and the building was monitored round the clock by security
cameras.) There was also a string of shorter entries: "Rifles with laser
lens ... snipers ... pineapples" (slang for hand grenades).

Nor did Hayakawa's military shopping list end there. In 1993,
Aum's Moscow branch requested a meeting with Viktor Mikhailov,
minister of nuclear energy. Nobody quite knew why, least of all
Mikhailov himself, whose office turned down the request. But one
scrawled entry in Kiyohide Hayakawa's notebook provided an
ominous clue about Aum's latest obsession. It read: "Nuclear
warhead. How much?"

16

THE GURU'S LOVE

Kotaro Ochida checked the knapsack's contents for the last time. One roll of thick masking tape. One small canister of tear gas. One Molotov cocktail. "This should surprise them," he said, passing the petrol bomb to Hideaki Yasuda.

The two men had broken one of Aum's holiest precepts: they had fled the cult. Now they had decided to fight back using the cult's own tactics. They planned to break into Aum's largest compound and rescue Yasuda's ailing mother.

It was past 3 a.m. on January 30, 1994, and the air was deadly cold. The sun had yet to rise from behind Mount Fuji's massive bulk. Yasuda and Ochida changed into Aum robes in the public toilets. Yasuda's father and younger brother waited anxiously outside in the family's Toyota Crown – the getaway car. When they were ready, the two ex-followers said their farewells and walked off down the bleak country lane.

Soon the Aum facility loomed in the half-light before them. Yasuda saw his companion take out a long commando-style knife. "Just in case," Ochida said.

Aum's Utopian dream had turned into a Kafkaesque nightmare. Cult leaders whipped up hysteria among ordinary members, claiming the state was planning an all-out attack on the group. The constant drumbeat of impending doom, together with Aum's mind-numbing way of life, was enough to blind most believers to one crucial fact: their real enemy was the cult itself.

Inside the busy compounds, lack of sleep and poor safety standards caused untold accidents. At least one believer was crushed to death by heavy machinery, and others perished in traffic accidents. Whenever possible, the cult did not report these fatalities to local authorities; it dealt with its own dead. Bodies were cremated in cult incinerators and the ashes secretly scattered in Mount Fuji's foothills.

Fatal accidents were just "the tip of the iceberg," according to one devotee. Aum's sealed community had become a mini-police-state. Those who broke cult laws were dragged away for "thermotherapy." Some never returned. Other followers, battered by the cult's spartan lifestyle and brutal initiations, developed mental disorders and wandered around mouthing gibberish. They also disappeared. Older or unhealthy cultists grew weaker and weaker until, one morning, they were gone. Scores of believers were vanishing without trace.

Anyone brave or curious enough to ask after the missing followers received the same answer: they had gone home. But this explanation made no sense. From day one, Aum members had it drummed into them: nobody, absolutely nobody, left the cult. It was considered the most evil sin of all – "betraying the guru's love," they called it.

For Kotaro Ochida, the guru's love had been everything. A pharmacist by training, he joined Aum in 1990 and began working at Dr. Hayashi's Astral Hospital in Tokyo. He was a passionately loyal follower with high hopes for the clinic's medical techniques. "Many people will be relieved of their pains," he predicted in a 1990 cult magazine.

It slowly dawned on Ochida that he was horribly wrong. The patients around him were in appalling shape. The treatment by cult doctors – scalding baths, mantra chanting, dubious pills and potions – had only made them worse. Ochida couldn't recall a single Aum patient whose health had improved.

One of these unfortunates was Hideaki Yasuda's mother. She suffered from Parkinson's disease. Ochida struck up a friendship and soon realized that the treatment was, in fact, hastening the woman's death. He finally left the cult in disgust and tried to forge a new career in the outside world, but couldn't – not while Yasuda's mother wasted away in terrible conditions. So Ochida contacted her son Hideaki, a former member of Aum, and presented him with a plan to bring the woman home.

Yasuda was reluctant at first – he had only recently left the cult and had no desire to return. But Ochida said the woman had now been moved to Aum's Mount Fuji HQ. Yasuda needed no more persuasion. If he did nothing, his mother would surely die.

Ochida and Yasuda crept past the gatehouse and hurried inside the Aum clinic. They searched the dim honeycomb of tiny rooms until they found Yasuda's mother on the third floor. She was lying in a bed with electrodes attached to her head and tubes snaking from her nose. The two men heaved her to her feet – she could barely walk – and began to carry her off.

Then another believer spotted them. Ochida hit him with a squirt of blinding Mace but too late to silence his cry for help. The cult's security guards arrived minutes later. Ochida sprayed the Mace wildly in all directions, but was quickly overpowered by five believers. Yasuda, pinned to the ground by five more, was screaming, "Give me my mother back!" The men were beaten and handcuffed. Then they were led to a meditation room.

The guru was there. He sat in a chair next to his wife Tomoko. Yasuda crouched before them. Behind him stood a group of cult leaders, among them Hideo Murai and Tomomitsu Niimi, the sadistic 29-year-old head of security. Ochida also lay handcuffed on the floor, his face drained of color.

Asahara's voice was slow and emotionless. "You will no doubt sink to hell," he said to Yasuda. "You now have two choices. One, you kill Ochida. Two, if you can't kill Ochida, you will be killed on the spot."

Chilled by the guru's tone, Yasuda couldn't find his voice. "Decide!" shouted Asahara. "Don't you know that Ochida forced your mother to have sex? That he made her drink his semen and told her it was part of an initiation?"

"No," replied Yasuda quietly.

"So you think that it's good that Ochida had sex with your mother?" asked Asahara.

"No, I don't," said Yasuda. Then he broke down. "I want to go home now," he sobbed.

The guru said he could – after he had murdered his companion.

"And then I'll actually be free to go?" asked Yasuda cautiously.

The guru smiled paternally. "Have I ever told you a lie?"

With undisguised relish, security chief Niimi prepared the execution. Ochida was forced to sit on a plastic sheet. Yasuda's handcuffs were unlocked, then locked again, this time with his hands in front of him. Then Niimi brought out a piece of rope. It was decided Ochida would be strangled to death.

Yasuda looked down at Ochida and shivered. The pharmacist stared back, his eyes wide with fear.

Yasuda looked away. "I can't kill him while he's watching me," he said. "Please, someone cover them."

"Do it yourself!" Asahara cried.

Yasuda was handed the roll of masking tape. He walked over to Ochida. "I'm sorry," he said.

Ochida tried to reply but Yasuda didn't catch it. He leaned closer.

"I'm ready," Ochida repeated. "I'm sorry to have got you into all this."

Ochida might have hoped for a swift execution, but Asahara had other ideas. He remembered that Ochida had brought a canister of Mace with him and ordered Yasuda to use it. But first, to stop the gas affecting the others in the room, a plastic bag was put over Ochida's head. Then Asahara gave the order. Cringing, Yasuda put the canister under the bag and pushed the nozzle.

Ochida began to writhe with pain. Several members – including science chief Murai – rushed forward to pin him down. One of them wound the rope round Ochida's neck and began to tighten it.

"Stop!" Murai shouted. "Yasuda has to finish this!"

Yasuda grabbed both ends of rope and began to pull. The noose tightened around Ochida's neck. But with handcuffs on, Yasuda couldn't pull hard enough. Minutes passed. He pulled the rope harder, and Ochida began to flail violently. Still Yasuda couldn't muster enough strength.

By this time, Niimi had seen enough. It was taking far too long. He snatched the rope from Yasuda and wound it a second time around Ochida's neck. He bound one end around Yasuda's foot, the other round Yasuda's hand. "Now," Niimi told him proudly, while Ochida moaned in agony, "if you pull the rope down, you can easily strangle him."

Yasuda tugged the rope with all his might. He held it until Ochida's body slipped face down onto the vinyl sheet. A cult doctor stepped in to check for a pulse. There wasn't one. The pharmacist was dead.

Yasuda stood over the corpse, staring with disbelief. A puddle of Ochida's urine formed at his side. Then Asahara spoke again. "Tell your father this: 'My mother's condition is getting better. Ochida decided to stay here.' " Then Niimi and his troops led Yasuda away.

Asahara turned to his wife. "I didn't want you to have to see this," he said to her.

"It can't be helped," his wife replied. "He violated the cult's precepts."

Then the guru pointed to the corpse. "Dispose of it," he ordered two members. "Murai knows the details."

Ochida was rolled up in the blue vinyl sheet and carried down to the basement.

Shoko Asahara had a thing about incinerators. He even claimed to have invented one himself. It was called the Final Cleaner.

Asahara had patented the incinerator in 1992, under his original name Chizuo Matsumoto. It generated temperatures of up to 1,500 degrees Celsius by blasting air through a floor covered with red-hot sand. The resulting combination of heat and attrition could reduce even a damp, heavy object – say, a human being of average weight – to two pounds of unidentifiable ash within thirty minutes.

But the Final Cleaner hardly satisfied the warped scientific curiosity of the cult's scientists. It was too cumbersome, too messy – too low-tech. So under Murai's direction they dreamed up another one. It was called, simply, the Microwave.

Aum officials had bought a refrigerator-sized microwave-generating unit for $23,000 from a legal supplier. They paid in cash, and told the sales agent they intended to use the equipment to dry instant noodles. This seemed convincing: microwaves can be used to dehydrate instant food and tea leaves.

The unit was ten times more powerful than a domestic microwave. Aum technicians had connected it to six sealed metal drums, which formed the ovens themselves. These could only be used once; the microwave unit generated so much energy that the drums were fragile and stank foully after use.

Aum was not merely interested in a giant oven; they were researching the weapons applications of microwave radiation. Murai and the other scientists had remodeled the unit to direct the microwaves into a cylindrical tube, using it to focus a high-energy particle beam in one direction. From this principle, Murai explained, one could create plasma weapons that would revolutionize warfare. "This is very clean compared to nuclear weapons," gushed Hayakawa in a Radio Moscow interview. "Under good circumstances, a microwave weapon will penetrate concrete and steel. Therefore, it can kill living things wherever they are. It can kill human beings, cows, cats, or dogs with high temperature. Nobody can escape it. So this is the ultimate weapon."

For now, though, Aum found a more immediate use.

Ochida's corpse was probably still warm when two followers stuffed it into one of the sealed drums that served as their giant oven. When the switch was thrown, the lights in the room dimmed slightly. The power-hungry microwave unit rumbled directing the microwaves in a narrow, invisible beam toward the drum. The followers tried not to breathe through their noses.

Inside the metal drum, the corpse cooked from inside and crumpled. What the followers later chipped from the drum they dropped into a solution of nitric acid. The remains of Kotaro Ochida were then flushed down a toilet.

Aum was not yet through with Yasuda. Ochida's reluctant killer was ordered to return to Mount Fuji within a week. Yasuda had other ideas, however. In a panic, he moved from his home outside Tokyo and hid out in a far-away northern prefecture.

Within two weeks of the murder, Asahara's goons had tracked him down. Yasuda knew far too much to be free, the guru said. He then dispatched a team to recapture the errant follower and haul him back to the cult. Murai and Niimi had gone, as had Dr. Hayashi, who prepared an injection to make their victim more agreeable.

Yasuda was sure the cult would come for him. His doors and windows were bolted, and he refused to answer the calls of his old friends. Determined to drive him from the house, the cultists stopped up his gas pipe, filling the house with fumes. Yasuda finally called the police, and the others left hastily. There were no arrests.

Ochida's disquieting end meant that yet another had died at Asahara's command. Yasuda, too, no doubt barely escaped with his life. But even as Asahara released hit squads to abduct and murder his enemies, individual killings no longer concerned the guru very much. His mind was fixed on far more grandiose schemes of death and destruction. For by the fall of 1993, the cult's most ambitious plans for Armageddon were nearly complete.

17

SATIAN 7

From the distance, Satian 7 looked unremarkable, a windowless three-story warehouse surrounded by dirt and rubble.

But as one drew closer the structure began to reveal itself. On one side, a dark tangle of huge pipes and wires descended the wall, emptying into a rectangular metal machine – an "air purifier," cult members said, to guard against poison-gas attacks. Strewn behind the building were piles of empty boxes, some marked with the word "sulfuric."

Shoko Asahara had named the buildings at Aum compounds Satian, derived from the Sanskrit word for "truth." Satian 1 served as an office building, with rooms upstairs for confining errant cult members. Satian 2 was a printing factory, the center for Aum publishing. Satian 4 was the guru's home, Satian 10 a hospital, and so on. But it was Satian 7 that held the most mystery at Aum's Mount Fuji headquarters. Even long-time monks were barred, for the building was said to be so holy that only a chosen few were admitted. At the entrance, security guards stood beside a steel door. Each visitor was checked carefully for a special permit badge.

Behind that steel door, they entered another world. A labyrinth of narrow corridors snaked between thin, dimly lit walls. The first passage led to a mezzanine, in the center of which stood a golden image of Shiva, the Hindu god of destruction that served as Aum's chief deity. To the left of Shiva stood an altar, on top of which were placed "the bones of Buddha," which Shoko Asahara claimed to have brought back from Sri Lanka.

It was all a grand deception.

Hidden in the ceiling above was the "Room of Genesis," where steel tanks held a noxious array of solvents, acids, and organic phosphorus compounds – the basic ingredients for nerve gas. They lay in the floor below as well. The entire structure, in fact, was a vast and intricate chemical plant, a complex of reactors, injectors, piping and circuitry. Behind Shiva's many arms rose a two-story distillation machine, which in turn reached into three chemical laboratories and a sophisticated computer control center.

Aum had spent over $10 million on this, its factory of death. By June 1993 Hayakawa's construction crews had completed work on the structure; by September cult scientists were running experiments there. The Supreme Truth Research Institute of Science and Technology – Aum's hi-tech division – had moved to the new building, leaving their makeshift labs and offices at Clear Stream Temple. At the same time, Asahara and Murai ordered the ranks of the institute sharply expanded, pushing the number of scientists, engineers, and technicians from eighteen to over a hundred.

The heart and blood of Satian 7 were on the building's second floor. The maze of twisting corridors opened into a complex of five reactors – steel vats used to contain chemical reactions. Around them hung a cat's cradle of thick piping, heating elements, wiring, and ventilation ducts. Technicians in full-body chemical suits took samples and checked for leaks, as close-circuit TV cameras monitored each step of production.

Virtually the entire system was automated, computerized, and geared toward mass production. The fifth and final reactor anchored the $200,000 system Aum had imported from Switzerland. This versatile device could run experiments in synthesizing chemicals, analyze the results, and keep electronic records on every test. Computerized controls automatically adjusted the temperature inside the system and the amount of chemicals used. From the final reactor, the chemicals flowed into an industrial packaging machine. The device automatically measured a specified amount of the chemical, then injected and heat-sealed it into nylon polyethylene bags.

Overseeing the system was a powerful computer in a central control room next door. Inside, Aum scientists moved with quiet intent, their clothing spiritual white, their heads hugged by electrode caps. In the background came the chatter of print-outs and the hum of industrial power generators. Down yet more twisting passageways lay a series of three independent chemistry labs, fitted with state-of-the-art equipment: an infrared spectrophotometer for chemical analysis, and a gas-chromatography device for analyzing and separating compounds. Each unit cost at least $10,000. One accessed the laboratories through steel hatchways that sealed in case of accident. Also nearby stood a decontamination chamber. Posted on the wall was a notice: "Do not use this shower. It will flow into a river."

Aum's young science corps tackled the job of producing sarin with enthusiasm. On their laboratory walls hung plaques celebrating the Sanskrit "holy names" of their top chemists. Workers gave the nerve agent nicknames – Magic, Witch, and Sally – as if referring to an old friend. And Satian 7 they simply called the Wizard.

The Wizard resembled the handiwork of a government, not a religious cult. A military specialist who later inspected the plant called it "seemingly larger, more sophisticated, and of better quality than Iraq's chemical gas plants." Each production run was designed to yield 17.6 pints of liquid sarin, or, by day's end, two tons of the deadly nerve agent. Aum's initial goal – to manufacture 70 tons – would be enough to kill off millions.

The engineers of Armageddon kept their offices on the third floor, packed into twelve small rooms divided by thin partitions. Lab equipment, computers, and notebooks filled the desks and tables. Lining the shelves were texts on chemistry and weapons technology, books crammed with dense characters of English, Chinese, or Cyrillic (the Russian alphabet). Stacks of floppy disks lay about, packed with megabytes of data on chemical agents and lasers. Among the top workers were a former researcher at Japan Wireless Company, an electronic engineer from Mitsubishi Electric Corporation, and a Ph.D. in computer science from Hiroshima University.

The key figure in all this was Masami Tsuchiya, the cult's chief chemist. Tsuchiya looked the part of the mad scientist. His goatee and crew-cut hair framed a broad face with eyebrows that arched high above piercing eyes. At Tsukuba University, he had earned a Ph.D. in organic chemistry. A professor there called him "brilliant," but others remember him as an introverted fellow with a barren room and no social life. His one passion seemed to be science. Tsuchiya was a true nerd who raced through books on chemistry, even in his spare time.

His graduate work focused on cutting-edge research: the application of light to change the structure of molecules. But in his second year of grad school, Tsuchiya suddenly announced his intention to become a priest. He had thought about the origin of universe too much, suggested a classmate, and had questions his science books could never answer.

Now in charge of Aum's chemical-weapons effort, Tsuchiya had his own laboratory named after him, a hundred workers to manage, and a vast chemical plant at his feet. He had studied the most comprehensive texts available on chemical warfare, and at last he was ready. For his master Asahara, he was prepared to build an entire arsenal – not just sarin, but a vast stockpile of nerve agents, blister gas, and more.

In the trenches of World War I, on a fateful spring day, Allied troops were suddenly overcome by a yellowish-green cloud rising from the German front lines. Soldiers clutched their throats, gasping for breath as their eyes filled with terror. Hundreds collapsed on the ground, writhing in pain and coughing blood from their tortured lungs. It was 1915, and the Germans had introduced the first chemical weapon – chlorine gas – into modern warfare.

The use of chemical agents escalated until, by war's end, they had caused 1.3 million casualties, including 91,000 deaths. Many victims were crippled for life. Despite their failure to influence the outcome of the war, chemical arms aroused a persistent fear among military powers that they might emerge as the ultimate weapon. So widespread was the revulsion against the effects that the 1925 Geneva Protocol outlawed their use.

During World War II, the fear of their return to the battlefield led every major combatant to develop huge chemical arsenals. Only the concern over retaliation stopped their deployment, leading to a balance of terror that foreshadowed the nuclear age. The Japanese Imperial Army alone felt unconstrained, using poison gas repeatedly in their war against China. The Japanese left behind as many as 2 million shells, which the Chinese claim have killed or injured some 2,000 people since the war's end.

The Imperial Army ran chemical warfare plants in the south of Japan, where they manufactured some 9 million shells, most containing mustard gas. One plant, in the city of Kitakyushu, was to be the second target of the atomic bomb, which, owing to cloud cover, was diverted to Nagasaki. Another plant, near Hiroshima, disappeared from maps for a decade or more. Many Japanese would still like to forget about the place. Fifty years later, 6,300 former plant workers received government payments for injuries resulting from their work there.

The superpowers maintained their own chemical stockpiles, but by the 1960s it was clear the world was changing. Egypt deployed mustard gas against Yemeni rebels in the mid-1960s. Starting in 1983, Iraq used mustard and nerve gases against its Kurdish minority and the Iranian army. By 1990, the Iraqis were producing at least 200 tons of mustard gas and 50 tons of sarin per month – enough to impress even Shoko Asahara.

The United States and the Russian Federation have pledged to destroy their chemical arsenals by early in the twenty-first century. But the expertise and interest in chemical weapons has spread even faster than that in biological agents. By 1993, the number of nations thought to hold chemical arms tripled over the previous twenty years, according to a U.S. Congressional study. Among the members of the chemical club are Burma, Vietnam, India, Pakistan, Israel, Egypt, and both Koreas.

Terrorists, too, have found occasional use for chemical arms. Grapes from Chile have been poisoned with cyanide and Israeli oranges laced with mercury. In one notable case, thieves in 1975 stole fifty-three canisters of mustard gas from a U.S. chemical-weapons stockpile in West Germany. The terrorists, thought to be tied to the Baader-Meinhof gang, failed to use the gas – but only a portion was later recovered. More recently, in 1992, a neo-Nazi skinhead group plotted to use cyanide to murder children in a Jewish day-care center in Dallas, Texas.

Like biological weapons, chemical agents are indiscriminate killers and relatively cheap to make – the poor man's atomic bomb. Chemical weapons, however, possess certain advantages over human pathogens: they are generally easier to handle and they are not contagious. Moreover, nations wanting a chemical arsenal have a long and deadly menu to choose from. There are nerve agents like sarin and its sister compounds, tabun, soman, and VX; blister agents like mustard gas, so called for its moldy, mustard-like smell; blood agents like hydrogen cyanide, favored by Nazi death camps and American gas chambers; and choking agents like phosgene. All are exceedingly lethal.

Chemical nerve agents kill by shutting down the body's nervous system, much like biological neurotoxins. They have been described as "doing to humans what insect sprays do to insects," and, indeed, there is a parallel. Both are part of the family of organophosphorus chemicals, discovered in Germany in 1936 in the insecticide labs of I.G. Farben. The Nazis quickly recognized their military use, classified the work and began mass production. By war's end, the Germans had synthesized huge amounts of three compounds for use in combat: soman, tabun, and sarin. They were never used.

Aum Supreme Truth chose the nerve agent isopropyl methyl-phosphonofluoridate – sarin. Cult scientists had opted for sarin because of its relative ease of production and the wide availability of raw materials. The agent would certainly be deadly enough. One expert called it "one of most aggressively lethal substances known to chemical science." Odorless and colorless, a single drop of pure sarin is enough to send a person to an early and agonizing death. For a person of 132 pounds, all it takes is 6 milligrams on the skin. That's .0002 ounces.

Most nerve agents are dispersed like tear gas, spreading out into a vaporous cloud. People die by inhaling the evaporating mist. Under the right weather conditions, a single 500-pound sarin bomb could wipe out half the people of central Washington, D.C., according to one study. The deaths would be gruesome.

At first, victims notice a runny nose, drooling, and tightness in the chest. The vision narrows as their pupils contract to the size of pinpoints. Muscle spasms, excessive sweating, and nausea kick in, and then vomiting, difficulty breathing, and uncontrolled defecation and urination. People begin to twitch, jerk, and stagger, lost in confusion with pounding headaches. As the paralysis progresses they lapse into convulsions and coma, and finally death, usually by suffocation. Those fortunate enough to survive may suffer permanent damage to their central nervous systems.

And sarin is relatively benign compared to the newer nerve agents, which are more persistent and easily absorbed. Aum Supreme Truth and Masami Tsuchiya were developing those as well.

"I am working in a dark room, day and night," Tsuchiya confided to a friend. "I can't remember the last time I saw sunshine."

Aum's chief chemist was not happy. The weeks spent inside Satian 7 had taken their toll on the young scientist's health, he complained, because of the toxic substances everywhere. Moreover, he was having trouble "getting people to accomplish things" owing to their lack of training.

Making chemical weapons, it turned out, was not easy work. The ingredients themselves were quite toxic; a series of accidents had struck Satian 7, injuring several workers. Fumes in the plant had given Tsuchiya and the others nosebleeds and irritated eyes. Odd smells emanated from the building, while outside, plants began to wilt and die.

Even the guru's blessing was no longer assured. As experiments began in the fall of 1993, Aum's chemists encountered setback after setback. An angry Asahara pulled Tsuchiya aside and scolded him for wasting so much time and money. The Master warned again of the coming apocalypse and demanded results soon. "I want you to do it," he commanded. "Although it is dangerous, just think of this as training in a solitary cell."

In his sermons, Asahara now spoke urgently of the conspiracy by American and Japanese authorities to attack Aum – ironically, with the very weapons the cult was then trying to make. "There have been continuous poison-gas attacks, especially in recent days," he announced that fall. "Wherever I go I have been sprayed from helicopters or planes. The hour of my death has been foretold. The gas phenomenon has already happened. Next time it might be an atomic bomb."

"I've been patient and never expressed my attitude towards our battle against the nation," he said in another talk. "However, if I don't show it, my followers will be destroyed.

"It was 1989 when my eyesight began to worsen and I became sick. Now I have a blister on my left temple and blisters in my mouth . . . I'm sure there is mustard gas . . . I repeat: there is a possibility that Aum Supreme Truth might cease to exist. The believers must take action."

But taking that action was proving difficult for the cult's young scientists. While formulas for various chemical agents are available in scientific textbooks, typically omitted is the so-called "alchemist's art," the how-to. Some instructions reportedly contain deliberate errors, to throw off madmen like Saddam Hussein and Shoko Asahara.

Modern chemical synthesis is an intricate science of molecules, compounds, process, and procedure. To create sarin, a set of chemicals must be combined in a specific and carefully ordered way, usually at high temperature. There are various techniques that will yield the nerve gas; Aum had opted for a Russian method, picked up probably from their fieldwork in the former Soviet republics.

Satian 7 stood essentially complete by October 1993. For weeks Tsuchiya toiled day and night, mixing in the methanol, adding the sodium fluoride at just the right moment. Finally, in November, cult scientists reached their goal: from the final reactor, drops of a colorless liquid spilled into an airtight receptacle. Aum had made sarin.

One experiment remained: Would it work?

18

THE OUTBACK

Banjawarn Station sits on a desolate plain in the arid expanse of Western Australia. In the Australian outback, the old sheep ranch is about as far out and back as one can go. Beyond lies only the vast, unforgiving sands of the Gibson Desert and the furnace of the Aussie interior. The nearest city of consequence, Perth, is 400 miles away.

Unkept roads with names like Gunbarrel Highway and Canning Stock Route scar the land, leading to a world of ghost towns and sleepy settlements – places with names like Yalgoo, Cue, and Meekatharra. The entire region once teemed with the rush of gold fever. Now those towns, some dead a half-century, bake in the sun, littered with acid vats and the detritus of an era gone past.

There is still mining here, but the gold has given way to other minerals: coal, diamonds, nickel, iron, copper – and uranium. And that is what first brought Aum Supreme Truth to Banjawarn Station.

In Russia, Hayakawa had wondered if Aum could actually buy a nuclear bomb. Back home, Aum's scientists were figuring out how to build their own. To develop a nuclear explosive, nations spent billions of dollars and built huge plants to enrich uranium to weapons quality. But Murai and the others thought they had found a short cut, using laser technology. Aum's first step, however, was getting its hands on some uranium.

Hayakawa helped here as well. Aum's chief engineer had located one of Japan's few deposits of uranium ore, in a rural area about 150 miles from Tokyo. He even sent someone to negotiate for the land. But locals there blocked the sale, leaving Hayakawa to look overseas. He soon zeroed in on Australia, one of the world's leading exporters of uranium. Beginning in April 1993, between jaunts to Moscow, he made repeated trips Down Under to set up Aum's Australian operation.

Hayakawa moved quickly. Within weeks he had arranged for legal representation, a mining consultant, and a realtor. By May, he had established two Australian companies – Clarity Investments and Mahaposya Australia Pty. Ltd., with Shoko Asahara as a director. Guided by a Japanese-Australian realtor, he and another cultist toured sheep ranches in the west and south of the country. The cultists wanted property to "improve soil for the betterment of the world," they told the realtor. At these remote spots, the agent watched with interest as the two men went off by themselves for hours, holding electronic testing gear with electrodes they stuck into the ground.

As he traveled the length of the vast country, Hayakawa checked off places in his notebook: "4/28, silver, bronze, gold all together. In South Australia, better uranium . . . On the border there must be some. But haven't searched yet. Search is $1,000."

Eventually he found what must have seemed the perfect place: Banjawarn Station. The isolated ranch was huge, sprawled over half a million acres of hard rock and scrub. About a dozen buildings stood at its center: a large ranch house and barracks, a holding pen, and several trailers and prefab storage units. Not only did Banjawarn have uranium deposits; the place would be ideal as an Aum refuge during the coming apocalypse.

In early September, Hayakawa returned to Australia, intent on closing the deal for Banjawarn. He paid over $400,000 for the ranch, and then gave the state government $110,000 more for eight mining leases on the land. "They wanted to do a bit of prospecting and a bit of farming," said a local attorney who advised on the deal. But Aum had more than "a bit of prospecting" on its mind. Shortly after his return to Perth, Hayakawa met with the cult's consulting geologist. How much would it cost, he asked, to move a shipload of 44-gallon drums with uranium ore to Japan?

Within days, the guru himself was coming to visit, making Hayakawa a busy man. He hired three planes, six four-wheel drive vehicles, and arranged for supplies and accommodations. On September 9, Asahara and his entourage arrived in Perth. Once again, Aum's travel overseas was hard to miss. On the flight from Japan, the group's pushy behavior prompted the crew to point them out to airport authorities. Going through Immigration, the cultists must have been a sight. There were twenty-five members in all, eighteen of them men, five of them girls under fifteen traveling without parents. Chief scientist Murai was there, as were Endo, the bioweapons specialist, and Dr. Nakagawa. At the center stood the blind and bearded figure of Shoko Asahara, clothed in flowing purple robes.

The group held one-month tourist visas in their passports, but Customs officials found the accompanying baggage rather odd. The Japanese brought in two huge crates of chemicals and mining equipment, for which they paid the airline a whopping $24,000 in excess baggage fees. There were picks, shovels, generators, a mechanical ditch digger, respirators, and gas masks. The officials were puzzled, as most of the gear could have been bought more easily and cheaply in Australia.

More troubling than the mining gear were the chemicals. On closer inspection, officials found several large glass bottles marked "hand soap." The contents would have cleaned off not just the dirt from hands but also about an inch of flesh. Inside was hydrochloric acid. In addition, Customs found a whole range of "assorted chemicals, acids, and chemical solutions." The chemicals were for gold prospecting, the cultists explained.

To Aum's surprise, Australian authorities were not as easy to dupe as their Japanese counterparts. Endo and Nakagawa claimed they were the responsible parties, prompting the Aussies to charge them with carrying dangerous goods on an aircraft, fine them $1,800 each, and confiscate the chemicals and equipment. For bringing in the mining gear, the group was fined an additional duty of some $15,000. To ensure they'd made their point, the cultists were told that, after this trip, the entire party was barred from re-entering Australia for six months.

Undaunted, the cult went about its business. There was much to do, and money was clearly not a factor. In Perth, the group replaced their chemicals and mining equipment. For two 25-gram bottles of thioacetamide, a chemical reagent not available in Perth, Aum even flew one member cross-country to Melbourne, a 4,000-mile journey. The two bottles cost $140; the airfare $800.

Hayakawa had spent another $22,000 to charter the three aircraft to fly everyone to Banjawarn. Aum showed the same poor attention to safety as they did back home, loading down the prop planes with passengers, equipment, chemicals, a generator, and extra fuel. "The planes were flying bombs," said one Australian investigator. "If any of the chemicals had leaked in flight, there would have been a massive explosion."

Once at Banjawarn, the cultists got busy. Using the machinery they'd flown in, the group succeeded in extracting small amounts of uranium from the parched rock. The ore was apparently packed in suitcases bound for Japan, where Aum scientists would attempt enrichment.

After a long week at the ranch, Asahara and the others left for home. Plans were made to return the following month, but the Australian authorities were not being cooperative. Aum members applied for new visas, only to be flatly turned down. Apparently, the Aussies did not take well to Japanese cultists smuggling hydrochloric acid into their country. By now, however, Aum had invested nearly $1 million in their Australian operation, and was not going to give up easily. In late October, two cultists managed to sneak through by getting visas from Australia's Osaka consulate.

The ranch soon attracted the attention of state officials. In November, an Agriculture Department inspector reported that Banjawarn Station was a mess: sheep were dying from inattention, most troughs contained foul water, rangeland had deteriorated. Feral goats had increased on the land, yet the owners refused to shoot them. "The lessees are of a religious cult that forbids killing," bemoaned the report. Moreover, secluded on the hot, isolated ranch, the pair of Japanese "face high personal risk in the bush" and needed experienced help, the report warned. A month later, the state ordered Mahaposya to appoint a manager within days.

To assuage local authorities, the cult complied, appointing an Australian fellow, Neville Brosnan, to oversee the ranch. Brosnan thought the Japanese hopelessly naive about survival in the outback. "They knew nothing of station life," he told the *Western Australian*. "They wanted to make Banjawarn a center of healing and worship."

Still, it occurred to Brosnan that something odd was going on. One day he came across a locked door to one of the prefab huts; inside, the room looked like a kitchen. Brosnan busted open the bolt and found a fully equipped laboratory, stocked with Bunsen burners, glass beakers and tubing, laptop computers, digital equipment, and ceramic grinding and mixing bowls. On the floor were limestone and other rocks. Nearby stood a small rock-crushing machine and two electric generators. On the shelves stood bottle after bottle that had once held Japanese whiskey, now filled with hydrofluoric acid. "I'm a prospector," Brosnan said later. "I've used the stuff. It's so deadly that a few drops spilt on your skin can kill you."

"What's the story on this?" he asked the Japanese. They quickly grew agitated. "No touch!" he was told. "Master say no touch."

Outside were gallons of other acids and toxic chemicals. Most were fairly standard items used in mining, but some could have been used to make phosgene, a World War I choking agent. Brosnan never quite figured out what his employers were up to. Prospecting, of course, was one explanation "Another story was they were going to use it for soil analysis," he said. "They came up with half a dozen ideas. Nobody knew what they were really doing."

Back in Tokyo, top Aum officials applied yet again for visas. Evidently, they had pressing, unfinished business at Banjawarn. But again they were turned down. No visits for six months, said the Australian embassy. Even after six months had passed, Asahara was having trouble getting his people to Banjawarn. At issue this time was the guru's request to be accompanied by seventeen "bodyguards." If you're that worried about safety, said the embassy, hire a bunch of burly Australians.

Exasperated, Asahara himself wrote three-page letters to Australia's minister of immigration and minister of land, using his passport name. With broken English and tortured logic, Asahara explained why he and his bodyguards must be allowed to re-enter Australia.

DEAR SIR

HELLO, MY NAME IS CHIZUO MATSUMOTO, ALSO A PRESIDENT OF COMPANY CALLED MAHAPOSYA AUSTRALIA INC . . . MAHAPOSYA INC THAT I MANAGE IN JAPAN IS ALREADY YEARLY TURN OVER REACH TO 30 MILLION US DOLLARS BY 2 YEARS ACTIVITIES. (NEWS WAS REPORTED BY A FEW FAMOUS MAGAZINE). BUT ON THE OTHER HAND OF THESE EXPANSION, DISTURBANCE IS GETTING INCREASE. RECENTLY A FEW PEOPLE TRY TO AIM MY LIFE.

EVEN BEFORE MISCHIEVOUS RINGINGS OR WINDOWS BROKEN DOWN WERE MAIN THINGS BUT THESE DAYS ESCALATE TO MORE DANGEROUS WAYS LIKE VIOLENCE INCIDENT. ON THE TOP OF IT, STARTS ATTACKING BY HARMFUL GAS.

FOR EXAMPLE DILUTED HARMFUL GAS HAS BEEN SPRAID AROUND TOKYO HEADQUARTER, FACTORY AT YAMANASHI AND EACH SHOP WE RUN . . . ALSO VISITING RUSSIA TO HAVE LECTURES & ACTIVITY, WE HAD THREATENING CALL THAT SETTING BOMBS AT A HALL, IN FACT INCENDIARY FIRE OCCUR, SO THAT I HAD TO CANCEL OUT ALL SCHEDULES AND LEFT FOR HOME. ON THE WAY TO THE AIR PORT FROM HOTEL WE WERE CHASED PERSISTENTLY, BUT GOT THROUGH SAFELY WITH PROTECTION FROM ACCOMPANIED BODYGUARD FROM JAPAN.

I AM BLIND BY NATURE, I CAN'T DO ANYTHING BY MYSELF. AS I SAID I WAS ATTACKED BEFORE. THAT'S WHY I SELECT BODYGUARD FROM OUR EMPLOYEE . . . WITHOUT THEIR HELP, I WOULD HAVE INJURED MANY TIMES. IN SPITE OF THESE FACT, ACCOMPANIED BODYGUARD ARE NOT ABLE TO COME ALONG WITH, MEANS JUST LIKE SAYING YOU CAN COME TO AUSTRALIA FOR EXCHANGE TO THE LIFE . . .

AS IT IS, MANAGEMENT OF MAHAPOSYA AUSTRALIA WILL BE
NEGLECTED, ALSO INFLUENCE BADLY TO INVESTING PROJECT. THIS
DAMAGES NOT ONLY MAHAPOSYA BUT ALSO YOUR COUNTRY IN SEVERAL
WAYS.
WE WOULD LIKE YOU TO CONSIDER ABOVE MENTIONED STATEMENT,
AND PLEASE HELP AND SUPPORT OUR VISAS.
THANK YOU VERY MUCH FOR YOUR LISTENING.

In a P.S. to the Minister of Land, Asahara suggested he would sell the
ranch unless visas were issued immediately. Yet somehow the tales of
purple-robed cult leader targeted by assassins, chased by Russian
thugs, and attacked by poison gas failed to impress Australian officials.
The visas were denied. Legal niceties, though, had never stopped
Shoko Asahara before. Aum was not yet finished with their sheep
station in the outback.

At the ranch, meanwhile, Neville Brosnan continued to wonder
what his employers were up to. His wife Phyllis thought the Aum
members harmless. "They were totally opposed to killing of any
kind," she later told the press. "They would not kill a mosquito on
their arm, even if it could give them river virus."

Back home in Japan, the crash program to mass produce sarin
continued at an alarming pace. By mid-February 1994, Tsuchiya had
synthesized 66 pounds of the nerve gas at Satian 7 and in his own
laboratory, an airtight, double-walled facility next door. As cult
scientists grew more adept at managing their chemical plant, plans
were made to increase production. The target remained the same: 70
tons.

Later that month, Asahara gathered together more than a dozen
of his top people. The guru was clearly impatient about progress at
the plant. He wanted Satian 7 ready for mass production by April 25.
War was coming, he stressed yet again, and Aum must be prepared.

His scientists asked for more workers, and Asahara obliged. But
at the same time he ordered tighter security around the project. Dr.
Nakagawa had obtained a polygraph and was told to test everyone at
the plant. One by one they came to Nakagawa's desk. "Are you a
spy?" he asked them. "Are you faithful to the guru?" In Aum's
increasingly violent state, failure may well have meant death.
Everyone passed.

Asahara then ordered the new workers to assemble before him.
"Are you prepared to risk your life for this work?" the guru asked.

"You must honestly tell me if you can't. Those who can't, say so honestly, and I will transfer you to other work."

Asahara was frank about the consequences of their new job. "The work that I am assigning you is rather dangerous, and if we use it, a metropolis somewhere will be destroyed. This work is worth forty days of religious training in a solitary cell. Afterward, you will be promoted to a higher rank."

Then Nakagawa spoke. "Things related to Satian 7 are a secret. Tell no one about this. From now on, you will be living in Satian 7, and once you enter, do not ever leave."

The extra help gave Tsuchiya time to experiment with other chemical agents. Again the young chemist proved a success. His work on mustard gas went so well that the group drew up plans to mass-produce that as well. By now, cult front companies had also obtained a stockpile of chemicals to create cyanide gas and at least two other nerve agents.

To his disciples, Asahara had claimed the weapons were for self-defense. But his real purpose was now becoming clear: to give Aum the means to wage war. With 1996 fast approaching, Asahara would look like a fool if signs of Armageddon failed to occur. With a growing arsenal of deadly agents, the guru now had the means to jump-start the apocalypse. Even more worrisome, he had begun setting a precise time for the beginning of the end.

"We will start a war in Japan in August," Asahara told his medical chief, Dr. Hayashi. "Casualties are expected, so you must be prepared." Puzzled, Hayashi asked others what the Master had meant. On learning of the cult's growing stockpile of nerve agents, he began buying huge quantities of PAM, an antidote. As sarin and its sister gases belong to the same family as insecticides, the drug was easily obtained through agricultural suppliers.

A key test remained for Aum's scientists – would their chemical agents work, and how effectively? That spring, Asahara decided on a worthy first target: Daisaku Ikeda, leader of the Buddhist sect Soka Gakkai. Largest of Japan's "new religions," the rival Soka Gakkai was a frequent target of Aum's wrath. A cult publication accused Ikeda of "selling his soul to the devil." A sarin attack seemed a convenient way of showing what happened to false prophets.

The boys at Clear Stream Temple, Aum's huge weapons plant, had rigged an industrial spraying device onto the back of a truck. Attached to the sprayer, inside an airtight container, they had placed two pounds of sarin solution. The cult had chosen the evening of an

Ikeda lecture, and maneuvered their truck beside the building where he spoke. The sprayer failed to work, however, so the cultists returned a second night. But then something went terribly wrong; the sarin leaked onto Niimi, the security chief, who soon fell to the ground in convulsions. Only quick action by Dr. Nakagawa stopped the man's nervous system from completely shutting down.

The sarin seemed to have worked, but on the wrong target. Aum still needed to test the agent in the field, but an attack in Japan now appeared too unpredictable. What the cult needed was an isolated place far removed from home – a site so distant and deserted that no one would think of looking there.

A toxic mist of sarin blew across an isolated corner of Banjawarn Station, settling on a herd of merino sheep. As if part of some strange ritual, the animals were tethered to the ground in a semicircle. Not far away stood a cluster of human figures, clad in full-body chemical suits in the blazing sun.

Before long, the sheep began to twitch and salivate, then stagger and lose bodily control. One by one, they collapsed on the ground, writhing in convulsions until, finally, they were still.

As remote as Banjawarn was, even Aum had its neighbors. And it was about this time that Phyllis Thomas, leader of a nearby Aboriginal community, happened by the ranch with her companions. Thomas hailed from the Mulga Queen Aboriginal settlement, about 35 miles away. She and her companions were driving past Banjawarn's private airstrip when they saw a scene that seemed out of a science-fiction movie.

"We saw four or five people wearing white or cream protective clothing and helmets," she told Reuters. "They were standing next to a light plane. I think it was twin-engined, and there were some other people in the plane."

"I was frightened," she said. "I thought they looked like wild, savage people. I thought to myself, they're doing something they're not supposed to be doing."

When it was over, twenty-nine sheep lay on the ground, slaughtered by Aum Supreme Truth in a nerve-gas attack. The experiment had been a success. Sarin worked.

One of Tsuchiya's technicians, a female believer, now realized that her efforts had gone into producing a toxic gas. She approached her boss with a question: Would further animal tests be necessary?

"Killing animals is wrong," the head chemist replied. "Men have committed more misdeeds than animals. It will be tested on men."

PART TWO

ARMAGEDDON

19

A CHEMICAL CHANGE

In the sixteenth century, the town of Matsumoto stood at the heart of a nation racked with civil strife. Attempts to pacify feudal lords and unify Japan had ended in assassinations and reckless military adventurism overseas. In 1592, Matsumoto's powerful Ishikawa clan ordered an impregnable moated castle to be built. It was constructed of wood and situated on a plain surrounded by snow-capped mountains. The Ishikawa samurai could spot their enemies approaching from any direction.

By the time the castle was completed in 1614, Japan had been consolidated under the government of the shogun Ieyasu Tokugawa in the city of Edo, known today as Tokyo, some 100 miles to the southeast. All contact with the world beyond Japan's shores was forbidden on pain of death. Landlocked Matsumoto was an inaccessible part of an insular country, yet it flourished in isolation. With civil war over, the swords of the samurai lay idle. Matsumoto castle was built for war, but its soaring turrets presided over an age of relative peace and prosperity.

The castle still stands in Matsumoto today as one of Japan's finest examples of feudal architecture. Now only a three-hour train ride from Tokyo, this resort town of 200,000 people is a favored destination for tourists seeking hot springs, alpine hiking, year-round skiing and pure mountain air. Near Matsumoto station, a large electronic display proudly counts the days to the 1998 Winter Olympics, which will be held in the surrounding Japan Alps. This event, locals hoped, would put their town on the world map. But global recognition came early to Matsumoto.

On the evening of Monday, June 27, 1994, a refrigerated delivery truck rolled into the ancient heart of the city. The two-ton vehicle lumbered past the floodlit castle and, near the district-court house, turned off into a quiet residential area. In a supermarket parking lot, the truck came to a halt.

It was there, at around 10 p.m., that a local housewife spotted the truck. It's unclear why she considered it noteworthy. Perhaps the vehicle seemed curiously unwieldy. Or maybe the driver and passenger seemed unusually jumpy. Whatever the reason, she later mentioned the truck to a police officer. He shrugged it off. "Oh, it was probably just making a delivery to the supermarket," he told her.

The officer was wrong. The truck did not contain food and drinks for the supermarket shelves, but another kind of inventory altogether. Crammed into the vehicle were thirty batteries, one atomizer, six makeshift gas masks, six religious fanatics, and 44 pounds of one of the world's deadliest chemical compounds.

Aum Supreme Truth had learned bitter lessons from land disputes in the past. It was extra-cautious in Matsumoto. In 1991, a food firm bought a plot of land there and began constructing a processing plant. Then locals discovered the truth. The food firm was in fact an Aum dummy company. And the two-story structure rising from the acquired land was the cult's new Matsumoto branch.

The original owner of the land immediately filed a civil suit to invalidate the sale, and the case began to grind through the town's district court. Meanwhile, Aum launched another of its well-rehearsed harassment campaigns against locals. "I was hounded by a flood of telephone calls," recalled one Matsumoto resident. "Sometimes they said things like, 'We're not going to let you get away with this.'"

In December 1992, Aum's new Matsumoto branch office was complete, and Master Asahara delivered a sinister sermon. He began by condemning the "unreasonable pressure" the court had applied over the disputed land. Then, in an apparent warning to the three judges presiding over the case, Asahara quoted from one of his favorite sources of apocalyptic thought – Nostradamus, the sixteenth-century French astrologer.

According to Nostradamus, he said, the world's judicial authorities would be "out of control" by the end of the twentieth century. "By being out of control," Asahara explained, "I mean that they will not know how to tell right from wrong." And judges who cannot distinguish between right and wrong, the guru continued, would suffer "a chemical change unthinkable in normal circumstances."

By this time, Shoko Asahara's wild sermons were littered with clues to what that "chemical change" might be. "The law in an emergency is to kill one's opponent with a single blow," he said two months earlier. "For instance, in the way research was conducted on soman and sarin during World War II." There were, in fact, references to sarin in Asahara's sermons going back more than a year, but no one seemed to notice.

The Matsumoto land trial finally ended in May 1994. The court's three judges were expected to hand down a ruling two months later. At this time Aum's lawyer visited the guru with some bad news. There was a strong chance that Aum would lose the case, he said. If the judges ruled against Aum, the cult would be forced to abandon their new Matsumoto outpost. That, the guru decided, would not happen.

Early the following month, Asahara summoned senior Aum members to his spacious chambers in Satian 2. Among those present were Hideo Murai, the cult's deceptively unassuming science chief, and Tomomitsu Niimi, the ruthless security chief. The details of the meeting remain sketchy, but its outcome was clear: a plan was hatched to rid the world of three troublesome judges. At the meeting's end, the Revered Master gave the order. Murai bowed obediently. "We'll go as soon as possible," he said.

Aum's vast Mount Fuji complexes soon saw a surge of secret activity. At Murai's command, Satian 7 stepped up its production of sarin. Work also accelerated on creating an effective delivery mechanism, which had so far eluded the team. That month, Aum scientists went shopping for travel clocks, double-sided adhesive tape, and containers for chemical time bombs. One unusual cosmetics case seemed ideal – it came with a portable perfume dispenser, into which the cult could place liquid sarin.

For a major attack, however, they would need a larger, more sophisticated device. Murai ordered a five-strong technical team to customize a refrigerated truck. The sarin would be kept in a large container bolted to the truck's load platform. The container was attached to a powerful electric heater run on thirty large batteries. The nerve agent would drip onto the heater and vaporize, then a fan system would blow the gas through a small window in the truck's side. The technical team had already tested the fan on a flood plain near the Fuji River estuary – using real sarin. Still, the vehicle's redesign was imperfect. The batteries that powered the atomizer weighed a total of 1,000 pounds and filled a third of the truck.

Two Aum lieutenants were dispatched to Matsumoto to scout the area around the district-court building. Another hired a black eight-seater minivan from a rental firm in front of Matsumoto station to serve as a lookout vehicle on the night. The number plates on the van and truck were altered.

The only task left was to choose the hit squad. This was done by the guru himself. He hand-picked each follower for a combination of qualities: physical strength, driving skills, and – above all else – loyalty. Among the chosen ones were two men in their late twenties, renowned as karate experts and die-hard followers of the cult.

By mid-June, Aum's chief chemist had stockpiled 44 pounds of sarin at Satian 7. It was then that he phoned an old friend. "Stay away from crowded places," the chemist warned him. "Aum Supreme Truth is out of control."

June 27, 1994, in Matsumoto brought a welcome respite from the damp and relative cool of Japan's rainy season. The crippling humidity dropped, the thermometer soared to 86 degrees, and a slight breeze picked up. It was a Monday morning and, across the town, residents threw open windows and hung out washing. As every housewife knew, the hot, dry weather was ideal for airing laundry. As every Aum scientist knew, hot, dry weather was also ideal for spreading chemical munitions.

Despite the military preparation, Aum's mission began badly. Somehow, the devout science chief Hideo Murai overslept. It was afternoon by the time his squad left Mount Fuji, and the deadly convoy – Murai and five cultists in the truck, five others in the lookout van – made slow progress. Weighed down by the batteries, the aging truck's top speed was only 30 miles per hour. As planned, the drivers avoided Japan's expressways, where automatic cameras often record license plates, and opted for a slower route along back roads. By the time the cultists arrived in Matsumoto, the judges had left the court building.

But Murai did not postpone the attack. Instead, he made a decision that would have a critical effect on hundreds of lives. He ordered his team to target a nearby dormitory where the three judges were known to live. The dormitory sat in a densely populated residential area.

At 10 p.m., the convoy parked in the supermarket lot. A team was dispatched to gather information on weather conditions. It returned soon after with its report: the neighborhood was deadly quiet, and a light easterly wind had picked up. Murai made some calculations. If the truck was moved to another parking lot nearby, this breeze would carry the nerve agent toward the judges' lodgings some 60 yards away. It would also have to drift past one house and two apartment blocks, but they could live with that. Casualties were inevitable in the righteous war against the forces of state persecution.

Final preparations were made. The team doctor gave his colleagues injections of sarin antidote. Afterwards, each man pulled an inflated plastic bag over his head. These makeshift gas masks were connected by tubes to oxygen cylinders. Then the two vehicles pulled out of the supermarket lot and slowly drove to the car park nearer the judges' quarters.

At around 10:40 p.m., the attack began. The window was opened and the fan switched on. Power surged from the batteries, raising the heater to critical temperature. Then a valve was twisted open and the sarin dripped onto the hotplate with an angry hiss of deadly steam. Almost immediately, however, the chemical reaction seemed to go wrong.

The sarin in the tank was cobalt blue, apparently the result of too much isopropyl alcohol being added. The temperature rose and created hydrogen chloride, which evaporated into a white mist. The truck was quickly lost in a deadly cloud of gases. Soon Murai and his team could see nothing through the windows. In the truck's sweltering confines, one cultist began to panic. "It's lucky we're doing this at night – everyone can see us," he thought, biting back his fear.

The cultist was right to worry. Around 11 p.m., a junior high-school student passed the parking lot as he took garbage down to a nearby dump. Strange, the boy thought: there's a van with its lights off and its engine running. He could hear muffled voices from inside.

On his way back from the waste dump ten minutes later, the student saw the van shoot out of the parking lot and drive away. Now its headlights were on and, for a second, its beams illuminated a fine white mist hugging the ground up to waist level.

Then the easterly wind changed direction.

20

MURDER AT MATSUMOTO

For machinery salesman Yoshiyuki Kono, June 27 was a pretty normal evening until the dogs died.

Kono returned home from work at 8 p.m., parking his Nissan Sunny outside his gate. The dark, sweeping roofs of his traditional wooden house brooded conspicuously among his neighborhood's concrete apartment blocks. The first character of Kono's surname was stamped on its eaves, a proud echo of the days when the area was home to samurai who served at the castle nearby. Kono was forty-four years old, a family man with one son and two daughters. He was also something of a loner. Rather than chatting with neighbors, he preferred tinkering with the VW Beetles which lay in various states of disrepair around his yard.

Kono removed his shoes at the door, then walked down a hallway lined with Japanese-language Western classics. He made his way to the living room, a cramped space cluttered with books and bric-a-brac. His wife Sumiko was a piano teacher, and Mendelssohn often seeped from the room's refrigerator-sized speakers. Kono sat at a low table at the room's center. On it was a cracked coaster with the inscription: "Bless this house, oh Lord we pray, make it safe night and day."

Sumiko served her husband Thai rice pilaf for dinner. Their son joined them, and the three Konos ate while watching a samurai drama on TV. After dinner, Kono read the newspaper while Sumiko washed the dishes. At 10 p.m., a television cabaret began, and the couple settled down in the living room to watch it.

Outside the Konos' living room is a modest garden with two miniature ponds and a small grove of trees. At the bottom of the garden, obscured by greenery, is a parking lot. Even with the living-room curtains open, the Konos wouldn't have noticed a refrigerated truck and black minivan pull in.

When the TV program ended, Sumiko turned to her husband. "I feel a little bit sick," she groaned.

Kono looked at his wife. She seemed fine. "Maybe you should lie down for a while," he replied.

Then Kono was distracted by a noise outside – a scratching sound from the kennels on the house's north side. He went out to investigate.

Kono discovered his setter bitch in the dog yard, convulsing and foaming at the mouth. "Hold on, girl," he murmured, and hurried off to fetch some water. When he returned, the setter was dead. So was her puppy, who lay motionless nearby.

Poison! thought Kono. Somebody threw poison over the fence and killed my dogs.

He shouted for his wife. "Mother! I think we should call the police. Hey, Mother!"

There was no reply. With a twinge of impatience, Kono trudged back inside.

He found his wife on the living-room floor, her body shuddering with violent spasms. Kono dropped to his knees and immediately began loosening her clothes, but the convulsions only grew stronger. At 11:09 p.m., he called an ambulance, then shouted for his children to come quickly. By the time they emerged from their rooms, Kono himself was on the verge of collapse.

His head was pounding. His vision was breaking up into kaleidoscopic fragments. When the lights in the room suddenly seemed to dim, Kono began to panic. This is it, he said to himself. I'm dying.

He grabbed his son's hand. "Mom and Dad might not make it through this," he told the boy, waves of nausea washing over him. "Please take care of everything, won't you?"

Then Kono slipped into a deathlike trance. His world rapidly disintegrated into a series of nightmarish scenes. Knocking in slo-mo on the ambulance window, hearing his disembodied voice say, *I-ate-Thai-rice-pilaf-for-dinner.* Vomiting uncontrollably in the back of the ambulance, watching through pinhole pupils while paramedics pumped his wife's failing heart. A blindingly bright hospital seething with casualties. A woman on the next stretcher screaming, over and over again. *What's happening to me? What's happening to me? What's happening to me?* His voice saying to his son, *If the police don't need the dogs for evidence, bury them under the lilac tree.*

Then the spasms began again, whipping through Kono's body.

*

Seven of Yoshiyuki Kono's neighbors died in agony on the night of Monday, June 27, 1994. In one apartment, police found *tatami* straw matting in shreds where a gas victim had writhed to death. Three others perished in their homes, three more on the way to the hospital. Throughout the neighborhood, residents with pounding heads had vomited and groped for light switches as their pupils shrank and the world dimmed.

Matsumoto's emergency services struggled to cope with over 150 casualties, many of them suffering from permanent injuries – clouded vision, erratic temperatures, acute damage to the lungs and digestive system. To Matsumoto's doctors it was clear that this was no ordinary gas leak. Blood tests on patients revealed a shocking lack of the cholinesterase enzyme, suggesting organophosphate poisoning of some kind. Doctors prescribed injections of atropine.

Kono didn't die, as he had expected, but was hospitalized along with his two daughters. All three would recover. His wife, however, was less fortunate. She arrived at the hospital in a deep coma. The nerve agent had begun to shut down her lungs and heart, and she suffered massive brain damage caused by oxygen starvation.

As paramedics fought to save the Konos, Aum's two-vehicle convoy roared out of Matsumoto. In their panic to leave, the cultists left the truck's gas outlet open. The last of the vaporized sarin wafted through the back streets, poisoning more people. Back at the Mount Fuji headquarters, the squad incinerated their clothes and dismantled the truck's gas-delivery system. Then they scrubbed the truck and rental van with a sarin neutralizer.

For Murai and his men, the Matsumoto attack had been a catalog of errors. The last-minute change in wind direction meant the three judges had not received a direct hit. They all survived. One was hospitalized, along with his wife, while the others suffered only mild symptoms. Even so, the hit squad had achieved one objective: the judges were too ill to attend court, so the ruling on the land dispute was postponed indefinitely.

And there was an unexpected bonus. The Matsumoto police clearly did not suspect the cult's involvement in the attack. Quite the opposite. The following day, investigators visited the hospital to interrogate a man who had first raised the alarm that night. Police chemists had identified the poison as sarin, but that's as much as they got right. Authorities announced they had confiscated nineteen types of chemicals from his house and that the man had inadvertently produced sarin while mixing a home-made herbicide in his back garden.

The police's chief suspect was no killer, however. He was a machinery salesman called Yoshiyuki Kono. Incredibly, the flatfoots at Matsumoto police station had fingered the wrong man.

Hideo Murai later punched a secret number into his mobile phone and reported the mission's success to Asahara. The guru was pleased – so pleased that he promoted two members of the hit squad.

"Thank you for your trouble," Shoko Asahara told them. "You guys did a great job."

Three months later, Yoshiyuki Kono remained the prime suspect. He spent thirty-three days in the hospital suffering from hyperactivity and irregular body temperature caused by minor brain damage. Every day, without fail, he spent time at his wife's bedside. Often he would play her Mendelssohn on a portable cassette player, praying that a well-known melody might lure her from the depths of her coma.

When Kono wasn't piecing together his shattered family, he was battling against a police version of events that seemed immune to the facts. He said he bought the chemicals for his hobby, photography, not to make a herbicide. As specialists later stressed, the odds of "inadvertently" producing sarin even while mixing a herbicide are extraordinarily remote. More damning, Kono simply lacked the range of chemicals to produce nerve gas.

The police weren't buying it. They needed a criminal and Kono was their man. In bedside interrogations, Kono said, the cops lied and shouted insults to force a confession out of him. "You're the criminal!" they yelled. "Be honest!" They reduced Kono's sixteen-year-old son to tears by falsely saying his father had confessed and that he'd best do the same.

Kono tried to tell a largely unsympathetic nation of his innocence, but the media, taking their cue from police, delivered a torrent of libel and abuse. One TV network flew over his garden in a helicopter, spotted places where Kono had pulled out weeds, and reported them as "chemical burns." Others announced Kono's imminent arrest and dug into his past. Prompted by the coverage, Kono received over one hundred threatening phone calls. An anonymous graffiti artist altered one streetside map in the neighborhood, so that Kono's home was now identified as the "House of Dr. Gas."

Kono and his daughters had been hospitalized. His wife was a vegetable. If he knew enough chemistry to mix his own herbicide, Kono argued with conviction and dignity, wouldn't he have known he was putting his family at grave risk?

At least one group of people believed him. In September, Kono received a parcel. Inside he found four books written by His Holiness the Master Shoko Asahara, along with a letter inviting him to bring his wife for treatment at an Aum-run hospital. There was also a questionnaire. If he filled it out, the letter promised, he could receive a free tape of the guru's "astral music" which would help his wife regain consciousness.

Japan's major media organizations also received a package that month. It contained a mysterious eleven-page document entitled "Some Thoughts on the Matsumoto Sarin Attack." The sender's identity was unknown. The only signature on the document was a string of cryptic initials: "H. to H. & T. K." Whoever the writer was, he or she was surprisingly familiar with the fine details of the Matsumoto attack.

"It is impossible to make sarin from the chemicals seized from [Kono's] house," the document read. "Despite the police theory that sarin was made at the scene, the perpetrator very likely brought in sarin that had been made elsewhere." The anonymous writer had no doubt about the real perpetrators of the attack. "Aum Supreme Truth is guilty of the sarin attack . . . It has the manpower, materials, money and motive to deal with this mad weapon."

What was the writer's true identity? The document's detailed analysis of June 27, 1994, suggested someone very close to the crime. A renegade Aum follower appalled by the cult's insanity, perhaps. Or a police investigator anxious to change the probe's direction.

No media organization published any part of the report at the time. In fact, Japanese journalists were still speculating intensely about the document's origins when the next letter arrived from 'H. to H. & T. K." This time, the message was abrupt.

"P.S.," it read. "Matsumoto ws definitely an experiment of sorts. The result of this experiment in an open space: seven dead, over 200 injured. If sarin is released in an enclosed space – say, a crowded subway – it is easy to imagine a massive catastrophe."

21

DYNAMITE

Two weeks after the attack on Matsumoto, disaster struck Satian 7. In the rush towards full sarin production, Aum's scientists had been less than diligent about plant safety, and now they would pay for it.

The alarm rang out just after midnight. Shouts filled the plant ordering everyone to evacuate, as a deadly, foul-smelling mist drifted through labs and hallways. It was chlorine, the same gas used by the Germans eighty years ago at the dawn of modern chemical warfare, and which Aum was now using to manufacture sarin. The gas had leaked from a faulty weld, then combined with moisture in the air to form hydrochloric acid.

Workers scrambled from the exit, their eyes stinging and noses bloodied. Some collapsed on the ground, gasping for breath. Followers appeared in gas masks to haul victims away to the cult hospital. Within minutes, the toxic cloud drifted across Aum's compound to the surrounding community. Four neighbors of dairy farmer Norie Okamoto fled to his house, vomiting and nauseous. Others complained of a rotten, sweetish odor and then dizziness, headaches, and trouble breathing.

The next morning, firemen and police checked the area around Aum's facilities, finding tanks labeled "sulfuric acid" and open bags marked "caustic soda" strewn about. But as they approached Satian 7, five or six Aum guards blocked their way. "Why are you trespassing on our property?" one asked. "It has nothing to do with us. We are the victims." Unwilling to confront the cult, the officials took their search elsewhere.

The cult's relations with local residents had never been good. Now they plummeted to an all-time low. An Aum spokesman blamed the smell on a poison-gas attack directed at the cult. Their neighbors thought otherwise, especially after spotting followers the next day at a public toilet, filling plastic drums with water. Apparently the contamination had spread to the cult's water supplies.

For years Aum Supreme Truth had wreaked havoc in Kami-kuishiki, the farming hamlet of 1,700 in which the cult's largest compounds stood. Cultists had driven over their neighbor's crops, abandoned empty chemical drums in their fields, played mantras through loudspeakers at night, and made twenty-four-hour construction noise. "Once, hundreds of them marched through the village wearing white hoods," said 65-year-old Okamoto, whose back door was barely ten yards from an Aum facility. "They looked like the Ku Klux Klan. It scared the hell out of the children."

Okamoto, a longtime resident, became a staunch member of the village's Aum Countermeasures Committee. The group erected large roadside signs, reading, "Admit it, Aum, you're not welcome here!" and "Stop ruining our property!" Other notices barred cultists from the local supermarket and public toilets, and a sign by a lawyers' group offered $200,000 for information on the missing Sakamoto family. Parent after parent visited Okamoto, asking for help in finding their lost sons and daughters. He kept their photos in a poignant album of young, innocent-looking kids in high-school uniforms or their Sunday best.

The foul odor emanating from the Aum compound, then, was just the latest in the villagers' long list of grievances. And the list would grow even longer. One week after the chlorine leak at Satian 7, another accident hit the plant.

Again came the reports of poisoning, toxic clouds, and gas masks at the Aum facility. By now, the leaves on trees around Satian 7 were discolored, the plants withered and brown. Farmer Okamoto's garden began to shrivel and die. Still, officials took no action. There was no direct evidence the gas came from Aum, and dealing with the cult was trouble, as everyone knew – including the cops. Aum was aggressive, confrontational, and quick to strike back with lawsuits and charges of religious persecution. All in all, not the kind of group handled well by most Japanese, who prefer an indirect, less confrontational way of getting along.

Yet in retrospect, it seems incredible that authorities failed to move against the cult. By now, Aum had committed a list of crimes that grew longer and more frightening each month: commercial fraud, land fraud, medical malpractice, extortion, drug abuse, firearms and explosives violations, manufacture of biochemical weapons, kidnapping, mass murder. With seven killed at Matsumoto, at least twelve had died by Aum's hand, while hundreds more had suffered terribly.

The authorities had clear reasons to suspect the cult of a number of these crimes. An obscure nerve gas called sarin had been publicly mentioned in Asahara's sermons and in cult literature, and residents complained of chemical leaks from cult facilities. Yet after all this, police responded by fingering the wrong man for the Matsumoto attack. Meanwhile, nearly five years after the Sakamotos had disappeared in Yokohama, cops there were still scratching their heads. "We're still not sure it's a criminal case," said a police spokesman in 1994. It was a sad time for Japanese law enforcement.

The lack of expertise in solving big crimes continued to dog police. One key factor was that Japan's decentralized police system has no national investigative authority like the FBI – a reaction to its prewar Gestapo-like Thought Police. There is a National Police Agency, but its purpose is largely administrative; investigations are conducted by local authorities. The absence of a national effort left the task to prefectures like Nagano, scene of the Matsumoto attack, where the 2,000-man police force spent much of its time rescuing lost hikers in the mountains nearby. The cops in Yamanashi prefecture, the site of Aum's Mount Fuji center, similarly handled at most one or two murders per year. Worsening matters, traditional rivalries meant that Tokyo and prefectural police shared little information on the cult's activities.

The nation's Security Bureau, an intelligence unit usually focused on leftists, had taken note of Aum's Russian contacts, but they also failed to share information. Even had there been a coordinated attack, authorities faced other difficulties investigating a tight-knit group like Aum. In another reaction to the bad old days, police were unwilling to do wiretapping or undercover work, leaving them few ways to gain intelligence from inside the cult. The nation, in effect, had a nineteenth-century police force trying to fight twenty-first-century crime.

The gas leaks at Mount Fuji offered another chance for Japanese authorities to scrutinize Aum. But again there was no follow-up. Within weeks, Satian 7 engineers had ironed out kinks in the production process. New batches of sarin soon dripped off the Satian 7 assembly line, which Murai confidently predicted would produce 70 tons of nerve agent within forty days. The failure of police to investigate left an open road for Aum's race towards apocalypse.

"Terror will be terror in the true sense of the word only if it represents the revolutionary implementation of the most advanced technical sciences at any given moment." The year was 1909, and a proponent of "dynamite terrorism" was giving an address to the Fifth Conference of Social Revolutionaries.

There was, it turns out, an earlier generation of hi-tech terrorists, who looked to dynamite, the premier scientific explosive of their time. In a fascinating 1981 paper, "The Mindsets of High-Technology Terrorists," two Rand Corporation analysts reveal how enthusiasts imbued dynamite with special, even mystical powers. "When the revolution comes there will be millions of dynamite bombs and they will flash and crash all over the civilized world simultaneously. That's what will happen," predicted Albert Parsons in an American anarchist journal in 1887.

Nitroglycerine had been discovered in Italy in 1846, but the chemical had a nasty habit of blowing up in its user's face. It was Alfred Nobel who found that by mixing in wood pulp and sodium nitrate, one could stabilize the explosive and make it widely available. Nobel called the invention dynamite.

Revolutionaries and terrorists seized on the explosive as the ultimate weapon. "Dynamite! Of all the good stuff, this is the stuff," wrote another anarchist in 1885. "In giving dynamite to the downtrodden millions of the globe, science has done its best work." The explosive captured the imagination of Irish Fenians fighting for independence, who called it a "gift of science" and threatened to level London with it. Armed with sticks of TNT, they staged attacks against the Tower of London, Scotland Yard, the House of Commons – and the London subway system.

Over a hundred years later, a Japanese death cult would engage in its own search for the ultimate weapon. By the summer of 1994, Aum pushed ahead with R&D on a dozen different weapons systems. Dynamite would be just one component of a devastating armory.

At Satian 7 and Tsuchiya's private lab, cult scientists had now succeeded in synthesizing a range of chemical-warfare agents. They had produced VX, a postwar nerve gas more persistent and penetrating than sarin, and had stockpiled pounds of mustard gas, the World War I blistering agent. To protect against more leaks, Aum purchased new gas masks and some 600 mask filters, telling suppliers they were for cleaning semiconductor parts. The fact that Aum had no semiconductor plant seemed not to occur to anyone.

Endo, the mad microbiologist, now boasted two biolabs, with equipment rivalling that of a major pharmaceutical company.

The half-blind Shoko Asahara spreads his unique gospel of mysticism and apocalypse. Asahara shopped the world's religions to form Aum, taking Hindu deities, yoga and Buddhism from the East, and Armageddon from the West. (Sankei Shimbun)

Left Buildings of Aum's Mt Fuji headquarters, at the base of the great mountain. From a one-room yoga school, Aum grew into a multi-million dollar empire with more than 40,000 members in at least six countries.
(Andrew Marshall)

平和と友好のきずな
麻原彰晃尊師と
ダライ・ラマ法王の親交

海を越え、届けられる
真理教信徒の善意と布施

今年度ノーベル平和賞に、
チベットの政治・宗教の最高指導者ダライ・ラマ法王の受賞が決定した。
非暴力によるチベット解放闘争が国際的に高く評価されたもので、
少数民族問題に悩む多くの難民に勇気と希望を与えるものとなろう。
そして、この亡命チベット人達とチベット伝統文化を支援している一人が、
宗教法人オウム真理教開祖、麻原彰晃尊師、その人である。

宗教法人 オウム真理教
お問い合わせ 富士山総本部道場 TEL 0544(54)1267・東京本部道場 TEL(03)3277(8595)

Right Aum guru Shoko Asahara with the Dalai Lama in the late 1980s. The Tibetan Buddhist told him he had 'the mind of a Buddha,' Asahara said, which Aum then used as a holy endorsement.
(Kyodo News Service)

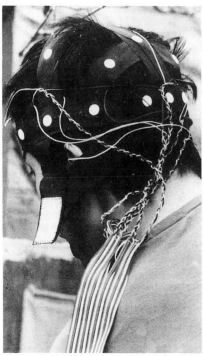

Above Aum members with Asahara masks, campaigning to elect the guru and other cultists to the Japanese parliament in 1990. Their loss at the polls led to spiralling violence and the complete rejection of society. (Sankei Shimbun)

Left Aum's electrode cap, called the PSI or Perfect Salvation Initiation. Worn by hundreds of devotees, the battery-driven headgear delivered six-volt shocks to the scalp to 'synchronize' one's brain waves with those of the guru. (Kyodo News Service)

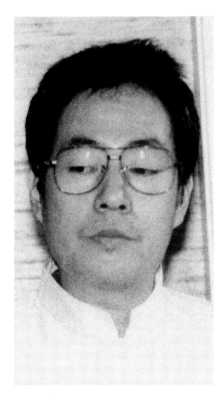

Left Kiyohide Hayakawa, who vied with chief scientist Murai to be Asahara's top lieutenant. As Aum's Minister of Construction, Hayakawa travelled the globe setting up facilities, buying weapons, and trying to obtain a nuclear bomb. (Kyodo News Service)

Below Dr Ikuo Hayashi, the cult's own Josef Mengele. As director of Aum medical services, Hayashi presided over a horror-shop of human experiments, drugging and crackpot medicine.
(Kyodo News Service)

Tomomitsu Niimi, Aum's sadistic Minister of Internal Affairs. As security chief, Niimi personally enforced the guru's law by kidnapping, imprisonment and murder.(Kyodo News Service)

Yoshihiro Inoue, Aum's Minister of Intelligence. The young disciple proved adept at recruiting new members, infiltrating the military, and plotting mass murder.
(Mainichi Shimbun)

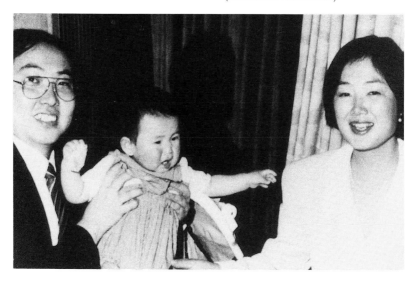

Tsutsumi Sakamoto, the gutsy, activist attorney who took on Aum, shown here with his wife and one-year-old son. Sakamoto and his family were among the cult's first victims. (Kyodo News Service)

Left Hideo Murai, a brilliant astrophysicist who became Aum's powerful Minister of Science and Technology. Under Murai's direction, the cult developed an extraordinary range of exotic weapons.
(Kyodo News Service)

Seiichi Endo, Aum's biological weapons chief. Armed with a Ph.D in molecular biology and state-of-the-art lab equipment, Endo cultured some of the deadliest organisms on Earth.
(Mainichi Shimbun)

Masami Tsuchiya, Aum's top chemist. Led by Tsuchiya, cult scientists synthesized a frightening array of nerve gases and other chemical agents.
(Kyodo News Service)

Left The remains of sheep killed by nerve gas at Banjawarn Station in the Australian outback. The remote ranch proved an ideal spot for Aum's experiments.
(Australian Federal Police)

Below One of the world's safest cities turns into a killing field as Aum launches a nerve gas attack on the Tokyo subways. The Monday morning, rush-hour assault signalled a new era in modern terrorism.(Asahi Shimbun)

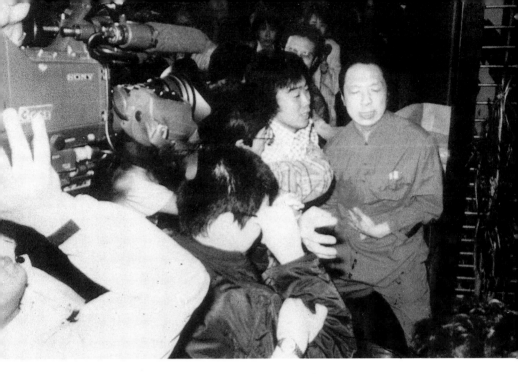

Above Chief scientist Murai clutches his abdomen after an assassin's attack in April 1995. He was stabbed repeatedly with a butcher's knife outside Aum headquarters. (Mainichi Shimbun)

Left Police belatedly raid Aum's Mt Fuji headquarters in spring 1995. Authorities found huge stockpiles of more than 200 chemicals, enough to build a devastating arsenal of biological and chemical weapons. (Yomiuri Shimbun)

Electron microscopes and hi-tech incubators replaced the old gear his team once used. So brisk was the rate of experimentation that Aum ordered 160 18-liter cans of peptone, the protein used for culturing bacteria. By contrast, university research classes usually use one liter of peptone per year.

Endo had amassed a library of some 300 books on biochemistry, including texts on how to culture the world's most virulent bacteria. The reading had paid off. He was finally close to perfecting a weapon using botulin toxin, and had purchased large quantities of the bacteria that produces it. At the same time, Endo had obtained spores of a poisonous mushroom species and, perhaps inspired by his Australian foray, began culturing Q fever, or North Queensland fever. A highly contagious rickettsia, Q fever knocks people on their backs with a terrible flu lasting up to three months. During the 1962 Cuban missile crisis, U.S. officials considered spraying it across Cuba as a "softening-up" attack before invasion.

At the cult's firearms plant at Clear Stream Temple, gun production progressed with initial runs of triggers, safety catches, and other less complex parts. Asahara had ordered a prototype AK-74 to be built by the end of 1994 "by all means," and cult scientists worked desperately to meet this deadline.

The cult also shared the Fenian fascination with explosives, but took it to new heights. Through the cult's construction jobs, Hayakawa apparently gained access to small explosives used in building demolition. The four-inch cylindrical charges were so easy to get, he bought 600. Other purchases brought in four tons of potassium nitrate, five tons of sulfur, and charcoal – the basic ingredients for gunpower. If Aum were going to mass-produce automatic rifles, they would need ammunition.

Cult chemists succeeded in synthesizing a whole range of powerful explosives. An early success was trinitrotoluene, better known as TNT. Another was RDX, or cyclonite, a vibration-sensitive chemical used to mix with other charges. The cult also made cellulose nitrate, the raw material for smokeless gunpowder, but failed with azide lead, used in detonators. Hayakawa was so satisfied with the cult's success that he set up plans for an explosives factory. "5/5 TNT plant, plan, plant engineer, illegal, 88 million yen," he scribbled in his notebook. And then, "30,000 tons TNT," followed by a chemical formula.

Aum's scientists showed their usual flair in researching delivery vehicles. What the cult wanted most was a highly efficient way to disseminate sarin and the rest of its biochemical arsenal. For that, Asahara decided, they would need an air force.

First, the guru sent two disciples to the tropical grounds of a private flight school in Opa Locka, Florida. On October 31, 1993, Aum's budding air force had its first top guns: the two received helicopter-pilot certificates and headed home for Japan. Then Aum reps contacted helicopter makers and importers across Japan, looking for the right deal. One French chopper, listed at nearly $100,000, looked promising. Aum offered cash but the company wanted nothing to do with a religious sect.

At the same time, cult buyers began picking up other aircraft for Aum's air cavalry – a blimp and two remote-controlled mini-choppers. The drone helicopters, used for photographing sites like active volcanoes, could stay aloft for ninety minutes with speeds up to 85 m.p.h. Even better, they could handle a payload of 18 pounds – enough sarin to kill off a small town. The cult paid $36,000 for the two drones, telling the vendor they would use them to develop a remote-controlled crop-duster. The vendor thought his customers so dubious he reported the sale to police. The cops never followed up.

For the guru's infantry, Aum turned to military surplus suppliers. The cult got itself on the mailing list of the U.S. Defence Department's Reutilization and Marketing Office, and began receiving sales notices for everything from gas masks to battleships. The cult eventually amassed a collection of used bomb casings, shells, missiles, and at least one rocket launcher. Some of the gear was marked "USA" or "Air Force."

Inexperience was perhaps the greatest factor standing in Aum's way. The cult's weapons experts took the remote-controlled helicopters for a test drive. They promptly smashed the first into a tree; the other plunged into an uncontrolled nosedive and crashed to pieces.

But such setbacks could not shake the faith of a scientific death cult and its priests. Under Murai's careful direction, research was launched into applying various points of the electromagnetic spectrum to weapons development. Electromagnetic radiation – the movement of energy in waves and particles – stretches from the lowest-frequency brain waves to the highest-level cosmic particles. Aum's scientists were already at work on two points of the spectrum: microwaves and lasers. Now they began exploring what truly seemed out of science fiction: how to short-circuit human brain waves using electronic pulses.

Emboldened by their ever-growing arsenal, cult leaders felt more and more confident they could actually fight and win a war. As the summer of 1994 gave way to fall, Asahara could wait no more. The apocalypse, he announced, was no longer scheduled for the end of 1996. The final battle was suddenly at hand.

22

HOLY MONK EMPEROR

"The time has come," wrote Hayakawa in his notebook. "We have to fight . . . Defeat means death for the guru."

To spark the final war, Aum began planning the coup d'état its leaders had dreamed of for more than a year. Their first strike would be seizing control of Tokyo, and then all of Japan. The operation was to be known as X-Day. In a series of lightning blows, Aum would stage a brilliant coup and wrest control of the Japanese capital.

"We'll arrange fifty past and present members from the Self Defense Force," Hayakawa wrote, referring to the Japanese military. Two hundred others would be put in a special strike force, backed up by units of Japanese gangsters and Russian troops. "One day before X-Day, Russian special team leaves for Sea of Japan by ship ostensibly to have training. Use doctors and chemical agents as disguise. On X-Day, they land in Niigata pretending to aid victims of sarin attack." Led by Aum commanders, the invading force then moves on Tokyo.

X-Day was planned for the first session of the new parliament. Emperor Akihito himself would be in attendance – what better day to show there was a new emperor in town? As Aum's shock troops stormed military units around the capital, its air force would launch a devastating attack on the government. Cult helicopters would spray the legislature and bureaucracy with sarin, killing thousands and paralyzing the state.

Aum would then declare itself in power, announce the establishment of a religious state, and declare Asahara leader of the new nation. Practice for the coup was to occur in Russia. Aum units would fly over and drill with Russian special forces until ready for the final assault on Tokyo. A leading cultist, Yoshihiro Inoue, summed up the plan in his notebook: "Sarin to be sprayed in major city, Russian navy assault squad to land in Japan, Aum to take over."

Russian forces alone were not enough to ensure the coup's

success. Aum needed its own army. Its membership in Japan now topped 10,000, some 10 percent of whom lived in cult compounds. In Russia, membership was already double that and still growing quickly. But most of Asahara's disciples knew precious little about combat and soldiering. To remedy this, Aum strategists did two things.

First, cult recruiters increased their efforts at grabbing past and present members of the Self-Defense Force, Japan's 230,000-strong military. Dogged by issues of constitutionality, the SDF has never been a popular group in postwar Japan. Even today, soldiers are wary of wearing their uniforms outside base. Despite this, the SDF has grown into one of the world's largest, best equipped militaries. Asahara was unimpressed with the SDF's prowess ("Japan would be wiped out in a third world war if its military remains as it is now," he once said). But the force nonetheless became a prime target for Asahara's army of God.

Of special interest to Aum was the First Airborne Division, the nation's most combat-ready unit, charged with defending Tokyo in case of coup or attack. Aum recruiters obtained internal lists of personnel and sent young female believers to a bar frequented by the soldiers. So successful were they that dozens of members from the Japanese military joined the cult, as well as many veterans.

That was only a beginning. To stage a coup, the cult needed a highly trained strike force. So began the Soldiers of White Love, Aum's army in the making. For training, Aum turned to the military veterans within its ranks. For troops, the cult hired itinerant construction workers from Japan's big cities.

It was a strange start for what Asahara claimed would become a military superpower. In May and July 1994, the cult ran at least two boot camps in isolated regions of Japan, where dozens of recruits marched, jogged, and drilled for combat. At one mountain retreat, cultists hired fifty recruits, some of them plucked from the skid rows of Tokyo and Osaka. The men were told they would be "extras" in a movie called, fittingly, *The Soldiers of White Love*, but needed a bit of training first. The group was finally evicted in August after locals grew uneasy about the shaved heads, martial-arts clothing, and strange chants.

At Aum headquarters, the cult established a fifteen-man "commando unit" camped in tents at the base of the great mountain. The group trained daily from 8 a.m. to midnight, with Chinese-style exercises using *chi* energy, weightlifting, and martial arts. Most were

SDF veterans, described by one admiring member as being "deeply tanned with highly developed muscles." Another said, "Their minds were so fixed I felt certain the cult was preparing for war." Hayakawa, meanwhile, scrawled in his notebook about plans to set up "a course on guerrilla warfare in urban centers."

Hayakawa ended his notes with one last appointment, a final date for the great terror to begin. "1995, November," he wrote. "War."

A religious sect seizing control of a world economic superpower – it was a delusion of fantastic proportions. But for Aum's doomsdayers, the coup plan was real, or as real as anything else in their twisted cartoon world.

In cult publications and radio broadcasts, Aum experts described in macabre detail the weapons of the future and how their followers alone would survive Armageddon. Murai spoke admirably of the plasma cannon, which concentrates microwaves into a single beam of 4,000 degrees Celsius. The weapon burns away living tissue while leaving structures intact. Such a weapon has been researched by the Pentagon, but Murai claimed the Americans had already deployed it in the Gulf War, evaporating Iraqi soldiers by the thousands. That was why, he said, only 8,000 bodies were found, while Iraq claimed it had lost 100,000.

Murai also claimed the superheroes of Aum would survive this devastating attack. "Enlightened believers produce an electromagnetic field," Murai explained. "This is plasma . . . When the plasma from outside affects your body, you can take it as your own energy, and you will be more powerful."

Another "ultimate" weapon was the "fixed-star reflection cannon," which Aum swore Russia was then developing. A stationary satellite focuses solar energy onto an earthbound target. The intense heat melts everything in its path – except Aum believers. "Enlightened believers can separate their bodily senses from their consciousness," an Aum text explained. "So they can withstand the high heat that would burn ordinary people. That's why they have trained by submerging for fifteen minutes in hot water of 50 degrees Celsius."

Similarly, Aum disciples could survive attack by vaporization bombs, powerful airborne explosives which burn liquid fuel, consuming all oxygen. "When enlightened believers are in deep meditation, their breath is very shallow or suspended," the cult said. This ability enables them to wait until the effects have passed. "Evaporation bombs create a low oxygen state, but only for a short time." Even worldwide devastation would pose no problem for those with the Master's training. "In the event of starvation, Aum trainees' metabolism is very low, so they don't need food. Aum believers can survive by opening their *chakras* and not breathing."

Like the indestructible comic-book heroes of their youth, Aum followers believed that they alone would rise from the ashes of Armageddon. Then, as Asahara prophesied, they would build the millennial Kingdom of Aum. But what would the kingdom look like? How would it be governed?

Endowed with superpowers, armed with weapons of mass destruction, Aum lacked only one thing: a state. That summer, Asahara ordered a sweeping reorganization, setting up the cult as a shadow government. At least on paper, Aum now resembled a cross between a medieval theocracy and postwar Japan. A constitution was drafted, spelling out the structure of the new nation and the duties of its subjects. Citizens, for example, "shall be liable to military service in order to protect the sacred law."

To govern the republic, Aum set up twenty-four ministries that eerily reflected the Japanese state its members were so eager to destroy. Murai became Minister of Science and Technology. The other appointments were not without irony. Hayakawa, the engineer, intent on giving Aum the means of mass destruction, was made Minister of Construction. Seiichi Endo, who spent his time culturing bacterial weapons, rose to Minister of Health and Welfare. And the cult's lawsuit-happy attorney Yoshinobu Aoyama was named Minister of Justice.

Aum Supreme Truth was of course no democracy, nor was the state it sought to create. The millennial kingdom was from here on dubbed the Supreme State, leaving no doubt about who would inherit the world. And on top of the great empire, ruling serenely over the cosmos, sat Shoko Asahara, now deemed the Holy Monk Emperor.

Asahara was a great admirer of Hitler, and shared the Führer's dream of a thousand-year Reich. As his power grew, however, Aum's increasingly corpulent guru resembled not so much Hitler as Caligula, the first-century Roman emperor remembered for his debauched and tyrannical rule.

23

SEX AND DRUGS

One day, a female follower was approached by an Aum leader. She had been summoned by the Revered Master, she was told, and should go immediately to see him at a nearby hotel. Unquestioningly, she stopped what she was doing. She arrived at the hotel to find her guru sitting on the bed of a twin room.

"Why did you summon me?" she asked.

"Sit down," said Shoko Asahara, pointing to a nearby chair. Then the questions began.

"Are you sexually experienced?" he asked the woman.

She replied that she was. He asked how many men she had slept with. She told him. Then Asahara said, "Take off your clothes."

The woman was shocked. "What, all of them?"

"Everything."

The woman began to undress. She tried to reassure herself. Maybe it's some kind of naked ritual, she thought. But when she was naked, Asahara began touching and kissing her body. Then they had sex. Afterwards, he swore her to secrecy.

The Master summoned her several more times, according to the account in Shoko Egawa's *Ambitions of a Messiah*. The woman dreaded each liaison, but went anyway. "We were told to obey the guru always. Once, he tore off my clothes. He said, 'This is a Tantric initiation. Your energy will rise quickly and you'll achieve enligthenment faster.' " The woman suspected she was not alone in her ordeal. "I heard other young women say, 'The Master has conducted an extreme initiation on me.' "

To his wide-eyed new recruits, Asahara had risen above what he termed "this filthy world of desires." The cult's oldest members knew better. In fact, Aum's Holy Monk Emperor had a libido of truly imperial proportions. In his private quarters – situated in a separate compound from his wife and family – Asahara had a bath big enough for ten people, and filled it with a steady stream of young women from the cult's Dance Department.

For a man who had already twisted a justification for murder out of Buddhist scripture, lechery was easy to legitimize. Ceremonies such as Blood Initiation had promoted Asahara's bodily fluids as magic potions, and sex with the guru was merely another way of receiving them. As a supremely enlightened being, Asahara of course derived no sexual pleasure from such "initiations." One top cultist explained, "He has this strong power to shut out worldly desires."

Ordinary Aum members had no such powers, however, and were therefore expected to observe a strict code of celibacy. They were ordered to channel their sexual energy into achieving enlightenment, rather than squander it between the sheets. Believers who had sex were forced to wear dog collars, walk around on their hands and feet, and eat the leftovers of other followers. A male and female cultist were forced to confess where they had made love, then were hanged there by their feet on Asahara's command. Anyone caught masturbating earned a week's solitary confinement.

It hadn't always been this way. After all, sex sells. Asahara understood and exploited this ancient truism from his first days in business. His Tokyo acupuncture clinic employed two young female assistants with short pink skirts. His first book, *The Secret to Developing Supernatural Power*, contained testimony from an Aum yoga practitioner whose superpowers included the ability to see through women's clothes. Asahara would later preach that pain and suffering were the only paths to enlightenment. In the early days, however, there was a much easier way: sex.

"It's the quickest route to learning how to have out-of-body experiences," he wrote in his first book. One chapter draws heavily from Tantric practice and provides an insight into Asahara's more sensual side – a sort of guru's guide to good sex.

"Masturbate daily, but do not ejaculate," Asahara begins. "Continue this for ten days. Then start masturbating twice a day . . . Find a picture of your favorite entertainment star, preferably nude. Use the photo to activate your imagination, and start masturbating four times a day." The number of times a man must masturbate – still without ejaculating – increases until week six. Then comes the payoff – the hot date.

"You must create a good atmosphere before sex," the guru advises. "For instance, dine in a restaurant with good food and ambience. Make sure your partner drinks a little alcohol. It's also helpful to see a foreign movie before dinner." Asahara doesn't explain what kind of foreign movie (Fellini? Costner?) because by now the bedroom beckons.

"I advise you to do some petting, starting at the tip of her toe," he writes. The man should caress his partner's belly and whisper sweet nothings into her ear "about three times." But he shouldn't get too carried away. "You've only just begun," Asahara cautions. "Hold the woman and kiss her lips. Then kiss her neck, and gradually move downwards, flicking your tongue across her nipples and stroking her clitoris with your palm."

Then the long, lonely weeks of self-denial come to an end. "After attaining the deepest insertion possible, don't move out right away but instead perform 81 *muhrabandas* [a kind of tensing technique]. Then slowly move in and out nine times. Then do another 81 *muhrabandas*. Then 18 in and outward thrusts. 81 *muhrabandas*, then 27 in and outs . . ."

At some point during this mathematically challenging routine, an out-of-body experience presumably occurs . . . but only if the man has obeyed the guru's last advice to the letter.

"Never use a condom," Asahara warns. "And always let her come first."

This racy chapter was deleted from the book's subsequent editions after Aum Supreme Truth was registered as a religion. But sex remained a tried and trusted sales tool for the cult. The campaign staff during the ill-fated 1990 election bid deliberately included photogenic beauties. There was also an unwritten rule among Aum recruiters: male recruits must be smart, young, and qualified; females need only be young and good-looking. The cult set up cut-price fortune-telling booths in Tokyo's busiest shopping areas to recruit pretty girls, who in turn were used to lure qualified males. Flyers for a men-only recruitment drive in Tokyo read: "Do you know that Aum has chaste, beautiful, celestial maidens? Why not visit our training center and listen to their songs?"

The cult's strict sexual code only applied to Aum's rank and file. Its leaders were allowed to live with the opposite sex in their own rooms. Dr. Hayashi, although married, generously shared this privilege with his female nursing staff. But the biggest exception to the rule was the guru himself. His tastes were conservative. He liked women with long hair, wide eyes, strong noses, and no make-up or jewelry. "Look at women of the Aum staff," he said in one lecture. "They don't make themselves up a lot. The beauty of their minds shines around them." Not that Aum's women had much choice. Those who wore make-up or accessories had their faces smeared with mud for a week.

The son of a straw-mat maker was now the sultan of his own harem. Tearing his own page from Japan's venerable geisha tradition, Asahara threw parties where beautiful female acolytes mixed drinks and mingled with male guests. Believers who donated large sums were summoned to a nearby guesthouse to find the guru surrounded by women dressed in dazzling robes.

Asahara usually chose the members of this harem himself. Aides also presented him with updated lists of the cult's prettiest believers. One sycophantic lieutenant even presented his girlfriend. "If she and the guru fuse together, her mental level rises," the devotee explained, before "offering" her to Asahara. "By sacrificing himself, he pours his energy into a woman. It's better than fusing with me."

Asahara's first love was his wife Tomoko. But his second was a follower called Hisako Ishii. She was a former "OL," or "office lady," at a major Japanese insurance company who joined Aum's yoga classes in 1984. With long, black hair and pretty looks, Ishii scored high on Asahara's feminine check list. She also proved a hard-core devotee, running for office during the election and getting arrested the same year in Aum's land-fraud case. Asahara rewarded her with the post of cult treasurer – a key position in Aum's billion-dollar empire.

Asahara and Ishii were inseparable. "They were together every hour of the day," said one believer. "He cared for Ishii much more than for his wife." Their relationship was an "open secret," a fact that distressed Asahara's wife. Tomoko and Ishii argued often. When Ishii gave birth to twins, Asahara was presumed to be the father.

Tomoko, however, had the last laugh: her husband's interest in Ishii faded after motherhood. He switched his attentions instead to a seventeen-year-old girl known as Sumeida, who was often spotted supporting the guru on his way from shower room to bedroom. With classic understatement, one follower described the relationship as "something more than just guru and follower." But few believers spoke openly about Sumeida – even mentioning her name was taboo. Asahara would eventually promote his Girl Friday to Aum's highest executive rung.

Sex was not the only worldly urge that Asahara worked hard to gratify. A former driver of the guru's $200,000 Mercedes Benz had one word to describe Asahara's appetite for food: "unbelievable." The driver often accompanied the guru and his family to restaurants, where they ordered "dish after dish" – onion soup, sautéed pork, raw tuna, and salted salmon roe, followed by ice cream, which believers were forbidden to eat. The once slim and ascetic guru now ballooned to an overweight sloth. Still, Asahara had his peculiar tastes. According to a six-page cult guide called "The Guru Welcome Manual," he loved sweet melons, insisted that his food be served on plates washed with natural soap, and hated instant, frozen, or microwaved food. (Aum's enterprising members had other plans for microwaves.)

The driver also ferried Asahara's kids to amusement parks and to mammoth spending sprees at toy shops. Once, the Mercedes was so full of toys that Asahara ordered the driver out, and drove off himself. Which raises the question: How could Asahara, near-sightless from birth, see well enough to drive a car? "I found it difficult to believe he was blind," the driver said.

The man, however, kept his doubts to himself. It was safer that way. Once Asahara had found a nail in the tire of the Mercedes, and accused him of being a spy. The driver was sent to the cult's doctors for a large injection of truth serum.

Asahara's driver was just one among many at Aum getting doped up. The guru himself had taken a liking to drugs, and ensured that their use grew quickly within the cult. His favorite drug was lysergic acid diethylamide, or LSD.

The original idea had come to cult physician Nakagawa, who recommended a new chemical weapon for Aum's growing arsenal. Nakagawa had read that just .025 milligrams of LSD was enough to trigger hallucinations, and he suggested that spraying it from the air might prove effective. Asahara and his aides thought the idea brilliant.

Decades earlier, the U.S. Army had similar thoughts and conducted a series of secret tests to find the best "incapacitant," as the generals called it. They tried LSD, but their top choice was BZ, a powerful hallucinogen that leaves victims dazed for up to four days. The Army manufactured 100,000 pounds of the stuff, but decided against deployment; further tests showed the drug's effects were simply too unpredictable.

Around May 1994, Aum ran its own tests, giving LSD to unwitting members about to undergo cult initiations. Once they saw it could be used safely, Asahara and other top members tried it themselves. Asahara's "trip" was so strong that the guru wet his pants and hallucinated wildly. "This is excellent," he exclaimed upon coming down. "I became high, perhaps the highest ever." Thrilled with the effects, Asahara ordered mass production.

So enamored was Asahara of LSD that he planned to use it not only as a weapon but as a short cut to enlightenment. The drug seemed an ideal recruiting tool. By doping the youth of Japan, Asahara hoped to triple Aum's 10,000-membership within two years. "Make all the drugs we can," ordered the guru.

A cult lab was soon refining enough "acid" for millions of people. So potent is the drug that a single gram can produce 50,000 doses. Aum manufactured at least 115 grams, or enough for over 5 million trips. That was a lot of dope. So much, in fact, that by the time Aum was done, it had produced nearly half of all the LSD seized worldwide since 1990.

By mid-1994, drug use at the cult exploded. That summer, Aum companies were ordering so much sodium thiopental, or truth serum, that suppliers were balking. Undaunted, cult chemists again took matters into their own hands, and by October were producing thiopental along with their LSD, nerve gas, and dynamite. One technician later confessed that she alone sealed 1,200 vials of thiopental.

Other drugs quickly followed. By that fall, Aum was running what now appears to have been one of the world's largest underground drug labs. Endo's "Ministry of Health," when not producing biological killers, was fielding a ten-person team synthesizing some ten different drugs. Along with the anesthetics and sedatives, Aum produced an illicit pharmacy of hallucinogens, stimulants, and other psychoactive drugs. Aum chemists synthesized at least 22 pounds of mescaline, a hallucinogen drawn from the peyote cactus of northern Mexico. That was good for another 20,000 doses. The labs also turned out a quantity of phencyclidine, better known as PCP or angel dust. First developed as an anesthetic in the 1950s, PCP was found to have hallucinogenic qualities which pushed it off the market for human use. Yet another drug was methamphetamine; the cult made batch after batch of the well-known stimulant. Long the drug of choice in high-pressure Japan, meth is known on the back streets of Tokyo and Osaka as *shabu*.

Where, again, were the Japanese authorities? In 1988, Japan signed a UN convention on illegal drugs, joining nearly a hundred nations in a bid to control "precursor" chemicals used to manufacture dope. Finally, in 1992, the government published a list of 22 chemicals that officials vowed to monitor, ensuring they did not fall into the wrong hands. But no enforcement measures were ever taken, and the regulations were quietly forgotten. On the list were sulfuric acid, ergotamine, acetone, nitric acid, hydrochloric acid, and phenylacetic acid – all chemicals found in abundance in Aum laboratories.

As a result, by fall 1994 drugs were woven into the fabric of Aum Supreme Truth. Special attention now went to finding the best combinations for mind control and mystical experience. In their research, cult doctors mixed dangerous cocktails, blending the hallucinogens with stimulants and hypnotics in various amounts. Afterward, they took blood and urine samples, and had their subjects write accounts of their psychotropic journeys.

As Asahara hoped, the wholesale introduction of dope into Aum gave the cult a powerful new tool in recruiting followers. Native Americans, hippies, and Harvard psychologists have all attested to the spiritual, revelatory aspects of hallucinogens. But most Japanese knew little or nothing about that. While Japan had its version of the sixties, drug use never caught on as in the West. Much of Aum's membership, besides, was too young to know.

Shinosuke Sakamoto, a doctoral candidate in anthropology at Tokyo University, was one who found out. And the experience, he told the press, changed his life. Sakamoto spent twelve hours "meditating" in a small, dark chamber, where he was struck by visions both colorful and transcendent. "I felt as if I had ascended to a higher stage," he said. "A bright light fell from above and entered me."

Like others, Sakamoto was won over. "What's wrong," he asked, "with having such a wonderful experience with the help of drugs?"

Aum would introduce thousands to the mind-altering giddiness of LSD. The intense hallucinations of cult rituals took on almost legendary status; by year's end, Aum Supreme Truth had become a colony of acid freaks. Drugs were now given every way from drinks to injections, I/Vs, cookies, and candles. Asahara himself offered many of them during "initiations" of importance. "Drink this," the guru said to one participant. "Don't worry, it's not poison." At other times, a nurse read this simple message: "You are about to relive your past and see your future. To raise this experience to sublime heights, you must remain calm and refrain from vomiting."

Testimony by Aum users point to the variety of dope the cult was putting into its membership. Some reported the vivid colors and distortions of time and space so common to hallucinogens – although they would ascribe this to the mystical power of Asahara's training.

Other experiences suggest the heavy presence of anesthetics and hypnotics. "I was given an intravenous injection and fell asleep in a minute or two," recalled one follower. "I had multicolored dreams and woke up seven or eight hours later. I felt dizzy for hours after that."

At one initiation, a member recalls his heart pounding and hands trembling after he drank white wine – a sign not of alcohol but of methamphetamine. At another rite, the Candle Initiation, a group sang meditative songs while sitting around a large candle. "It smelled like burning flesh," recalled a participant. "I felt nauseated and then fell asleep." Others became disoriented and violent, thrashing about until they were restrained. Still another drank "strawberry wine" that left him dizzy for days.

Aum borrowed not only dope from the sixties, but also the trappings. "I was taken to a small meditation room which had a huge speaker," one initiate recalled. "Loud music was pumped into the room. My hands and legs were tied and I was left alone. After that, I started seeing brilliant colors and a spiritual vision." It seems almost quaint today, but in some rooms Aum put on its own, surprisingly low-tech "light show." Hidden in the next room, members projected multicolored beams onto the walls, using cellophane filters atop flashlights.

Cult leaders developed a manual to cope with the drugs' unpredictable effects. For those who complained of a burning sensation, the book prescribed telling them they felt the pent-up energy of Shoko Asahara, and that this demonstrated "the leader's greatness." Those wanting to return home were warned against such a rash act: "Because you have entered the astral plane, if you enter the secular world in such a state, it will cause problems in your life." And for those who grew scared and asked to leave: the fear was a throwback to their "animal karma," and if they fled now they would never transcend their present lowly state.

Always in search of new money-making schemes, Aum soon turned to its growing underground pharmacy as a source of cash. The market for LSD in Japan was not great, but among those who cared, Aum's acid was a welcome sight. The cult's meth failed to impress the marketplace, however. By fall 1994, Aum members were peddling it to the nation's largest crime syndicates, where it was known simply as "Aum stuff." "Everyone knows Aum's stimulants are just garbage," complained one gangster. "They only keep you awake."

It seems fitting, at least, that Aum was forging contacts with the underworld. More and more, Aum seemed not so much a cult as an organized crime syndicate. Under U.S. racketeering law, the cult could have been prosecuted as a "continuing criminal enterprise."

Aum had taken on Asahara's personality: obnoxious, greedy, intimidating, violent. The cult found it could get its way simply by pushing and taking what it wanted. Parents, attorneys, and neighbors all had tried to rein in the cult, to no effect. The obvious line of defense against a cancer like Aum – law enforcement – had gone to sleep.

Ironically, the only force left able to stand up to Aum was a group the cult increasingly resembled: the Japanese Mafia.

24

ENTER THE YAKUZA

A brilliant tattoo stretched from Kiyohide Nakada's neck to his calf, the classic mark of a Japanese *yakuza*, or mobster. Simply rolling up his sleeve and baring part of the design was enough to get trucks moved, doors opened, and bills paid. Not that Nakada needed to show the tattoo much. With his shiny, shaven head, clipped mustache, and piercing eyes, he was a man most fellow Japanese already tried hard to avoid.

Nakada was the real thing. For years he headed a gang affiliated with the Yamaguchi crime syndicate in Nagoya, one of Japan's largest cities. He served three years in prison on a firearms charge, and once quipped that "stabbing people is like stabbing tofu." But there was another side to the gang boss.

Nakada was fascinated by mysticism. He often told friends how he once had an "out-of-body experience." Organized religion, though, was not for the hard-headed *yakuza* – at least not until his wife got involved. While Nakada was serving time, she had joined a religious cult, hoping to use prayer to heal her son's eye ailment. Nakada disapproved, and on his release demanded that his wife abandon her new faith. She refused.

That was before Nakada's liver began to fail. So serious was the disease that a doctor gave him a mere three months to live. Desperate, he turned to his wife's cult for a cure, and with its help he claimed a miraculous recovery. That was enough for the gang boss. In 1988, Nakada, then forty, dissolved his gang, donated his assets, and joined a new syndicate called Aum with Shoko Asahara as godfather.

Like Aum, the *yakuza* could be entered easily enough, but getting out was not that simple. So when Kiyohide Nakada joined Aum Supreme Truth, he took his Mob ties and underworld ways with him. The cult was delighted.

The Japanese *yakuza* rank among the world's largest, richest, and most influential crime syndicates. Like the Italian Mafia, the *yakuza* boast a history dating back nearly 300 years, to medieval bands of gamblers and peddlers. They are a proud and traditional bunch, who sport full-body tattoos and sever their fingertips as punishment. They have also become a thoroughly modern Mob, who today control a multibillion-dollar empire in drugs, gambling, extortion, and a hundred other rackets.

The *yakuza* also serve as a kind of alternative police force in Japan. Many Japanese, including the police, give them a certain grudging respect. "The one thing that terrifies Japanese police is unorganized crime," reflected one criminologist. "That's why there's so little street crime here. Gangsters control the turf, and they provide the security."

As Japanese struggled to rebuild their country after the war, it was the *yakuza* who were credited with protecting shopkeepers against ethnic Chinese and Korean gangs. Even today, should a group of delinquents start causing trouble in a neighborhood, chances are they will answer first not to the cops but to the local *yakuza* boss.

In Japan, so numerous and entrenched are the gangs that it becomes difficult to avoid contact. According to the country's National Police Agency, there are some 80,000 "made" members and associates of the *yakuza* – four times the size of the American Mafia. The gangs hold major interests in the construction, real estate, and entertainment industries, and wield influence within the nation's top political parties. They are also very turf-conscious, ready to fight over territory or, worse, loss of face.

So it was inevitable, perhaps, that the paths of Aum Supreme Truth and the Japanese Mob would cross. The first encounters were not auspicious, however.

In the early days of the Mount Fuji complex, Aum had bought a tract of land for a printing plant from a local *yakuza* gang. During the boom years of Japan's bubble economy, the gang had invested in the property, hoping to cash in during the explosion in golf-course construction. But with the bubble's collapse it now made sense to unload the land, and Aum was buying.

The deal went smoothly enough until Aum began building their factory. Gang members had left behind some belongings, which the cultists promptly threw out. On learning this, a group of mean-looking *yakuza* came by the site and began threatening the construction crew. The gangsters didn't know whom they were dealing with.

The crew quickly called for help, and out came an even meaner-looking group of Asahara's goons, among them several just-retired veterans of the Japanese military. The fight was no contest: the Aum followers promptly beat the hell out of the meddlesome *yakuza*.

This, of course, was just the start of trouble. The hoods were part of the much larger Yamaguchi-gumi, which was not just any gang, it was *the* gang. The Yamaguchi-gumi was the largest and most aggressive of Japan's national syndicates, a 23,000-man criminal cartel with its own board of directors and hundreds of affiliated gangs and corporations. Aum's leadership realized they would soon have a gang war on their hands unless amends were made. It fell to Hayakawa, increasingly Asahara's key troubleshooter, to sort things out. He made a contrite visit to the gang headquarters and, with a huge cash payment, settled the matter.

Shoko Asahara was preparing to wage war across the globe. But at that particular moment, a battle with the Japanese Mob was not one he wanted to fight. There was a better way. The *yakuza* were among the best warriors in Japan. Why not recruit them to join the holy cause?

Aum's main conduit to the underworld took the form of two ex-gang leaders who had joined the cult. The first, Nakada, had proved particularly devoted to the guru, and as Asahara launched his plan to militarize Aum, the former gangster's status within the cult grew. By 1994, Nakada was calling his old pals in the underworld, asking for weapons and offering big money, according to the magazine *Weekly Bunshun*. For a genuine Tokarev, a Russian handgun, he would pay $4,000, good even for the inflated prices usually fetched on Japan's black market. He was also interested in automatic weapons and hand grenades, he said.

Over the course of four deals with the *yakuza*, Nakada reportedly got hold of eighteen handguns, including both Tokarevs and U.S.-made automatics. A fifth deal, involving a shadowy Chinese gang, brought in twenty hand grenades. According to the weekly, Nakada was quite clear on why he needed the arms.

"The guns are for war," he told an underworld contact. "I will fight against the state with the guru. Although we don't have fighter jets or destroyers, we will arm ourselves as strongly as the Self-Defense Force and change Yamanashi Prefecture [home to Aum headquarters] into a military base.

"We've got a factory to make *shabu*," he went on, alluding to the cult's production of methamphetamine. "The *shabu* is for brainwashing and strengthening fighters." Nakada undoubtedly knew that the last Japanese soldiers to be given meth were the kamikaze pilots.

In true *yakuza* fashion, Nakada was prepared to go all the way. "We have scientists, doctors, and nurses, so we can survive if a big war breaks out. Ultimately, we will be armed with nuclear weapons bought from Russia. What I can say now is that I'll fight till the end, even if the only weapon I have left is a needle."

Nakada, though, wanted more than weapons out of the *yakuza*: he wanted men. On behalf of Aum, he offered thousands of dollars for introductions to key gang bosses, to ask if their men could be "rented" by the cult. He approached the boss of one of Japan's rightist gangs, which work closely with the *yakuza*, asking for "young, experienced soldiers to fight against the state."

Aum attracted at least one other prominent *yakuza*. Shinichi Hatano had served for years as an adviser to the Yamaguchi-gumi in Osaka. Hatano, too, boasted convictions for firearms, as well as narcotics. He joined Aum in 1993 at the age of forty-three but decided against a full commitment. He would prove most valuable to the cult as a gunsmith.

A former lathe operator at a foundry, Hatano was adept at fashioning makeshift guns out of models. In Japan, where guns are hard to come by, the *yakuza* have long turned to authentic replicas which, with some clever working, can be made to fire live bullets. Hatano's talents were quickly recognized by Aum's weapons engineers. Months would pass before the AK-74s began rolling off the assembly, and the cult needed firepower now. For his pals in the cult, Hatano began converting model derringers, a double-barreled, .22-caliber design of the old miniature pistol. The little guns were popular with the *yakuza*, and were met with admiring faces at Mount Fuji as well.

Gun making, drug dealing, extortion, murder – Asahara had lifted many pages out of the *yakuza* handbook. With a cash-hungry weapons program to feed, Aum leaders added more and more scams. A particularly lucrative one was insurance fraud.

Not just fraud, say police, but murder for insurance. On joining the priesthood, members were made to sign over insurance policies, making Aum the sole beneficiary. So profitable was the area that Aum formed an Insurance Project Team, made up of five women who had worked at insurance companies. If suspicious "accidents" or early deaths befell certain members, particularly the elderly, it was easy enough for cult doctors to fake their cause of death. Aum may have brought in as much as $5 million this way, say police.

Another lucrative scam was murder for inheritance. Again, the elderly were key targets. Typically, the victims ended up in one of Dr. Hayashi's chilling medical clinics. There was, for example, the wealthy 81-year-old woman who was admitted in April 1994, convinced by a grandson to move there from her regular hospital. Frail and suffering from heart problems, she underwent scalding bath treatments while the cult transferred over $1 million of her real estate to Aum's name. Four days later, she was dead.

Aum even took on the *yakuza* head to head in one business: debt collection, an area long dominated by the Mob in Japan. More as a recruiting technique than a money-maker, the cult set up its own consultation service, targeting Japanese with bad debts or credit trouble. On finding a likely candidate, Aum sent in the "Trouble Busters," leafleting nearby phone booths, public toilets, and street corners. "The Trouble Busters will free you from bad debt," read the friendly ad. "Consultation free." Nowhere was Aum mentioned.

Callers were directed to an unmarked office, where they filled out a questionnaire and had their fortune told by a resident psychic. If deemed worthy, they were offered a contract to go *johatsu*, or disappear, a traditional means of escaping debt in Japan. Soon they had left their homes, their families, and their bad loans behind, to live in what seemed a community of other debtors. In reality, they were living in an Aum compound. In group sessions, cult members criticized society ("You're not wrong, it's the system"), making them feel good about having fled. Next they were offered work, such as selling computers for Aum's Mahaposya front company. Then the pressure began to join the cult. At that point, cut off from their previous lives, they had little choice.

Nakada, the former *yakuza* boss, was useful for more than black-market weapons. He was a man accustomed to violence, who didn't mind threatening Aum's neighbors and bringing errant cultists into line. Like many *yakuza*, he was a career extortionist, able to intimidate local farmers and squeeze donations out of reluctant devotees. He eventually rose to become the number-two man at Aum's Ministry of Home Affairs, charged with enforcing security within the group.

Above Nakada ranked a man who also would have been at home in the underworld – perhaps in the Mafia's Murder, Inc. Tomomitsu Niimi was among Asahara's earliest and most devoted followers. He was a slender figure with a long neck, shaven head, and a reptilian smirk that seemed permanently etched upon his face. Like so many Aum members, he was a quiet kid. He read law at university, as well as the works of Nostradamus and esoteric Buddhist texts, and worked at a food company upon graduation. Six months later, he quit and joined Aum.

Once inside the cult, Niimi made up for what he lacked in size by sheer ferocity. It was Niimi who snapped the neck of Shuji Taguchi in 1989, and then months later helped slay the Sakamoto family. And it was Niimi again who in January 1994 helped strangle Ochida, the pharmacist. Now Minister of Home Affairs, he presided over an expanding security net that had turned Aum into a police state.

As paranoia grew about outsiders and Armageddon, cult members were encouraged to report potential spies and dissenters. The enemy within seemed everywhere; there were even rumors that the cult might split apart, driven by conflicts between Hayakawa's Construction Ministry and Murai's Science Ministry. The number of desertions, meanwhile, was growing markedly. In 1994, at least twenty-five followers successfully fled the cult.

To keep the guru's law, Niimi and others created a special ten-member team called, rather innocuously, the New Followers Agency. The group's job was anything but innocuous: abductions, confinement, spying, murder. As Aum bullied its way through 1994, business for Niimi's enforcers was booming.

Believers were demoted if caught calling or sending mail to family and friends. Violations of celibacy and other cult precepts were dealt with harshly. Niimi even meted out punishment for those with the wrong blood type. Sorting people by blood type is a peculiarly Japanese pop superstition. Adherents claim they can determine personality and behavior by a person's hemoglobin, much like charting stars in astrology. Among the adherents, unsurprisingly, was Shoko Asahara, who one day issued a directive warning cultists to be extremely cautious of followers with blood type O. Such people, he warned, were bound to break Buddhist laws.

The following day, Niimi issued his own notice. "I regret that six of the O blood-type sinners were under my suspicion," he reported. "They will do five days of severe penance."

Increasingly, severe penance could end in death. Homicide was becoming a way of life for the cult. Punishments for suspected traitors and enemies were swift and brutal. One of the guru's chauffeurs, a man in good health, suddenly disappeared one day. He died from a "lethal gas attack," followers were told. That fall, another fellow, aged twenty-seven, was abruptly summoned to a "disciplinary committee" and accused of spying and poisoning the cult's drinking water. He was given a polygraph, beaten, and sentenced to death. Niimi and another then wrapped a rope around his neck and squeezed the life out of him. Like so many others, his remains headed for the Microwave.

Earlier that year, Asahara had severely reprimanded a 32-year-old priest for falling in love with a nun, a violation of cult precepts. The man, a longtime member, responded by asking his guru for permission to quit the cult and marry the woman. It was an ill-advised request. Asahara agreed, but only if he submitted to a purification rite: immersion in 120 degree water for fifteen minutes. He agreed.

Niimi and others tied the man's arms and legs and plunged him into a drum of scalding water. Quickly overcome by the heat, he cried out, but Niimi ignored the shouts. When he tried to escape, Niimi held him down by the head. After seven minutes he passed out, but Niimi held him down for the full fifteen minutes. The man's unconscious and severely burned body was finally pulled from the water. A nurse looked at Niimi in shock. "He had a lot of bad karma," Niimi told her. The man was taken away to a cult hospital and never seen again. He died two weeks afterwards, Niimi later confessed, and was microwaved.

All this time, county officials near the compound never received a single death notice or burial request from the cult. Yet by year's end, some twenty Aum followers had disappeared. Their bodies would never be found.

25

THE GULAG

The scene had the eerie quality of a 1950s science-fiction movie. A woman in her thirties, clad in dirty clothes, makes her way to a train station near a great volcanic mountain. Suddenly three men appear; they are wearing white headgear studded with electrodes. They grab the woman and thrust her violently into a nearby car. The vehicle speeds away towards a fenced-off compound readied for Armageddon.

This was not the 1950s, of course, but the fall of 1994. Leaving Aum, followers quickly learned, was fraught with peril. "Fleeing Aum Supreme Truth is the most dishonorable act," commanded an Aum rulebook. "It betrays the guru's love. The person will never find the truth again."

Aum's escalating criminality created an increased need for secrecy – the sect did not want deserters blabbing to the police. This in turn created much work for security chief Niimi, whose goon squads grew adept at kidnapping and abduction. They had studied a KGB manual on nabbing people off the streets, armed themselves with stun guns, and practiced karate and other martial arts. Borrowing their technique from the Stalinist era, they rehearsed a method that was as effective as it was simple. Four men are required: a driver, a lookout/door opener, and two strong men to grab the victim. One lunges from behind and jerks his arm around the person's neck; locked in a chokehold, the victim cannot call out. Another grabs the legs and both men stuff the person into the car.

The response to those daring to leave became particularly barbaric. Runaways were no longer merely pressured to stay, but abducted and forcibly returned to cult centers. There they were subjected to psychological bombardment that seemed more suited to a North Korean brainwashing camp than a Japanese religious sect.

At the same time, the severity of the cult's "initiations" – its dominant rituals – increased markedly. The pressure to join Aum as a monk or nun, and donate one's life savings, was now almost constant. Followers who refused faced a lifetime (or more) of hell, they were repeatedly told. Once inside the cult, they were locked into a spiral of violence and destruction from which only the most determined followers escaped.

Yuko Tanaka (a pseudonym) was a nurse, a contented wife, and an expectant mother in 1992. At twenty-six she had much to look forward to. Her husband worked at a well-known computer company and he, too, had a bright future.

Around this time he began attending Aum yoga classes. Drawn in by the cult's mixture of science and spirituality, Yuko's husband became a member; she soon followed. What happened next is detailed in a series by Japan's daily *Asahi* newspaper and in *The 2,200-Day Pursuit of Aum Supreme Truth*, a Japanese-language book by Shoko Egawa, one of the few journalists to take on Aum.

In March 1994, the couple went to see Asahara speak to his minions. In a mesmerizing voice, the guru told them he was a reincarnation of Jesus Christ and that he had been crucified in a previous life. Aum itself was now on the cross, he told them, for even as he spoke, the group was under attack by poison gas. In a dramatic appeal, he called on those before him to renounce the world, to dedicate their lives to Aum before Armageddon was upon them.

Yuko's husband was deeply moved. He had made up his mind, he told her. He was joining Aum as a full-time monk. Yuko hesitated, but found it hard not to follow her husband. As she wavered, an Aum member assured her, "Don't think about anything. Just do it." Yuko gave in.

The young family donated their money and all their possessions, driving to Mount Fuji in a car they turned over to the cult. Within days, their heads were shaved and instead of hair there now sat electrode caps, including one on the couple's one-year-old son. Yuko was assigned to the cult's medical branch, while her husband helped install air purifiers to "guard against poison gas."

About two months later, cult leaders told Yuko she was ready for a "special initiation." She was led to the third floor of a building, where she found the guru himself, holding a vial of Aum's now famous yellow liquid. "Don't pass out," was all Asahara said as he handed over the drug.

After Yuko drank the liquid, she was left in a small cubicle and told to meditate for the next twelve hours. But she soon grew dizzy and panicked, forcing her way out of the room and then fleeing the compound. She remembered little more, except that she somehow ended up on a roadside before being dragged into a car. Once back at the compound, she was bound with rope until the initiation ended in a bout of Aum's blistering "thermotherapy."

A few weeks later, Yuko began to have doubts about her new life. Her son had been taken away, sent to a cult children's center somewhere. She had seen neither him nor her husband for weeks and was feeling lonely. A few days later, she witnessed the frightful scalding of another initiate in hot water. Aum leaders blamed the incident on "poison" put in the water supply. Amid rising paranoia, Yuko was sent with three cult doctors to check if children at another compound had been similarly attacked. There, at last, she found her son with seventy other children, living in squalor.

The conditions were hard to believe. The kids were sick, malnourished, and violent. Ten children had skin problems, four had fingernails missing, three were asthmatic. But this was not from poison gas, the nurse knew. It stemmed from spoiled food, lousy care, and dubious medicine. Then and there, she decided to leave the cult.

That evening, she took her son and sneaked out of the compound. Unfamiliar with the terrain, she soon lost her way in the mountains, stumbling around as the sound of howling dogs filled the night air. Two hours later, a cult member found her and escorted them back to the base.

Yuko returned to Mount Fuji with her son, but remained determined to leave. At the first opportunity she fled, finding her way back to Tokyo. But Aum's influence kept working even after she had left the cult. "As soon as I left the compound, I started feeling scared that I'm going to hell because I broke with Asahara," she recalled. "I thought I couldn't keep living without Asahara, so I called Aum that same day."

She phoned the Tokyo center, apologizing and asking for permission to become a lay member. Aum, of course, would have none of it. But on the phone that day, the voice at the other end seemed kind and understanding. "If that's what you want to do," she was told, "you owe it to the Master to tell him so in person." Yuko agreed. Within hours she was on her way back to Mount Fuji to meet with the guru.

When she arrived at the Mount Fuji center, the guru was nowhere to be found. Instead, Yuko was told the Master wanted her to undergo another initiation. Panicking, she fled again.

Back in Tokyo, a cult doctor phoned, asking her to return to Mount Fuji, saying that it all had been a misunderstanding. The Master was in fact waiting to see her. Reluctantly, she agreed.

Yuko returned, but again there was no Asahara. This time she was escorted to a building where senior cult members were waiting. She could not leave, they told her, until she had submitted to the Bardo Initiation.

In Buddhist scripture, *bardo* refers to a forty-nine-day period between the time one dies and the time one is reborn. For Aum, the concept became an excuse for psychological torture.

Yuko was placed alone in a small room with a television monitor. A videotape snapped on, with scene after scene of people dying: a brutal shooting, a car explosion, a bloody motorcycle accident, graphic death scenes from films. This lasted for a full hour. At the end, Asahara's voice came on. "You can't avoid death," the guru repeated over and over. "Everyone must die."

Another video began. This time there were simple cartoons, but then the screen went dark. On speakers somewhere in the room, voices began talking about Yuko's descent into hell. They described ghoulish scenes of torture, horrible creatures, fire and pain. In one scene, she is begging the Guardian of Hell for food; he forces open her mouth and breaks the jaw, her mouth filling with blood. Then the Guardian pours molten steel into her. Her body burns but still she is alive. This went on for five hours.

Yuko was then taken outside to another, smaller building. She was blindfolded and led to a tiny cell. Strange music played in the background; it sounded to her like a duet of Asahara and his ex-lover. "Do you know hell?" one asked. "Yes, Mr. Judge of Hell," went the response. "Do you know hell?" the voice asked again. "I don't know, I don't know hell."

Then came the sound of gales, of vast and mighty winds, with a woman screaming in the distance. By now, Yuko was frightened and worn down. Suddenly, a terrible pounding began just beyond her ears. Someone was there, beating a drum not more than a foot away. It was an Aum priest, acting as the Judge of Hell.

The Judge began to criticize her life. He knew all about Yuko from her previous confessions. "You still can't be a nun, can you?" he demanded repeatedly, pounding the drum with each question. "I can't!" Yuko kept responding. "Why can't you?" came the question, over and over, each time with the beat of the drum. "The guru will take over your karma."

This went on for three hours or more. The pressure was relentless, the drum beats more frequent. By the end, Yuko was in tears, apologizing, pleading for them to stop. She was exhausted. The priest then ordered her to sit in a lotus position, the traditional yoga posture. She complied, but suddenly other Aum members forced her onto her back, snapped on handcuffs, and painfully bound her lower body with rope. Her legs now locked into the lotus position, she was pulled back into a sitting posture.

There were others in the room. "Now you can't be a nun," shouted a male voice. "You don't notice your own karma. Now we've bound your legs in the lotus position. You feel pain, don't you? That pain is your karma. We are shedding your karma. You must be grateful to us."

The people walked away, leaving Yuko alone. Asahara's voice then droned from the speakers: "I will be a nun. I will be a nun. I will be a nun." This lasted for one hour.

Yuko had endured enough. The pain of the ropes was excruciating. She twisted her body and managed to free herself, but an Aum priest raced into the room. He held a *kendo* stick, a Japanese fighting staff, and pounded it against the walls and floors. "You are holding too much karma from hell!" he yelled. "A bitch like you would kill people." He then pushed her onto the floor. "You are a killer, a killer, a killer."

Yuko was a wreck. Her face was streaked with tears and snot, her clothes were rumpled, her body partly exposed. She was ordered to sit back in a lotus position. She refused. "Then I'll help you,' laughed another male, and forced her back into the posture. She resisted, but then another male joined in. By now she felt almost as if she had been raped. "Please stop them," she cried to another woman present, but the woman did not respond.

Thirty minutes later, Yuko was finally released. The Bardo Initiation was over. Twelve hours had passed since her ordeal in the cell began. As soon as she could muster the strength, Yuko plotted her next escape from Aum's clutches.

Others suffered Aum's peculiar brand of enlightenment for even longer. Yuko heard of one follower who had tried fleeing the cult but was caught. He, too, was forced to attend a Bardo Initiation – for three days. Yuko was determined it would never happen to her again.

*

After the initiation, Yuko's movements were closely watched. Fortunately, her handlers excused her for a moment to visit the bathroom. She quickly slipped away and fled from the compound.

Yuko vowed never to return to the cult. But Aum still held her son. In mid-August she met with Niimi, her husband, and others at the nearby village, demanding they hand over her child. The cultists insisted she return to Aum or face eternal damnation. "Even if I go to hell," she said, "I don't want to go back to the compound." The negotiations broke down.

Frustrated, Yuko began walking away through the parking lot. Suddenly, Niimi and the others lunged at her, slapping on handcuffs and bundling her into a car. So brutal were they that her husband cried out, "You're killing her!"

Yuko knew too much to be set free. She had worked closely with cult doctors, witnessing the horrors inflicted on those under Aum's care. Even worse, she had watched them use and abuse a pharmacy of powerful psychoactive drugs. Back at the compound, she was thrown into a tiny, windowless cell, with a small slot for food. A padlocked door ended any thought of escape.

For two weeks Yuko was imprisoned. Finally, Niimi's goons moved her to what appeared to be a freight container, the kind used on trucks and shipping barges. The cult had fashioned it into a prison and brainwashing center. Her new jail would prove even worse than the tiny cell.

Inside the steel container were five other victims held by Aum, all in handcuffs. A makeshift wall divided the place into two compartments; on the floor were weathered straw mats. The temperature outside hit record highs that August, worsening the swamp-like humidity that drenched everyone's clothing each summer. Inside, the heat was unbearable, climbing day after day above 100 degrees. Steam pouring in from an Aum "air purifier" made conditions even worse. The one place of near privacy, the toilet, stank so badly Yuko could hardly stand it.

The container was not simply a prison, but an "initiation" center. The prisoners were not allowed to sleep at night, lie down, or talk. Two dim fluorescent lights remained on at all times, and surveillance by guards was nearly constant. Meals were limited to meager provisions served once daily, and then a three-day fast, ensuring the captives were weak and cooperative.

Then there were the endless rituals. Yuko and the others were forced to sit cross-legged and recite nonstop vows of loyalty to the cult. "I am going back to Asahara," Yuko shouted until she was hoarse. In one rite, prisoners were forced to stand for four hours, and then given an hour's rest. In another, they were made to hold their breath as long as possible over the course of three hours, then given an hour's rest. Both rites were repeated three times a day.

Yuko was going crazy.

She was not the only one. Next to her was a man at least as bewildered, a 64-year-old innkeeper from southern Japan whose daughters had joined the cult. His trouble had started some six months earlier, when Aum followers began frequenting his business, urging him to donate money. Then in March, he was drugged and kidnapped by six cultists, including his two daughters and son-in-law. Confined in Dr Hayashi's Tokyo clinic, he was diagnosed with a stroke and given the full range of Aum's crackpot medical procedures: drinking and vomiting up pints of hot salted water, frequent enemas, and the cult's ever-popular thermotherapy. "It was hell," the man recalled. He was then transferred to the Mount Fuji prison, where the cult worked on extracting his $1 million in real-estate holdings.

By the time the innkeeper joined Yuko, the reeking container car held ten people. Yuko was unsure how much longer she could last. Then, six weeks after being thrown in prison, she was let out and escorted to a small room in another building. There, a medical worker hooked her up to an I/V.

"The initiation this time is based on Western medicine," she heard a doctor say before she passed out. She is unsure what happened next, but other cultists familiar with the rite say she was doped with thiopental and given subliminal suggestions. One described a similar experience in which earphones were put on with Asahara's voice, encouraging him to renounce the world.

A week later, Yuko was released from the container. It was now mid-October. As she came to her senses, Yuko realized she had been Aum's prisoner for three months.

She was given a job in the compound and, for the first time, was allowed to sleep undisturbed at night. But she remained under constant surveillance; female cultists even followed her to the bathroom.

After two weeks of this, Yuko managed to slip away, sprinting out of the compound and across a field to a neighbor's home. She arrived spattered with blood, her clothes torn from racing through the thorny underbrush. By now Aum's neighbors were used to harboring escapees from the cult. Yuko was placed under police protection and the next day returned to Aum with local residents, demanding that the cult release her son. Niimi met them at the gate. If she wanted her son back, he told them, Yuko should come inside by herself to get him. Yuko wisely refused.

Nine days later, the woman returned with a lawyer and other supporters, threatening legal action unless her son were freed. Dr. Hayashi and Aoyama, the cult attorney, tried again to persuade her to return, but Yuko would have none of it. The cult finally relented, and let the woman and child be on their way. Aum's best attempts at brainwashing had failed.

But like a battered wife who returns for more abuse, Yuko eventually went back to a cult center in Osaka. "Still I was scared that I was going to hell," she told journalist Egawa. But she refused to go near the Mount Fuji center again. Asahara himself personally called, offering words of comfort but then pressuring her again to become a nun. "Continuing your religious training to the end is the way to find truth," the guru gently argued. "It's a waste to give up now."

That was enough. Shortly thereafter, Yuko left the cult for good.

Yuko told the police that she had been imprisoned for three months, that others were held against their will, and that drugs were freely used on the compound. The cops listened with interest, but at the end seemed hesitant. If nothing else, the Japanese cops were a model of consistency. There wasn't enough evidence, they told her, to move against the cult.

26

ELECTRODES

"We have a new initiation," Dr. Hayashi explained. "Please drink this."

It was September 1994, and Aum was experimenting. The victim this time was a Japanese army veteran, a 25-year-old fellow assigned to Asahara's personal bodyguard. Hayashi had summoned the man to Satian 6, where the doctor handed him a glass used for urine samples. Inside was a yellow liquid. "Soon I got dizzy and was knocked out," the man recalled. "When I came to, I was on a bed and didn't know what was going on. It seemed many days had passed, but I had no memory.

"When I touched my head, there were swollen spots – they were so painful both inside and outside my head. It was a dull, aching pain."

The "spots" were in fact surgical incisions, made at four points in the man's skull – one at each temple and two in the back. Each cut measured one centimeter long and two centimeters wide. Fresh scars and swelling bald spots showed through what was left of his hair.

The man lost track of time. Weeks, then months passed by. "My whole body ached from lying on a bed so long," he recalled. "A tube was injected into my nose and into my urethra. I was hooked up to an I/V too. My arm was covered with needle marks." Perhaps from the surgery, and then from the drugs, he had trouble speaking and could barely move. Locked away in an Aum clinic, the ex-soldier began to waste away. Once a strapping 220 pounds, he lost nearly a third of his weight and looked on the verge of death.

At one point, a female doctor with white hair came by. "You leaked information to the outside," she said matter-of-factly. "That's why you nearly died."

The man later escaped and was nursed back to health. "When I went home I had a thorough exam of my brain," he said. "But a CAT scan showed nothing. As for the four scars . . . I think they might have put electrodes in my head."

"Electrodes in my head" – the phrase echoes, as if from some distant retrograde future. Aum, the hi-tech death cult, had met the cyberpunk world of *Neuromancer*, William Gibson's science-fiction classic. In Gibson's book, a "console cowboy" called Case prowls the holographic backstreets of Tokyo, and wires his mind directly onto computer nets. He might have felt right at home at Satian 7.

Aum's scientists were fascinated by electronics and the brain, seeking new ways to achieve mind control. Dogma, drugs, and brainwashing apparently were not enough to keep Asahara's legions in line. "Aum may have planned to create a human robot by modifying the brain," suggested a Tokyo magazine which investigated the topic. Asahara, it claimed, had asked Murai if the cult could produce followers who would obey his orders at any cost. The ever-obedient Murai promised to look into the matter.

Brain-wave patterns had always interested Aum's scientists. These were, after all, the basis of the electrode caps worn by the cult priesthood. But now the scope of their experiments expanded radically. In a new book, Asahara and Murai discussed the frontiers of mind control. "I heard a story that in Taiwan, police robots are beginning to work," the guru said to his chief scientist. "I feel now we are getting into the time of animation."

"Yes, you are right," Murai replied. "We cannot laugh at animation films anymore. I've heard that an electric wave of 840 to 890 megahertz can cause a sympathetic response in the human skull and have a big influence on the brain. In the U.S., the technique of mind control by electrical waves already exists."

As usual, Aum science was far-fetched – but not impossible. In medicine, electromagnetic waves have long been used to stimulate healing of wounds and broken bones, for pain relief, and as shock therapy in severe psychological cases. As any psychiatrist knows, electric shocks to the brain can have dramatic effects – including the complete interruption of mental functioning for short periods. Sensors implanted in the brain now enable victims of paralysis to send electrical signals to microchips in the shoulder, telling their muscle fibers to contract and lift the arm.

Military researchers have wondered if such technology could be deployed in battle. For years, scientists on both sides of the Cold War looked at using electromagnetic energy to influence the human brain;

that work apparently continues today. Studies have shown that various frequencies can cause effects ranging from drowsiness and shortness of breath to memory loss. Some question whether the brain, an electrochemical organ, could actually be switched off – whether the human nervous system could be short-circuited by the right combination of electromagnetic wave and frequency.

A 1982 U.S. Air Force review of biotechnology warned that electromagnetic weapons "may pose powerful and revolutionary antipersonnel military threats." Four years later, in a somewhat innocuously named book, *Low-Intensity Conflict and Modern Technology*, Captain Paul Tyler took a chilling look at their potential use against human beings. Tyler, who held a medical degree along with his U.S. Navy commission, wrote that such weapons "would be used to produce mild to severe physiological disruption or perceptual distortion or disorientation . . . They are silent and countermeasures to them may be difficult to develop." The devices might produce a beneficial effect as well, he added, making it easier for one's own soldiers to maintain peak performance with minimal rest. (The book's foreword, interestingly, was written by a then obscure congressman from Georgia named Newt Gingrich.)

Aum was not the first fringe group to contemplate electronic mind control. In 1984, members of The Order, an American band of white supremacists, spent $100,000 on their so-called Reliance Project. According to *The Order*, a book on the subject, a key member later told the FBI how the group was "in contact with two former government scientists who had been involved in a secret U.S. scientific experiment dealing with the transmission of electronic signals or waves at particular frequencies." The signals, he said, "serve to render people more docile and subservient."

Could Aum's scientists actually control people by planting electrodes in their heads? "Turning people into robots was a game for Asahara," said a former Aum member. "He fancied himself as god in a realm of robots."

What Asahara really created was a realm of zombies. One set of tests performed by Dr. Hayashi used electric shocks to wipe the memories of suspicious followers. According to Hayashi's detailed medical records, seven shocks of 100 volts each, delivered to the scalp, was enough to blank the short-term memory of one of Asahara's drivers, who had been branded a spy. The man couldn't remember he had ever driven the guru's car. A worker at Satian 7 who tried to escape received eleven shocks, and a male follower accused of sexual relations got nineteen. During one three-month period beginning in October 1994, Dr. Hayashi administered over 600 electric shocks to 130 followers. Afterwards, some of them forgot which cult they were in, what the guru was called, even their own names.

Nobody, it seemed, could stop Aum. Japan's police force was either unable or unwilling to follow five years of leads that all pointed to the cult. There were heroes, but they had suffered terrible fates: the attorney Tsutsumi Sakamoto, murdered with his family in 1989; Kotaro Ochida, strangled to death while trying to rescue a friend's mother; Yuko Tanaka, who escaped to tell police of the abductions, prisons, and drug abuse. And then there was Shoko Egawa.

Shoko Egawa is a slightly built, bespectacled writer who from the cult's earliest days thought something was rotten inside Aum Supreme Truth. Years before, while working as a Yokohama newspaper reporter, she had introduced a fleeing Aum member to Sakamoto, which started the attorney's investigation of the cult. Egawa never doubted Aum's involvement in the Sakamotos' disappearance, and doggedly pursued the cult over the next three years. By spring 1992, she had produced two books on Aum, *Ambitions of a Messiah* and *The Kidnapping of a Yokohama Lawyer*.

Egawa was virtually alone in her pursuit of the cult. Other reporters knew that taking on Aum meant lawsuits, harassment, and perhaps worse. Eventually, public interest in the cult waned, and with it Egawa's market. But then came the Matsumoto sarin attack, and she was back with a vengeance. Now a freelance writer, she produced story after story in Japan's lively weekly magazines, interviewing past members, exposing cult rituals, and enraging the Aum leadership. Despite receiving threatening phone calls, she fearlessly pushed ahead in looking at the cult.

At a gathering of Aum members in Asahara's private room, one of them read a story by Egawa ripping the cult apart. When the reading was over, Asahara grinned. "I wonder if Egawa has taken a fancy to me," he said. One follower in the room later told a reporter: "Asahara suddenly grew serious the next moment and assumed an ominous air, as if to order her murder."

The job to silence Egawa fell to Niimi. On September 20, 1994, Niimi and his hit squad drove to Egawa's Yokohama apartment. In his hands he held the latest weapon from the cult's laboratories.

Around 3:30 a.m., Egawa was woken by an odd noise. The newspaper box on her front door was rattling.

"I thought it strange and went to the living room facing the entrance," she later wrote. "The entrance hall was full of gas with a strange powerful odor. I guess I inhaled the gas . . ."

This time the lethal gas was phosgene, a World War I choking agent. Phosgene strikes at the lungs, swelling the tissue until the victim dies of asphyxiation. The chemical today is widely used in the plastics industry, where it is known as carbonyl chloride. Aum's technicians had loaded some in a small aerosol dispenser, which Niimi now pumped into his victim's fourth-floor apartment.

"Soon I felt pain my throat and I was seeing stars," Egawa recalled. Scared to go outside, she listened for footsteps but heard nothing. Then she ran into the corridor.

"When I looked down I saw someone dashing out of the building and jumping into the passenger seat of a large white car parked on the street. Then the car disappeared."

Egawa made her way to the hospital, where doctors found her bronchial system terribly swollen and prescribed two weeks of care. From her bed, Egawa had no doubt who was responsible. Aum, she said, was trying to commit murder yet again with chemical weapons. Aum's reply was as swift as it was predictable. "If the attack on Egawa is true, this must be a plot to entrap Aum Supreme Truth," read a cult statement on the attack. "Indeed, there have been other attempts to frame Aum."

An attack on so obvious an Aum critic should have rung alarm bells for the police. Surprisingly, it did. Like a slow student finally grasping a key concept, Japan's cops were at last starting to look at Shoko Asahara and his murderous cult.

The great awakening apparently began with police in Yokohama, site of the Sakamoto murders and now the assault on Egawa. The cops there had learned that for months before the Matsumoto attack, Aum had talked of sarin in their publications. Chemical weapons were, of course, an obsession with the cult, as any perusal of its literature would have shown.

About the time Egawa found phosgene seeping through her front door, authorities in Yokohama shared their relevation with the National Police Agency in Tokyo, which oversees the nation's 260,000 police. The NPA then assigned officials to begin gathering reports of Aum's crimes nationwide. On learning of the toxic leaks at Aum's Mount Fuji center that summer, the agency also decided to do some chemical work of its own. The NPA dispatched staff chemists to the site, who quietly passed alongside the compound, gathering soil and leaf samples where plants had withered and died.

In November, police had their answer. The samples contained traces of methylphosphine acid monoisopropyl, a residue left when sarin decomposes. The chances of that particular compound occurring naturally, said the chemists, were next to none. But the sarin residue by itself wasn't enough for the NPA's ever-cautious officials, who demanded more evidence before they would authorize a massive raid on a religious organization.

There should have been no shortage of cases to choose from. At one point, they considered the allegations of kidnapping and drug abuse by Yuko Tanaka, the ex-nurse. Then they thought about her former cellmate, the innkeeper, who after five months had escaped by promising a hefty donation, and then filed a complaint against the cult. Neither case, however, seemed to satisfy the bureaucrats at the NPA.

Badly in need of intelligence, the NPA's Security Bureau took the politically dangerous move of sending an undercover agent into the cult. Such a move would have been made long ago by most Western law-enforcement agencies. But in Japan, the NPA risked sparking a major scandal by misuse of police powers. Complicating matters was the difficulty of placing a deep-cover agent inside a secretive and murderous sect. The attempt would end in tragedy. According to a well-placed Security Bureau source, the agent was murdered by the cult.

As November turned to December, police were still deliberating how to go after the cult. And the cult, meanwhile, had infiltrated the police.

Like *Invasion of the Body Snatchers*, the classic 1950s sci-fi film, Aum's insidious influence seemed to reach into every corner of society. The cult reportedly counted among its flock as many as forty young bureaucrats from government ministries – education, post and telecommunications, justice, construction, transport – as well as tax collectors and regional judges. One judge was said to have donated $10,000 to the cult. There were also reporters and editors, including a program director at NHK, the national broadcaster.

Aum's membership list also included over a hundred experts in engineering, communications, computing, and other fields from companies like Toshiba, Hitachi, and IBM Japan – all firms whose latest technologies Aum coveted. Some eventually left their firms to join the cult full-time: others merely donated large sums of money. There were also those regarded by Aum as "sleepers" – nonmembers who perhaps only attended yoga classes but could, with the right plan, be recruited into the cult.

Aum's tentacles reached deeper into the Japanese military. By year's end, nearly forty active-duty members of the Self-Defense Force had enlisted in Asahara's army, together with sixty or so veterans. One member at the National Defense Academy slept under a large poster of Shoko Asahara and vowed to recruit others before graduation. Even more helpful was a first lieutenant in Japan's 2nd Anti-tank Helicopter Unit, who leaked reams of classified data to the cult.

The soldier became Aum's primary spy within the SDF, stealing an impressive array of classified military documents: a list of equipment and personnel assigned to anti-tank helicopter units; a description of weapons systems on the military's powerful new combat helicopters; and booklets on radio and communications, complete with circuit diagrams. Perhaps most useful to the cult was a training manual called *Special Weapons Defense*, which gave scientific data not just on nuclear weapons, but on the amount of biochemical agents – down to the milligram – needed to kill half the population in a targeted area.

When infiltration failed to get what Aum wanted, the cult turned increasingly to wiretapping. Like biochemical technology, the tools to conduct electronic eavesdropping are now within the reach of ordinary people – and Aum took full advantage. The first tap had been discovered as early as 1991 by NTT, the national phone company. Aum's technique was simple enough. They reportedly obtained NTT uniforms and ID badges, and put together a tapping manual for their security and recruiting teams. Favorite targets were rich potential donors and Aum enemies. Opponents claim at least seven wiretaps were found on homes belonging to relatives and others opposed to the cult.

As 1994 drew to a close, it was the police that most occupied the minds of top Aum officials. Fortunately for the cult, Aum's recruiting had paid off here, too – at least half a dozen members of Japan's finest had joined up. One top cop admitted that two of them belonged to the Tokyo Metropolitan Police Department. Computer networks offered another venue for intelligence. That fall, an Aum member named Light and Sky searched Japan's largest on-line service for a list of addresses for police stations nationwide.

The police contacts proved invaluable. Within weeks, Aum had learned of the NPA's secret sampling from their Mount Fuji center. The knowledge sparked a panicky round of meetings within the cult, as the leadership wondered whether a raid was imminent. Aum, they agreed, could always claim that Satian 7 was an agrichemical plant – that they were making pesticides, not nerve gas. But just as a precaution, containers holding the raw ingredients for sarin were relabeled.

As the weeks passed, nothing happened. Their police contacts told them there was no news. Cult leaders began to relax, confident they had escaped official scrutiny yet again. In a sense, they were right, as Japan's slow-footed cops wondered about how to best tackle the cult. At least for a while longer, Aum Supreme Truth was free to wreak havoc in the world.

27

NUKES

"Nuclear warhead. How much?" The guru was still waiting impatiently for an answer to the question Kiyohide Hayakawa had scrawled in his notebook. Asahara's right-hand man made eight trips to Russia during 1994 with a historic mission to fulfill: to arm Aum with the world's most awesome weapon of mass destruction.

The cult's Russian empire had continued its explosive growth. By the end of 1994, Aum boasted a staggering 30,000 believers in Russia – three times its Japanese membership. There were at least six branches in Moscow, and up to eleven outside the capital, including St. Petersburg, Vladivostok in the Far East, Vorkuta in the Urals, Vladikavkaz in the Caucasus, and Samana on the Volga River. There was also a core of followers in Kiev and Minsk.

Hayakawa had already served his master well. But Asahara's talk of Armageddon had heaped new pressures upon his lieutenant, chief among them the urgent plan to buy a nuke. Acquiring nuclear capability had long been an article of faith among cult leaders; the guru had warned in sermons that a final, apocalyptic war would be fought with nuclear weapons. While the cult was looking into mining uranium, Aum's influence in Russia opened the possibility of a short cut. Why build a bomb when you can simply buy one? The information on Hayakawa's activities is sketchy, but enough exists to raise troubling questions.

The safety of the former Soviet nuclear stockpile of some 30,000 warheads is a burning issue in the post–Cold War world. The possibility of terrorists acquiring nuclear weapons material is "the number one threat to American national security today," according to Graham Allison of Harvard University's Center for Science and International Affairs. "Americans have every reason to anticipate acts of nuclear terrorism against American targets before this decade is out," warned Senator Richard Lugar of the Senate Foreign Relations Committee.

By 1995, the CIA had received more than a hundred uncon-firmed intelligence and media reports that nuclear warheads and related material were missing. Russia and its former territories are the chief source of these reports. In 1993, 330 pounds of uranium were seized in Izhezk some 600 miles from Moscow. The following year, Russian police arrested two men who attempted to steal 21 pounds of highly enriched uranium from the Arzamas-16 nuclear-weapons research facility. Also in 1994, Prague police intercepted six pounds of weapons-grade uranium en route from Russia to western Europe.

These and many other disturbing reports – fuel rods missing from Russian nuclear plants, a chunk of uranium found in a discarded refrigerator in Frankfurt – have triggered concerns that a new black market in nuclear materials is emerging. Western law-enforcement officials fear the powerful Russian *mafiya* and other crime syndicates will cash in on a global trade in contraband radioactive material.

All this raises the critical question: How secure is the Russian nuclear stockpile? A senior scientist at the U.S. Natural Resources Defense Council described the lack of security at some of Russia's hundreds of nuclear facilities as "hair-raising." Fuel in Russian nuclear submarines and icebreakers is highly enriched, yet security at naval bases is particularly poor. There are also concerns about out-of-work nuclear-weapons experts finding lucrative new outlets for their skills. Or as Sam Nunn, one of the U.S. Senate's top defense experts, put it: "Literally thousands of nuclear scientists do not know how they are going to provide adequately for their families, but they certainly do know how to make nuclear weapons."

Russia officially plays down such concerns. A high-ranking member of Russian counterintelligence dismissed cases of smuggling of weapons-grade uranium as "speculation," labeling them part of a "far-reaching attempt . . . to establish so-called international control over Russian nuclear facilities." Such comments willfully underesti-mate the means, motives, and sheer determination of fringe groups like Aum – and of men like Kiyohide Hayakawa.

Hayakawa's notes contained "lots of references to nuclear warheads," according to an extensive summary of Aum's worldwide activities by Japanese police. A report by the U.S. Senate Permanent Subcommittee on Investigations, which scrutinized Aum's search for weapons of mass destruction, noted that Hayakawa also wrote down several prices for a nuclear bomb. Among the prices, say sources, was the bargain sum of $15 million. These references could imply that Hayakawa had merely discussed the prospect of acquiring a nuke with specialists. Equally likely, however, they could suggest a far more perilous situation: that Hayakawa was actually in the middle of complex negotiations to buy a nuclear device.

Aum's construction chief had plenty of experts he could have consulted on nuclear matters. As well as recruiting physicists from Moscow State University and other elite colleges, Aum had infiltrated the most prestigious nuclear research body in all of Russia. The I. V. Kurchatov Institute of Atomic Energy in Moscow is named after the late physicist Igor Vasilyevich Kurchatov, the father of the Soviet Union's atomic bomb and nuclear-power programs. With at least three research reactors, the Kurchatov remained a famous brain trust for nuclear studies – and a repository for plenty of weapons-grade nuclear material. A Kurchatov spokesman admitted there was "at least one" Aum follower at the institute.

John Sopko, one of the Senate investigators who looked at length into Aum and proliferation, thought it unlikely the cult could have acquired a nuclear warhead or mastered the technical skills necessary to build one. Far more plausible, he believed, was the threat of Aum acquiring highly radioactive material and developing a radiological or "dirty" weapon.

Such material – say, the plutonium core from a warhead – could be rigged with explosives and detonated, causing a highly carcino-genic mist. And unlike chemical agents such as sarin, radioactivity can endure for thousands of years. "Could you imagine [a radiological weapon] being set off in the Tokyo subway system?" asked Sopko. "Half of Tokyo would be uninhabitable for the next couple of centuries."

Aum stood at the dawn of a new age of nuclear terrorism, and there was nothing Shoko Asahara wanted to see more than a radioactive sunrise over Japan. Only Hayakawa knows how close the cult came in Russia to achieving this goal. The cult's intentions were all too apparent: it was willing to spend millions of dollars on gaining nuclear capability. Every Russian nightmare the CIA had warned of – the theft of nuclear weapons, the buying-up of scientists, the black-market trading in radioactive material – now seemed a step closer to reality.

Acquiring a nuke was not the only pressing task facing Kiyohide Hayakawa. Back at Mount Fuji, the cult's weapons factory at Clear Stream Temple was now producing hundreds of parts for the AK-74 automatic assault rifle. When assembled, these would provide Aum's infantry with firepower in the November 1995 coup. Before then, however, the cult's holy warriors needed to learn how to handle the rifles.

In September 1994, Hayakawa was one of fifteen cultists who attended a ten-day weapons-training program at a military base outside Moscow. The course was run by veterans of crack Russian units known as Spetsnaz, who taught Aum's soldiers the skills of self-defense, survival, camouflage, and shooting rocket launchers and assault rifles with live ammunition. Later Russian reports identify the "secret military base" as either the Kantemirovskaya tank division or the Tamanskaya motorized infantry division, both near Moscow.

As well as training the cult's infantry, Hayakawa's Russian contacts also provided the first manned aircraft in Aum's air force. A month before the Spetsnaz program, the enterprising engineer had finally gotten his hands on a military-class helicopter: a MIL Mi-17 from the old Soviet war machine. Hayakawa's delight was obvious. "We've found it at last!" he wrote in his notebook.

The Mi-17 was a twin-turbine, multipurpose chopper built in the Tatarstan capital of Kazan. It was mainly a cargo carrier, but could be equipped with 128 57-mm rockets, 4 Skorpion anti-tank missiles, and a flexibly mounted 12.7-mm machine gun in the nose. The seven-ton chopper was bought for $700,000 in the Caucasus republic of Azerbaijan. Then, with the help of an Austrian trading company, it was dismantled and ferried through Austria, Slovakia, and on to the Netherlands, where it was put on a ship to Japan.

Russian and Japanese media reports later alleged that a high-powered Russian helped the cult in its negotiations: Ruslan Khasbulatov, former speaker of the Russian parliament and one of the most influential men in Chechnya, that one-stop military hardware shop in the Caucasus. He had met Asahara during the Russian Salvation Tour – purely a meet and greet, he later insisted. In Hayakawa's notes, the "guarantor" on the deal is recorded simply as "untraceable person."

Sometime in early June 1994, the Mi-17 arrived at the port of Yokohama and passed easily through Japanese Customs, presumably because it was not equipped for carrying weapons. It was then trucked to Mount Fuji, where cult engineers began reconstructing it.

Perhaps heartened by his success, Hayakawa returned again to Russia a few months later to add another front company to Aum's global business empire. In November 1995, a new Moscow security firm called Aum Protect was set up. This would hardly have been headline news. With the city's rocketing crime and corrupt police, a gun was one of the most sought-after accessories for many Muscovites. If not a gun, then something else: among the city's most popular dogs was the Rottweiler. Meanwhile, the protection industry was booming. Nearly 800,000 people were employed in security businesses in the region.

Four of Aum Protect's twelve staff were highly trained veterans of the KGB's 9th Division. Their contacts, together with the fact that security guards can carry registered firearms, were very useful to the cult. Aum Protect was ready to act as a conduit for acquiring weapons and other materials, a familiar role already played by other cult front companies worldwide. "Aum could easily have used the firm to buy legally such weapons as Makarov, Tokarev, and Stechkin pistols, as well as Kalashnikovs and armored vehicles," believed Vitaly Savitsky, head of a State Duma investigation into religious sects.

The well-built men of Aum Protect quickly became a highly visible aspect of the cult's Russian operation. Anyone visiting the Moscow HQ would find the entrance barred by one of these man-mountains. Aum Protect staff would later flank cult lawyers and witnesses during court cases. They were also useful for putting pressure on disobedient followers.

Despite the cult's rapid growth, or perhaps because of it, Aum's Russian outpost was increasingly infected with the same paranoia now spreading through the Mount Fuji mother community. Aum Protect was a symptom of the cult's growing sense of besiegement. It was receiving frequent telephone bomb threats, devotees were told. Enemies of Aum lurked everywhere.

During a mass meditation session at Olympiski Stadium, stray dogs suddenly ran snarling through the crowd. Devotees claimed either the Moonies or the Japanese Buddhist sect Soka Gakkai had deliberately released the dogs to sabotage the meeting. The incident unnerved Asahara, who retreated to his suite at Moscow's Olympic Lufthansa Hotel and refused to meet Russian followers – they had "dirty energy," he said. Then, supposedly fearing for his life, he left Russia. He never returned. The first cracks were beginning to appear in Aum's Russian empire.

One very public threat to the smooth running of the Moscow operation was the Youth Salvation Committee. This increasingly vocal group of parents of Aum members had compiled some shocking evidence. In Russia, as in Japan, scores of followers were missing. At least two cultists had committed suicide. In spring 1994, one mother found her 28-year-old son hanging from a tree in Mozhaiski forest on Moscow's southwest fringes; he left no suicide note. A thirteen-year-old epileptic boy called Maxim joined the cult with his mother. Aum's monks allegedly tormented him for his lack of spiritual progress. The boy jumped to his death from the balcony of a Moscow apartment.

The parents' first attempt to prosecute Aum was quickly thrown out of court after the cult presented testimony from psychiatrists that their followers were mentally sound. The parents believed that police reluctance to investigate complaints against Aum had much to do with the back-room influence of the cult's high-level supporters in Moscow. "So many top people were interested in obscuring the truth about Aum," said parent Zinaida Zakharova.

The parents' campaign was headquartered in a shabby hall next to Moscow's Virgin of All Sorrows Church. Their spiritual focus took the formidable shape of Father Oleg Stenyaev. With his wild beard, piercing eyes, and enormous girth, Stenyaev is almost a caricature of the typical Russian Orthodox priest. But his methods were hardly typical. He decided that to beat Aum, he would have to join them. The priest signed up for yoga classes.

"Two followers tried to put me on my head," said Stenyaev, laughing at the memory. "Then they made me drink six liters of water. It was coming out of every hole in my body." Blinded by arrogance, cult leaders believed they could convert a Russian Orthodox priest, but Stenyaev proved to be a Trojan horse in Aum's ranks. He learned cult jargon and privately counseled believers. He held discussion groups with sect leaders, proving before the Aum flock how little these living Buddhas knew about either Buddhism or Christianity.

Cult leaders seemed to realize the threat Stenyaev posed. The priest was leaving his church one day when a car pulled up with four men inside. A Japanese man got out and, through a Russian interpreter, told Stenyaev they were "friends of Aum." Then they tried to push the priest into the car. Unfortunately for the aspiring kidnappers, the 220-pound-plus Stenyaev was simply too wide to manhandle into the back seat. Before long, a police car drew up and the friends of Aum casually got back in the car and drove off.

After several long months, Stenyaev had gained enough trust among Aum's Moscow following to lead over fifty followers out of the cult. Marina Romandina would not be among them, at least not yet. An alarmingly pale eighteen-year-old with ice-blue eyes, Marina was taking a year out from music college when she joined Aum in spring 1994. She shaved off her blonde hair, devoured Asahara's books in translation, and wore what the Russians knew as the "hat of salvation" – the cult's electric-shock headgear.

Although global in scope, Aum's overseas offices were run much like other multinationals from Japan; every executive post of importance was held by a Japanese. The Moscow office was no exception. The Japanese management found Russian names difficult to pronounce, never mind remember, and so gave every follower an identification number. Marina was number 92.

The lives of Marina and her fellow Russians were dominated by a man called Maitreya Saitaishi. His real name was Fumihiro Joyu, a smooth-talking 29-year-old with boyish good looks and a degree from a top Tokyo university. Joyu left a promising career at Japan's Space Development Agency to join Aum, where he became one of the guru's favorites. "He is absorbing my religious theories as if water soaked into the dry earth," Asahara once wrote.

Joyu had actually absorbed only Asahara's very worst qualities. He was a mini-guru, a cruel and arrogant man who later proved to be Aum's most accomplished liar. Joyu didn't try to hide his contempt for his poor Russian flock.

Firing out orders through ten interpreters, Joyu ran Aum's large Moscow center at Alexseyevskaya Square, where the cult owned one floor of an office block. Behind the permanently drawn curtains, some 300 followers slept, prayed, and attended to earthly concerns – updating huge computer lists of members, holding seminars, and recruiting, recruiting, recruiting. "We had no time to stop and think," said Marina. "In fact, we were encouraged to believe there was nothing to think about."

It was Marina's job to rent community halls for "Path to Freedom" seminars. These were physical and emotional roller-coasters, forty-eight-hour bombardments of "astral music" and mantras in which participants stood and chanted the same words for two hours: "I am happy to join Aum, I will always follow the guru, I will become a monk." There were two three-hour breaks for sleep, and a ritual called "sacrificing food to the guru." Says Marina, "We had to eat and eat until we felt sick. This was to make us understand that food caused pain. Anyone who threw up had to eat their own vomit."

The intensive seminars were an exceptionally effective recruiting device, perhaps due to the white candies which were handed out. The candy numbed the tongue and, said Marina, "tasted like mints." Zinaida Zakharova thought the candies explain Aum's lightning conversion rate. "We watched our children's personalities change abruptly. After three days, they begged to leave home and join Aum. To me, that sounds like a drug dependency, not a psychological one."

There is compelling evidence that in Russia, as in Japan, Aum systematically doped its followers. Cultists ate twice-daily meals of macaroni and porridge – the Russian version of "Aum food." They were told Joyu had sung a mantra and "injected the food with his energy." Marina suspects that Joyu's energy wasn't the only unusual ingredient. "After eating, I always felt sleepy and had vivid dreams," she said. The food was prepared only by "enlightened" women cooks, all of whom happened to be Japanese.

Then there were the pills. "Every month, we were given a package of small yellow tablets called 'sattva vitamins,'" Marina continued. "We took one every day. Afterwards, I'd feel so lethargic. I couldn't think ... I didn't want to think." Marina believed the "vitamins" were actually a type of prescription tranquilizer called Fenozepan.

Aum recruiters had promoted yoga as the answer to the bad diets, poor medical care, and myriad stresses afflicting so many Muscovites. But cult members suffered chronic health problems. Marina remembered one 55-year-old woman whose legs were paralyzed and skin hurt to touch. Joyu summoned her, said Marina. "She was screaming with agony as they carried her to him. Joyu just looked at her, smiled, and gave her a short lecture. All that pain for just a few words!"

Joyu constantly encouraged believers to recruit more, donate more, sacrifice everything. His one goal: to establish a Lotus Village, Aum's first Russian community, to be built at Klin outside Moscow. However, in late 1994, the Klin plan collapsed. The owner would not sell the land, perhaps owing to Aum's growing notoriety. Joyu clearly thought otherwise. "We were told it was our fault because we hadn't practiced hard enough," said Marina.

After the Klin failure, life inside the Moscow HQ plumbed new depths of misery. "Just about everyone was suffering from some kind of neurosis," Marina explained. "Monks would beat each other up. Women quarreled the whole time. There was a lot of talk of suicide." Close to breaking point, Marina went home for a brief visit.

When she returned to the Moscow HQ, she noticed something – a strange odor permeated the building's halls and corridors. "It wasn't

there every day, but I always smelled it during intensive seminars."
Marina remembered the smell from childhood trips to the country:
"It wasn't really a chemical smell. It reminded me of last year's hay."

Without knowing it, Marina was perhaps describing phosgene,
the World War I choking agent with the distinctive smell of mown
hay. Aum had already made phosgene in its Mount Fuji laboratory,
and used it to attack journalist Shoko Egawa.

Was Aum stockpiling chemical agents in Russia too? Investigators there later showed no eagerness to discuss that possibility. But
journalist and former KGB agent Konstantine Preobrazhensky claims
that one Moscow roofing company was actually an underground
Aum branch with fifteen live-in followers. According to an ex-believer
he interviewed, the branch's corridors were clogged with red and blue
chemical containers, and local residents complained of headaches and
skin irritations. Before this report emerged, said Preobrazhensky, the
barrels were removed in several trucks and the building boarded up.

Marina Romandina's own investigation into the strange smell at
cult headquarters was equally inconclusive. Her questions to cult
leaders were met with silence. "I began to think I was just imagining
it. It was hard for me to think rationally. Nobody was in control of
themselves anymore. Many of us had high temperatures and allergies.
My throat ached and my eyes watered." Marina said other followers
suffered sudden nosebleeds, vomiting, or severe headaches.

With her faith crumbling and her health shattered, Marina fled
the cult. Father Oleg Stenyaev's efforts, pending lawsuits filed by
parents, the living hell inside Aum's community – all these factors had
a profound effect on those who remained. There was also a strange
story filtering through to Aum's Moscow followers from Japan. The
details were vague, but it had something to do with some Russian
musicians, an Arabian princess, and a cold, cold night at Mount Fuji.

28

DEVIL MUSIC

A thousand dollars a month! To Sergei Evdokimov, it seemed too good to be true. He was looking at an advertisement in Moscow's Conservatoire announcing auditions for a new orchestra. In a good month, the 34-year-old flutist earned maybe $300 in various Russian orchestras. The ad offered the chance to make over three times that amount. Sergei noted down the details.

He wasn't surprised to find the auditions mobbed. Fifteen musicians competed for each place. "They came from all over the former Soviet Union," said Sergei. "Everyone wanted to be in this orchestra." By November 1992, Sergei had joined 120 of the finest instrumentalists from Russia and beyond; they now made up a new musical ensemble called Chyren – Sanskrit for "Divine Offering."

Shoko Asahara had just bought himself an orchestra.

Sergei would unwittingly help the Japanese guru fulfill a lifelong ambition. At school Asahara had performed in a band – as lead singer, naturally – but showed little musical talent. Later, however, he developed what he termed "the Divine Ear" – the ability "to hear the voices of gods and humans." With this holy skill, he began composing "astral music," the New Age tunes played at Aum meetings, often with the guru's own, off-key voice setting the melody. One room at the cult's Tokyo HQ contained a grand piano reserved for Asahara's personal use. With the Chyren orchestra, Asahara now had his own band again, albeit on a slightly larger scale. The total annual salary bill for Chyren's musicians alone was nearly $1.5 million.

The newly hired musicians were told Shoko Asahara was "a great Japanese composer." Not quite, explained Chyren conductor Vladimir Koudria. "Asahara would hum melodies to four or five musical assistants, and explain what kind of music he wanted. The assistants would go off and arrange it with computers and synthesizers. Asahara said he never thought of it as his music. He heard it from another dimension."

The guru "composed" a hundred different musical works in this fashion, including three full symphonies called *Christ*, *Genesis*, and *Message of the Saint's Skies*. "They were slightly melodic but very primitive," said Sergei, a lithe man with roguish good looks. "Some bits were stolen from Beethoven, some from Tchaikovsky. It's very unhealthy for a professional musician to play this devil's music. After a while, your skills began to degenerate."

Still, Sergei at first joined rehearsals with enthusiasm. The musicians practiced for four hours each day in a rented hall, then received an hour-long lecture on the gospel according to Aum. "We didn't really listen," said Sergei. "Some of us played games, read newspapers, drank vodka or champagne. We all knew the orchestra was run by a religious sect."

Soon, however, the musicians were expected to attend rehearsals for seven hours, only four of which were actually spent rehearsing. The other three hours combined lectures, videos, and "practical exercises." "Arms up, arms down, arms up, arms down – it was something like calisthenics," said Sergei. "Another time, we had to put our hands up and scream, 'Aum!' Then we had to scream, 'Shiva!' The louder we screamed, the better. It was like a madhouse." When the musicians were told this was a powerful ritual that could make women stop menstruating, Sergei piped up: "Can it make men start?"

The rehearsals were no joke for Boris Afanashev, Chyren's 61-year-old French-horn player. "When we prayed, we had to strike our head 1,000 times on the floor. I was forced to do it, even though I have a bad heart and high blood pressure."

The Chyren orchestra's first tour of Japan in May 1993 soothed away the musicians' doubts. During its well-advertised visit, the orchestra played twelve packed concert halls across Japan in twenty-four days. The first half of the concert program was Tchaikovsky, the second half Asahara. The orchestra also performed for monks and nuns at the Mount Fuji HQ. "They threw us a great Russian-style banquet, with borscht and everything," recalled Sergei. Afterwards Asahara presented each musician with the latest model of Panasonic camcorder.

Chyren toured Russia and the former Soviet republics at the end of that year. Then, in December 1994, it returned to Japan. The contrast with the previous tour was depressing. There was no publicity, and the musicians played to tiny audiences made up of cultists from different Aum branches. The men no longer wore tuxedos, nor the women evening dress. The musicians were now decked out in white robes.

There was no Tchaikovsky either. "We played only Asahara's devil music," said Sergei.

More bizarre than the musical program was the conductor. Vladimir Koudria no longer held the baton; a fifteen-year-old girl did.

"We called her Sheherazade, because she looked like an Eastern princess out of the Arabian Nights," laughed Koudria. "She wore a long, strawberry-colored dress with long sleeves, lots of rings, and a headdress." Koudria believed the girl could have been Asahara's teenage lover Sumeida, the latest accessory in the guru's shower room. "She and Asahara seemed very close. Every time she moved, followers would jump up to serve her. She conducted all the symphonies in Japan. Of course, the musicians knew the scores by heart. I told them not to look at her. They played perfectly."

But the tour was a total wash-out, said Sergei. "We couldn't work out why they'd taken 120 Russians all the way to Japan, paid for their food and lodging, and not profited from it in any way." They were about to find out.

December 15, 1994. The orchestra was on Japan's southern island of Kyushu, waiting to fly back to Tokyo. "At 7 a.m. we were taken to the airport," recalled Sergei. "We were each given a sandwich for breakfast. We arrived in Tokyo to be told we were going on an interesting tour of Mount Fuji. They said Asahara wanted to perform a secret initiation, which usually cost $10,000. For us, though, it would be free."

After a brief stop at Aum's Tokyo center, the musicians set off for Mount Fuji in three coaches. The journey took three hours. By the time the Russians arrived outside one of Aum's huge facilities, they were all ravenously hungry. "We asked if we could eat but instead we were taken on a tour of the Fuji lakes," explained Sergei. "Our Japanese conductor, Mr. Kamada, just said, 'It's better not to eat.' " Sergei remembered the last Mount Fuji visit – the banquet, the camcorders – and obediently suppressed his hunger pangs.

The tour ended around 9 p.m. It was dark by then, and a mountain chill had set in. The coaches parked outside one of Aum's facilities, and the orchestra was led up to a large hall on the third floor. Much to their disappointment, there was no Russian banquet, no pile of gifts. There was a group of Aum members there, but they didn't seem to be musical types. The hall was separated into scores of cubicles by wooden or cloth partitions. The floor was wet and filthy. Sergei and his colleagues were told to take off their shoes. Then each of them was led inside one of the cubicles.

"There were beds on the floor," recalled Sergei. "They all had wires coming from beneath them. Each bed also had a pair of earphones and a blindfold. I was very tired so I lay down on the bed. Immediately, I began to feel this vibration going through my whole body."

He noticed the wires led to a row of speakers beneath the mattress. Each one vibrated with a mantra sung by Asahara. The same drone came from the headphones. The whole system was controlled by a bedside box with several dials on it. Sergei, like many of his colleagues, turned the master dial off to stop the bed shuddering. But each time he did so, a vigilant cultist would turn it on again.

Some musicians began complaining of the cold and damp. Most of them had left their coats in the buses. And the buses, Sergei noted with a stab of panic, had long since gone. Eventually, around midnight, the cultists brought in some plastic coats. Many exhausted musicians wrapped themselves in the coats and tried to sleep. "The believers still insisted that they lie on the vibrating beds with earphones on," said Sergei. "Some musicians were just too tired to argue."

Meanwhile, cult physicians and nurses were visiting each bed, taking the musicians' temperature and blood pressure. It began to dawn on Sergei that Chyren's members were being used as guinea pigs in some sort of experiment. "They want to make zombies out of us," he thought. But after his blood pressure had been taken, all he could think about was rest.

"I lay on the bed and switched off the box, but a folllower came round and turned it on again. Eventually, I got out my cigarette lighter and burned the wires. Then I tried to sleep." After fifteen minutes, Sergei gave up. The room was so cold. He opened his eyes and looked up. Then he saw it. Something was dripping from the roof.

"I didn't know what it was but it had a strong chemical smell," Sergei said. "The roof was high so I couldn't work out exactly where it was coming from. It couldn't have been a leak, since it wasn't raining or snowing."

Through an interpreter, Sergei and some others confronted a Japanese cultist and asked him about it.

"The state attacked us with poison gas," the cultist replied. "We're just washing the gas out."

Boris Afanashev, the French-horn player, also noticed the droplets. He described it as "a liquid with a strange odor." After four hours, he pushed his way downstairs to get some fresh air. "It was then that I felt some kind of gas had been used on us. My body was shaking and I felt nauseous. I felt I wanted to scream and curse."

Back in the hall, cultists had brought in industrial heaters. Since the hall was poorly ventilated, this only made the situation worse. "It was unbearable to be inside the hall for more than five minutes," said Sergei. "You simply couldn't breathe. Many of the women were in hysterics. They were hungry and afraid. The earphones, the vibrations, the stink of chemicals – they didn't know what was being done to them."

"There were fifty monks and 120 musicians in the hall," said conductor Vladimir Koudria. "It wasn't designed for that many people. After half an hour, there was no oxygen in the room and the air was filled with the smell of the heaters." But being out in the open was a mixed blessing. Koudria had noticed a ventilation flue on the side of the facility. "A dirty green smoke spurted out of it. Then it turned blue. Whenever I stood close by, my thoughts, my whole body, turned incredibly heavy. If I moved away, I felt better in five or ten minutes."

Koudria had no time to investigate further, because a bitter argument had broken out between a group of musicians and their Aum keepers. "We want food and we want a motel," they said. Their demands were ignored. Despite their numbers, the orchestra members were powerless. "We were isolated in the middle of the Japanese countryside," said Sergei. "Nobody knew where we were. The facility was surrounded by Aum guards. They were karate experts, so we were afraid of them."

Then, sometime around 1 a.m., the guru arrived. Shoko Asahara stepped out of his Mercedes and into a swarm of bodyguards. He was accustomed to smoothing over difficult situations. He found 120 starving musicians a little harder to finesse.

"I'm presenting you with a free initiation," Asahara explained. "Normally it would cost $10,000. There are people who have been waiting years for their turn."

"We're not going upstairs anymore," shouted one musician. "We can't breathe up there."

"If you don't go upstairs again, you will all be fired," warned Asahara.

"You're violating our contract," said another musician. "We were promised three meals a day."

"*You* are violating the contract by not going upstairs," said Asahara. He added that if the orchestra still refused, "you can all walk to Tokyo and get back to Moscow at your own expense."

"We're cold and we're hungry," the musician said. "We could die here."

The guru's face went blank with rage. "Well, die then," he said. "I'll pray for you."

Sergei had heard enough. "We decided then and there to get the whole orchestra out of the hall," he said. Curiously, though, not everyone wanted to leave. "Some of them said, 'Leave us alone, we like it here. We like Asahara.' Others were talking gibberish. They had red eyes and their movements were sluggish."

Then, as Sergei and the others led their colleagues from the building, pandemonium broke out. The orchestra's ethnic Russian administrator began yelling, "We've got to get out of here, they're going to kill us all!" Panic spread through the crowd. Some musicians were screaming, others were shouting furiously at their impassive cult guardians. In the midst of it all, Boris Afanashev recalled one musician running around a nearby field, crying "It's wonderful here! I want to stay forever!"

"By 3 or 4 a.m. we managed to get the whole orchestra outside," said Sergei. "Then we said to Asahara, 'Fire us if you want to, just bring back the buses.' " And soon, with cries of relief from the orchestra, the buses arrived. But as the musicians climbed aboard, a violinist named Lobov darted off and sat cowering in the roadside bushes. "I'm not going back in there!" he screamed. "The drivers are all monsters! They're going to take us to the mountains and throw us on the rocks!"

"He was hysterical with fear," recalled Sergei. "His eyes were crazed and he kept staring at one point in the distance. He may have been hallucinating. It took three people forty minutes to coax him back onto the bus."

When everyone was aboard, a head count was made. Something was wrong. Where were Zontag and Bakanov? The cultists provided the answer. Two people had been caught by Aum security while fleeing across Mount Fuji's pitch-black slopes. Now Aum wanted conductor Koudria to come with them to identify the fugitives. Sergei sensed a trap. "Two Russians wandering around Mount Fuji at four in the morning – who else could they be but Chyren members?" he asked.

Despite Sergei's fears, Zontag and Bakanov were soon reunited with the rest of the orchestra. They had told their captors that they had reached a public callbox and phoned the Russian embassy in Tokyo. Sergei believed this was why Aum had decided to let the orchestra go.

The three buses finally drove away from Mount Fuji. "We still had some sandwiches left, so we shared them out among us," said Sergei. "It was like the war years." It was daylight by the time the group reached Tokyo, where they were taken to an Aum-run Chinese restaurant. Everyone was too tired and hungry to worry about what could be in the food. They ate in a cloud of depression. "We knew that as soon as we returned to Moscow, we'd all be dismissed," said Sergei. "Chyren was over."

Sergei was right. Aum disbanded the orchestra, and its talented musicians went their different ways. Sergei got work with the Moscow Symphony Orchestra, but he and his colleagues are still trying to work out what happened at Mount Fuji on that cold December night.

Aum apparently conducted some sort of test on the musicians. The group was probably drugged, as were so many others in Aum's clutches. But did the cult also try to gas them, or was it simply the asphyxiating effect of industrial heaters?

Vladimir Koudria believed they would never know for sure. But he said the members of Chyren did learn a valuable lesson. "We have a proverb in Russia," Koudria said. "Every messiah is a liar."

Aum's messiah would endure long enough to torture yet more souls. The Chyren episode ended in disaster, but Shoko Asahara seemed unfazed. He had more pressing matters on his mind than the fate of a mutinous orchestra.

29

MINISTRY OF INTELLIGENCE

The Mitsubishi Heavy Industries compound in Hiroshima is as massive as the name suggests. MHI's main building is a postindustrial goliath made of concrete and glass, and the physicists, engineers, and designers who work inside are part of a key engine in Japan's military-industrial machine. MHI is the nation's largest defense contractor and the leading repository of state-of-the-art weapons research.

To Yoshihiro Inoue, the 25-year-old chief of Aum's Ministry of Intelligence, it also held a virtual library of sensitive military secrets. MHI designed tanks, escort ships, and nuclear power plants, and its Hiroshima facility was a hi-tech goldmine – one that Inoue was about to plunder.

It was about 11:30 p.m. on December 28, 1994, a dead hour in the middle of the slow holiday season. While millions of Japanese lived it up at overseas resorts, Inoue's five-man team sped through MHI's front gate in a rental car. Sergeant Tatsuya Toyama, a member of an elite Japanese paratrooper unit, was at the wheel. Inoue sat beside him. There was another paratrooper in the back, and one more curled up in the trunk.

Also in the back seat sat Hideo Nakamoto, a 38-year-old MHI senior researcher. Nakamoto had provided Inoue's squad with the MHI uniforms they now wore, and his company ID ensured an easy passage through the twenty-four-hour security at MHI's gates. Once inside the compound, Sergeant Toyama stood guard, swinging a flashlight. The others walked swiftly into the building.

Then the thieving began. Inoue's team logged onto MHI's mainframe and downloaded megabytes of restricted files onto a laptop computer. What they couldn't fit on disks was photocopied or simply pilfered. Among Inoue's loot was a description of laser sighting devices for tank guns, and a document – marked "Top Secret to Company Outsiders" – containing data on laser technology to enrich uranium. Afterwards, Toyama helped carry cardboard boxes full of documents and disks out to the car. Then Inoue and his squad drove out the way they'd come in – through the front gate.

Breaking into MHI was so easy that Inoue returned again and again. The information he stole was funneled back to Aum scientists, injecting new energy into the sect's grandiose designs to develop a dazzling variety of futuristic weapons.

Chief among them was the laser, which Aum had been studying for several years. In fact, just two months before the MHI break-in, local residents at Mount Fuji had witnessed a bizarre sight: a sharp beam of red light streaking across the night sky. It was four inches wide and emanated from Aum's Satian 5 building. For two hours, the beam was locked onto another sect facility about a mile away. Cultists later told locals that Aum was merely conducting a "laser irradiation experiment."

The firearms factory at Clear Stream Temple had used laser cutters capable of slicing through iron plates since April. But the guru had long been obsessed with the dark beauty of lasers. "I believe that in the end a giant laser gun will be developed," Asahara preached in 1993. "When the power of this laser is increased, a perfectly white belt, or sword, can be seen. This is the sword referred to in the Book of Revelations. This sword will destroy virtually all life." The guru's passion for lasers was easy to understand. After all, what was a hi-tech cult without the classic "death ray" seen in a thousand sci-fi movies?

"Laser" is an acronym for "light amplification by stimulated emission of radiation." A laser is an intense, highly concentrated beam of electromagnetic waves, all of exactly the same frequency, phase, and direction. Albert Einstein predicted its invention in 1917, but it was two Americans and two Russians who simultaneously discovered the laser in the 1950s. One of the Russians was Nikolai Basov, the Nobel laureate with whom Shoko Asahara had sipped tea in Moscow during Aum's Russian Salvation Tour.

For such a young technology, lasers have seen rapid development. Thousands of low-energy lasers are used in weapons systems worldwide for range-finding, targeting, and guidance. But still to be perfected and deployed is the high-energy laser gun – a thermal weapon with potentially vast destructive capability. It would work by generating enough heat to bore holes through aircraft, melt buildings, and vaporize human flesh.

Laser beams are absolutely straight, usually silent and invisible. A shell from a tank gun travels at about a mile per second. A laser beam, on the other hand, travels at the speed of light. That's 186,281 miles per second. The effect is virtually instantaneous; aim and fire, and there is virtually no time for a plane, tank, or person to move out of the way.

During the Cold War, the U.S. and the Soviet Union spent billions of dollars trying to create such a "death ray." Aum was spending millions, too – and not just on thermal-weapons research. Cult scientists were convinced that lasers would help them develop a nuclear bomb.

The key to making an atomic weapon was obtaining enough enriched uranium. The concentration of U-235 in natural uranium is only 0.72 percent. Gas-diffusion methods and centrifugal separators are currently used to enrich U-235 to 80 percent, considered weapons grade. Next-generation uranium enrichment will probably use laser and plasma beams.

Japan is one of several countries studying laser-enrichment technology in the hope of commercializing it for use in the nuclear-power industry. However, a 1992 international conference agreed that each government should strictly control the research data since it could be used to develop nuclear or laser weapons. Aum had failed once in using lasers to enrich uranium mined from their Australian ranch. The raid at MHI provided the cult with enough data to try again.

Lasers were just one of myriad technologies preoccupying the sect's mad scientists. On one encrypted optical disk, they had compiled a wish list of cutting-edge research: studies in advanced liquid and gel explosives, blueprints of rocket ignitions, data on missile targeting systems for fighter jets – Aum wanted it all. Such sensitive information could not be bought, of course. But it could be stolen. And that was the job of Yoshihiro Inoue.

He was the son of a salaryman, a quiet boy of middling intelligence who devoured books on Nostradamus and the supernatural. He took up karate to compensate for his delicate build and shied away from girls. Yoshihiro Inoue was born to join Aum Supreme Truth.

Inoue attended his first Aum seminar while studying at high school in Kyoto. He was soon so absorbed in cult teachings that he meditated in the lotus position during class and Aum attitudes began to show in his school work. Here is one poem which Aum's future spy chief composed for a class project:

There's no salvation
If this is our tomorrow.
I want to escape
On a night train
From this filthy crowd.

But Inoue did find a kind of salvation. He became an Aum monk at the age of eighteen, taking the holy name Ananda. Few of Asahara's young acolytes were so obedient, so uncompromisingly loyal. "What makes me and others happy is carrying out the will of the guru," the teenager wrote in a cult magazine. The adoration was mutual. Asahara said Inoue was "a genius in training" who had been a Tibetan monk in a previous life.

Inoue also proved a genius in recruiting. Despite his unappealing exterior − lifeless black eyes, a thin, adolescent mustache above pouting, effeminate lips − he possessed an inner strength that helped attract 1,000 new believers and 300 monks, including many Tokyo University students. When his family tried to persuade him to leave the cult, Inoue listened, then convinced his mother and brother to join.

In the summer of 1994, Asahara appointed Inoue as chief of Aum's Intelligence Ministry. With his own private hotline to the guru, the cult's young spymaster was soon extraordinarily busy. Since his moral universe swung around only one rule − "The guru is law" − he regarded no activity as too radical or illegal. He directed the abduction of runaway followers, and kidnapped and confined potential cash donors to the cult. "Anyone who would have defied orders from Asahara or Inoue was sure to meet with torture-like punishment," said ex-cultist Takeshi Hayashi, who lived in fear of the Aum leaders.

Inoue's true expertise was not torture, though, but infiltration − of Japan's bureaucracy, of its hi-tech companies, and particularly of its military. One of Inoue's prime targets was the 1st Airborne Brigade, the elite unit that serves as Japan's most combat-ready force. This paratroop unit, charged with protecting the capital, had long been a recruiting target for the cult.

Inoue recruited and converted at least three paratroopers from the 1st Airborne. Now under Aum's command were Takahisa Shirai, Tatsuya Toyama, and Shinya Asano, all sergeants in their mid-twenties. Asano had undergone six drug-fueled cult initiations, during which he claimed to see "desert islands and outer space." The sergeants were apparently quite open about their beliefs, holding regular Aum meetings in their barracks, which were decorated with posters of the guru. Their commanding officers never realized that at least three members of Japan's premier paratroop unit now counted themselves loyal to a man intent on destroying the very country they were sworn to protect.

Under Inoue's direction, the paratroopers launched a series of bold intelligence-gathering raids. His squad clambered over the fence of a police driving-test center to steal personal data to help the cult forge driving licenses. They picked two locks to reach the laser-research lab of NEC, Japan's top computer manufacturer and the world's leading producer of semiconductors; once inside, the group copied disk after disk on laser-beam amplification. They stole a stack of documents by breaking into the home of an employee of Nippon Oil and Fats Company, which made rocket fuel for Japan's space program. Inoue might have explored other places as well; police later found in the cult's possession floor plans to six major electronics firms.

Inoue later ordered Sergeant Shinya Asano to bug the Chiba City apartment of a certain Masaru Yamamoto. It was an ironic touch. Yamamoto was the commander of the 1st Airborne Brigade, the sergeant's own unit. A transmitter was connected to the circuit terminal outside the apartment, and a receiver tape recorder buried nearby. Inoue hoped to obtain useful information: Commander Yamamoto was top of a list of ten high-ranking military men whom he wanted to recruit into the cult. Inoue also toyed with the idea of kidnapping a member of Yamamoto's family, and ordered his squad to trail the commander's 27-year-old daughter.

The Japanese military wasn't Inoue's only target. Japan is home to ninety-four U.S. military facilities and 44,100 personnel. Inoue chose to have a closer look at the naval base at Yokosuka outside Tokyo, where the U.S. 7th Fleet docked. Using Sergeant Asano's military ID, Aum's spy chief led a team of cultists on a walkabout inside the 560-acre base. Inoue noted the layout and studied – no doubt longingly – a visiting U.S. aircraft carrier.

The sergeants of the 1st Airborne Brigade were later summoned by Asahara. "A war will no doubt break out between Japan and the U.S.," the guru warned them. "You all have important roles to play." Afterwards, Inoue urged his squad to recruit new Aum loyalists from among their ranks. "Especially those with anti-U.S. views," he added. "They don't need to join Aum. When the time comes, they just need to fight with us."

*

As Aum scientists digested Inoue's freshly thieved data, chief chemist Masami Tsuchiya added yet another deadly nerve agent to the cult's chemical arsenal. The compound had the consistency of heavy motor oil and an equally weighty name: ethyl S-2-diisopropylaminoethyl-methylphosphonothiolate – better known in chemical warfare circles as VX.

Applied directly to skin, a mere 15 milligrams of VX – enough to fit on a pinhead – can kill or incapacitate an average-sized human. In larger quantities, it can penetrate boots and clothing. Stable, easy to disperse, and virtually odorless, VX acts rapidly when absorbed through the skin and lungs. Unlike sarin, it is nonvolatile and long-lasting. In cooler weather, VX persists in the ground for weeks, and continues to kill.

VX was developed in the West to improve upon and comple-ment existing Nazi nerve agents like sarin. The U.S. produced some 5,000 tons of VX during the 1960s. In 1968, thousands of sheep grazing near the army's Dugway Proving Ground in Utah suddenly died. After intense public pressure, the military admitted the sheep had been accidentally killed during an open-air test of VX some 28 miles away. Together, sarin and VX form the core of Western chemical-warfare strategy – a murderous combination of short- and long-term effects.

VX had never been used in either war or peace on human beings. Then Tsuchiya gave some to Tomomitsu Niimi, the cult's chief hit man. Niimi had already pumped phosgene through the letterbox of journalist Shoko Egawa. Now he had something even more lethal to put in his syringe.

Niimi's first target was Noboru Mizuno, an 83-year-old Tokyo parking-lot operator. Mizuno was an unsung hero who had sheltered five women who escaped from cult facilities that summer. Cultists often visited his house to persuade the women to return, but the elderly man chased them off with a wooden stave. On December 2, 1994, at around 10 a.m., Mizuno was putting out the garbage. When he went back inside his house, he collapsed and began vomiting. An ambulance was called and, as Mizuno sped towards the hospital, his pupils began contracting. He spent over six weeks in the hospital recovering. Afterwards he had little memory of the event, and no idea that he had just made chemical-warfare history – with the help of an Aum hit squad armed with syringes of VX.

Ten days later, Osaka police received an odd report. A 28-year-old man had collapsed in the street while walking to work. The man,

Takahito Hamaguchi, was rushed to Osaka University hospital. By the time he arrived, his heart and lungs had stopped. He was declared brain dead two days later and died after ten days in a coma. Doctors were so baffled by the cause of death that they froze a sample of the man's blood.

The actual cause of death was Niimi, armed with his VX syringe. While Inoue watched on from a nearby apartment block, Niimi and another cultist wearing tracksuits had jogged up behind their victim and plunged the syringe into Hamaguchi's neck. Hamaguchi had visited Aum's Mount Fuji HQ many times, but Asahara believed he was a police informer, since his judo club trained in a police facility, and ordered Niimi to execute him.

While "enemies of Aum" were rubbed out, the systematic kidnapping of former cultists continued without respite. On December 9, a former Japanese soldier accused of sowing dissent within the cult was abducted from his home near Osaka, drugged, and driven back to Mount Fuji. Two weeks later, a university student who had left Aum returned to a Tokyo branch at the cult's bidding to make a formal farewell. Big mistake. The student woke up two weeks later to find himself drugged, beaten, and confined in a Mount Fuji facility.

The supposed police raids on Aum had never materialized, so it was business as usual at Satian 7. By November, two shifts of scientists working round the clock had made tons of the final two sarin precursors. By the year's end, everything would be complete apart from the last mixing stage. Then the cult would have not kilos, but tons and tons of nerve agent.

It was reason to celebrate. In December, a cult science manual printed the words of a song. It resembled the company anthems sung by Japanese factory workers each morning, except this was a melody for the apocalypse. It was called "Song of Sarin, the Magician":

It came from Nazi Germany, a dangerous little chemical weapon, Sarin Sarin!
If you inhale the mysterious vapor, you will fall with bloody vomit from your mouth,
Sarin! Sarin! Sarin – the chemical weapon.

Song of Sarin, the brave

In the peaceful night of Matsumoto City
People can be killed, even with our own hands,
Everywhere there are dead bodies,

There! Inhale Sarin, Sarin,
Prepare Sarin! Prepare Sarin! Immediately poisonous gas weapons
will fill the place.

Spray! Spray! Sarin, the brave Sarin.

As Satian 7 moved closer to mass production, 7,000 miles away
Aum's New York office was also gearing up for war. For months,
Aum USA had used a Silicon Valley shipping and buying agent called
International Computers and Peripherals to help buy millions of
dollars in computer parts. Now, however, the cult's orders began to
change.

ICP was asked if it could procure thousands of "serum" bottles,
and hundreds of mechanical fans and camcorder batteries. An
ambitious plan lurked behind this strange request. Murai's scientists
apparently planned to construct hundreds of battery-operated gadgets
to release killer clouds of biological and chemical agents. ICP also
received inquiries from Aum about gas masks, survival gear, and laser
equipment. At one point, Aum asked the company if it could obtain
"arms," a plane, and "container ships." The arms, a cult official said,
were for a customer in the Middle East. ICP replied they were unable
to help, and directed Aum to the U.S. Chamber of Commerce.

Back in Japan, Aum continued efforts to produce its own
conventional weapons. The AK-74 program at Clear Stream Temple
was trying the guru's patience; the factory had yet to produce a single
rifle, despite his repeated calls to complete a working prototype of the
automatic assault rifle by the year's end.

Even as a radio broadcast in Clear Stream Temple chimed to
mark the New Year, scientists were assembling the final parts of the
prototype. As soon as it was finished, they rushed it over to Asahara's
quarters only a few hours behind deadline. The guru was delighted.
He encouraged them to accumulate more "virtuous deeds" and
ordered the creation of a new gun-research laboratory. With less than
a year before Aum's planned coup d'état in November, he urged
workers at Clear Stream Factory to fulfill the next goal – to produce a
thousand rifles and a million bullets by March.

For Shoko Asahara, his New Year's gift rounded off a year of
proud achievements. Satian 7 was on the verge of mass-producing
sarin, which had been successfully tested in Matsumoto's backstreets.
The cult had built a vast arsenal of biochemical and conventional
arms, including VX, mustard gas, anthrax, botulism, Q-fever and
TNT. The cult had become perhaps the world's largest underground

producer of hallucinogens and barbiturates. Its commando unit, the Soldiers of White Love, was soon to be armed with AK-74s, while Aum scientists continued researching lasers, nuclear bombs and other weapons of mass destruction. From a handful of members and one office in 1984, Aum's tentacles now enveloped the world. It had over 40,000 followers in over 30 branches in at least six countries, and a global network which had acquired sophisticated lasers, chemical reactors, and a Russian military helicopter.

Shoko Asahara had reason to feel invincible. The world, it seemed, was unfolding according to his master plan. "From the end of 1995, Japan will be repeatedly hit by great changes," the guru predicted in a year-end radio broadcast. "They will lead to Armageddon and World War III."

The guru was only half right. The first great change hit not at the end of 1995, but at the very beginning.

30

SLAUGHTERED LAMBS

One New Year's Day, 1995, the following story appeared on the front page of the *Yomiuri Shimbun,* Japan's largest newspaper:

> Traces of an organic phosphorus compound that could have resulted from sarin were detected in Kamikuishiki, a small village at the foot of Mount Fuji . . . Police suspect sarin could have been produced in Kamikuishiki about twelve days after Matsumoto's poisoning incident.

The report was devastating for Aum. Not only had the *Yomiuri* announced test results of the soil samples taken by police the previous fall. It had also made the crucial link between the sarin residue outside Satian 7 and the Matsumoto gassing. Reading between the lines, Aum was clearly implicated in both events. Every Japanese journalist knew the Mount Fuji hamlet of Kamikuishiki was Aum country.

As more police and an army of reporters headed for Mount Fuji to investigate, Asahara called an emergency meeting of cult leaders in his quarters. First, he verbally abused Hideo Murai – none of this would have happened if the chief scientist had been more careful. Then he barked orders at Kiyohide Hayakawa, his head of construction. "Turn Satian 7 into a chapel," the guru told him. "Do it quickly and make sure damage to the plant is minimal." Hayakawa immediately set about turning a death factory into a shrine. Vinyl sheeting went up around Satian 7 to hide the drastic remodeling going on inside. Sarin production was halted, and chemical equipment destroyed or trucked to distant facilities. The interior was washed down with neutralizer, and pipes were cut and removed to create space for a mammoth statue of Buddha, which was built and installed in two weeks.

On Asahara's orders, the sarin stockpile in Masami Tsuchiya's adjoining laboratory was also destroyed, and topsoil around the facility was replaced. Tanks of phosphorus trichloride were emptied and refilled with kerosene. Other chemicals, including some 10 tons of methylphosphon acid dimethyl, a sarin precursor, were dumped into a nearby well. However, cult physician Nakagawa was unwilling to part with the fruits of their labor. He spirited away three pounds of the precursor and buried it near Satian 6. It would come in very useful later on.

Aum had plowed some $30 million into its sarin program. Huge amounts had been spent on a corrosion-resistant alloy called hastelloy, used in machinery parts which distilled chemicals. Hundreds of thousands of dollars more went on fluorine treatment, a process so costly that most universities don't use it in their laboratories. Now cult scientists stood by as months of hard work literally went down the drain.

Remodeled as a shrine, Satian 7 was ready to meet the press – or at least parts of it were. Reporters who entered the facility soon after were shown a dimly lit room wreathed in purple clouds of pungent incense. The room was dominated by the huge statue of Buddha, behind which lay the scaled-down sarin plant. Reporters were told the Satian's second-story rooms were used for meditation and holding "treasures," while the third floor was storage space.

Another part of Aum's concerted cover-up was a massive media counterattack. On January 4 the cult held a press conference in Tokyo chaired by Yoshinobu Aoyama, Aum's young attorney. With poker-faced delivery, Aoyama insisted Aum was not the manufacturer of a nerve gas, but the helpless victim of it. "State authorities" of Japan and the U.S. had repeatedly sprayed sect facilities, he claimed, and now the police were "making moves" against the cult. It was the same old story: Aoyama was again playing the card marked "religious persecution."

Dr. Ikuo Hayashi was also on hand to offer his expert medical opinion. He explained that followers had first shown symptoms of poisoning two years before, but this was confirmed only after the cult had imported its Russian-made gas detector. "At a sect concert last year," the doctor continued, "a gas was sprayed into the hall and a four-year-old child died suddenly. This was despite the superpower and superhealth which have been trademarks of the Aum sect."

Then a nineteen-year-old follower called Kii Miyauchi addressed the packed room. "Ever since I became a follower, I have felt listless with a regular pulse of over 100 and continuous coldlike symptoms. Recently, everywhere we go, military helicopters spray poisonous gases."

A reporter threw out a question: "Are villagers in the area unaffected by the spraying?"

The villagers were not affected, Dr. Hayashi calmly replied, because "they very cleverly take into consideration the wind direction and timing" and thereby manage to avoid the air attacks.

"What is the function of the number 7 facility?" came another question.

"I cannot divulge the religious content," replied lawyer Aoyama, before quickly changing tack. "We are clearly the victims. I will discuss anything that can help clarify the truth."

Aoyama was actually doing the very opposite. As well as turning around the accusations against Aum, he sued several media organizations for linking the cult to the Mount Fuji sarin leak. He also filed a suit for attempted murder against the president of a local fertilizer factory, accusing him of "spraying sarin and other things" on Aum facilities. (One farmer had a simpler explanation for the foul odor emanating from the factory. "Of course it stinks!" he said. "It's a fertilizer plant!")

The media were also given a video and a press release to bang the cult's point home. The video was titled *Slaughtered Lambs*. Over a soundtrack of urgent, tinkly music, its narrator claimed that some 240 aircraft – including helicopters, prop planes, and military jets – had flown low over Aum's facilities, spraying sarin and mustard gas. As a result, eighty Aum followers had come down with rashes, runny noses, fatigue, headaches, and diarrhea. The video then showed Dr. Hayashi pumping followers with syringes full of atropine, a powerful sarin antidote.

Who was trying to slaughter Asahara's lambs? A "state power," the narrator concluded over grainy footage of cats twitching to death in laboratory gas experiments. He then cited several cases of states using human guinea pigs to test biochemical agents – Unit 731 of the Japanese Imperial Army was one example – and claimed the FBI had used poison gas in the storming of David Koresh's Ranch Apocalypse at Waco, Texas, in 1993. The video also tackled a fresh media allegation: that Aum had gassed the town of Matsumoto to kill the three judges presiding over the land dispute the cult was about to lose. The narrator explained that Aum had no motive to hurt the judges, since it was confident of winning the case.

"Aum survives these attacks because it is a mystical religion that goes beyond the boundaries of life and death," Asahara's voiceover began. "Aum is a mighty obstacle to the evil that rules this world." Then the guru appeared on a pedestal back-lit by a dying sun. "I am suffering the effects of mustard gas," he sighed. "I am now facing death."

He was not the only one. "The Japanese people are controlled by the media," read the accompanying press release. "Fast food and instant food are lowering their life expectancy and depriving them of their ability to think. The end of Japan has begun."

On the very same day Dr. Hayashi and company met the media, Tomomitsu Niimi was carrying out his own orders from the guru. Niimi's approach to crisis management went by a different name. It was called "execution."

His target was Hiroyuki Nakaoka, the 57-year-old head of a cult victims' support group founded with the help of Tsutsumi Sakamoto, the Yokohama lawyer whom Aum had murdered. Nakaoka was walking across his parking lot when Niimi hit him with a deadly stream of VX. Nakaoka was lucky: Niimi missed his face. After lapsing into a coma for several weeks, he survived. But worried that the attack would scare off supporters, Nakaoka hushed the incident up.

Niimi's latest target might have taken cold comfort. After all, he was one of an array of eminent people now regarded by the cult as sworn foes. "WANTED! Members of the Black Aristocracy who have sold their souls to the Devil," read an article in that month's edition of *Vajrayana Sacca*, a cult magazine. Beneath was a list of fourteen "enemies of Aum," starting with Emperor Akihito, who was nicknamed the "Puppet Emperor." Then came the Crown Prince's wife, Masako – or "Empress of the Nation Gone to Ruin." Her father, Japan's envoy to the United Nations, was "Ambassador to Hell." Political powerbroker Ichiro Ozawa was nicknamed "Denizen of Darkness" for his perceived ties to the U.S. And rival guru Daisaku Ikeda, whom Aum had twice tried to assassinate with sarin, was "the Sixth Satan."

Aum's intentions went well beyond name-calling. Cult members cased the home of politician Ozawa and videotaped the grounds of Ryuho Okawa, another rival guru. At a meeting of cult leaders in January, Asahara asked for a volunteer to attack the head of Tokyo's Metropolitan Police Department.

"Is there anyone here who can hit the TMPD superintendent general on the hip?" he asked.

One follower replied, "That's beyond my imagination, but I'll do it if the holy leader orders me to."

Cult intelligence chief Yoshihiro Inoue also compiled his own hit list. Headed "Top People in Government Terrorism," it named about fifty of Japan's leading figures, including the prime minister, cabinet members, other politicians, and key members of Japanese intelligence and law-enforcement services. Before Inoue's career as spymaster was over, one of these men would lie bleeding outside his apartment, cut down by a hail of bullets.

Not even the Emperor headed Aum's hit list. Asahara had long predicted a "final war" between Japan and the U.S. After the news of the sarin residue, cultists repeatedly tried to pin the blame on the U.S. military. It made sense for the cult to target that military's commander in chief, President Bill Clinton.

"Clinton will be without doubt a one-term president," predicted *Vajrayana Sacca*, the cult magazine, in ominous tones. "At best, he will not be re-elected. At worst, it would not be strange if he were assassinated, making it appear like an accident."

How to stop the American president? One hint was provided by the always enterprising Inoue. Just two months before, the Aum spy chief had asked Dr. Hayashi if he would go abroad to pick up a package. "I'm thinking of sending sarin to America," he said.

The leaders targeted by Aum were not merely agents of hell, the cult revealed. They were Freemasons and – worse yet – tools of the Jews.

Aum had at last discovered the Great Satan, the cabal of evil behind the coming apocalypse. Not surprisingly, it sounded much like the conspiratorial nonsense of a thousand other fringe groups.

The cult journal attacking the Emperor and others actually comprised a book-length treatise entitled *Manual of Fear*. The contents were a frightening if predictable mix about Jews and Freemasons running the world, bent on destroying Japan with Hollywood movies, rock music, junk food – and world war. Inside, Aum issued a "declaration of war" on that slippery but menacing target, "the world shadow government."

Behind it all lurked the Jewish people. For nearly 100 pages, Aum writers recited a tired litany of anti-Semitic text, quoting at length from *The Protocols of the Elders of Zion* and similar racist tracts. The Talmud, Aum related, was in fact a murderous work. Jews were responsible for mass murder in Cambodia, Bosnia, and Rwanda, and meant to kill off 3 billion people by the year 2000.

Most Japanese, of course, have never met a Jew; that has not stopped them from buying shelves of best-selling anti-Semitic books on how Jews run the world and secretly subvert Japan. Such crackpot notions were a natural draw for the Aum gullible, who added Jews to the top of a long list of demons to exorcise. But it wasn't the Jews alone who troubled Aum – it was "Jewish Japanese." As scholar David Goodman points out in his paper on Aum and anti-Semitism, this apparently meant anyone tainted by the world outside Japan, including Japanese political and religious leaders. Even rival groups like the Moonies' Unification Church and the Buddhist Soka Gakkai were viewed as "Jewish" sects by the cult. "The object of anti-Semitism in Japan has always been the Japanese, not Jews," wrote Goodman.

Aum was merely part of a long a reactionary tradition of xenophobia in Japan. It was Aum Supreme Truth as the Black Dragon Society, the ultranationalist savior of a Japan gone to ruin. Asahara, admirer of Adolf Hitler and military might, would have felt at home among the war criminals of the 1930s and 1940s. Even the literature now resembled that of wartime Japan.

"The enemy's plots have already torn our lives to pieces," screamed Aum's treatise on the Jews. "It murders countless numbers of people and, under the guise of high-minded words and lofty principles, plans to brainwash and control the remainder. Japanese, awake!"

To fight the Jews – who now apparently included the Japanese emperor, President Clinton, and Madonna – Aum needed more and more weapons. Biochemical agents, laser beams, and nuclear bombs were simply not enough. Aum's scientists were at work on yet another futuristic weapon capable of wreaking havoc. This one was called the rail gun.

The rail gun is, in effect, the next-generation cannon. It fires a shell not by detonating a charge, but by accelerating a shell along a rail by electromagnetic force. The U.S. researched this technology as part of the Strategic Defense Initiative, known popularly as the "Star Wars" program. The Americans planned a 100-meter-long rail gun capable of firing a shell at nearly seven miles per second – about six times the speed of a tank shell.

Aum's research on the rail gun had begun the previous fall. A special three-member team was set up in Satian 16 and code-named Time Tunnel, perhaps after the old American sci-fi series of the same name. The team of three scientists included both a dropout and a graduate from Tokyo University, and a graduate from the applied-physics department of National Defense University. Their primary task was to develop the gun's sophisticated power unit, complete with revolving electric generator and high-capacity condenser. This task was nicknamed "beating the demon."

To build a rail gun of SDI proportions requires an enormous electric generator. Aum's Time Tunnel team aimed to build a portable, serial-firing rail gun with a semi-automatic release. By early 1995, they had produced a two-meter-long prototype that fired 20-mm-caliber shells. It was unwieldy – a two-ton truck would be needed to move it – but it worked. The scientists test-fired it several times in a bid to improve the shell speed. The first test achieved 218 meters per second, or mach 0.8 – nowhere near the 4.5 mach needed to destroy a tank. But Aum's rail gun was already deadly enough to kill a human target.

Shoko Asahara had high hopes for the project, visiting Satian 16 to egg on the Time Tunnel team. "I'll give you freedom to do as much as you like," he told engineers. "Just try harder to steadily increase the shell speed." More than anything else, Asahara wanted an immensely powerful weapon that would silence his enemies and give them a taste of Armageddon.

But then the extraordinary happened – Armageddon came early. And it arrived, of all places, in a Japanese city called Kobe.

31

NIKORATESURA

At 5:46 a.m. on January 17, 1995, an earthquake of awesome power struck Kobe in central Japan. Fifteen seconds was all it took to transform a thriving port city of 1.5 million people into a scene from hell. Expressways cracked and toppled, apartment blocks crumbled or sank into the liquefied earth. Huge fireballs cut swathes through entire neighborhoods, burning those still trapped beneath the rubble. As lists of the dead scrolled endlessly over television screens nationwide, emergency services struggled to cope with Japan's worst disaster since World War II.

Over 5,500 people perished in the Great Hanshin Earthquake. Tens of thousands more lost their relatives, friends, homes, and everything they owned. But for Shoko Asahara, the Kobe quake was no tragedy. Quite the opposite. It was a godsend.

The disaster – which the guru later claimed to have predicted – benefited the cult in several vital ways. As Kobe became the number-one national priority, the attention of both Japanese authorities and the media was diverted from Aum. The apocalyptic scenes from Kobe also confirmed for cultists their guru's predictions of impending doom, as well as exposing how ill-prepared the government was when faced with a major crisis. Asahara's status as prophet was boosted, and his sense of invincibility began to return.

Not long after the quake, Aum published a new book. "The war has already begun," wrote Asahara in *Disaster Nears for the Land of the Rising Sun.* "Today we have no other choice but to fight." This war, Asahara wrote, was being fought with "new types of weapons, such as those using microwaves and lasers." Clandestine gassing runs by Japanese and American aircraft were only one kind of attack the cult had supposedly suffered. "Asahara's drivers sometimes suffered pain in their eyes, so I gave them special glasses to protect against lasers," chief scientist Murai was quoted as saying. "Then the pain went away. This proves that Aum has already been attacked with lasers."

The book also featured a bizarre conversation between Asahara and Tiropa, the holy name of his construction chief Hayakawa. This doomsday dialogue starts with a seemingly innocent question:

ASAHARA: Tiropa, I'd like to hear your observations of social trends, since you've been studying them closely.

HAYAKAWA: War is the only way to get rid of panic. Present-day conditions clearly show that society is on the verge of panic. The next step is war. There is no other choice.

ASAHARA: Tiropa, you're what you'd call a secret-weapons expert, or at least you know a lot about them. What do you think?

HAYAKAWA: Plasma weapons can be activated instantly at a temperature of about 4,000 degrees. You can kill living creatures, no matter where they are.

ASAHARA: Tell us more, Tiropa.

HAYAKAWA: There are no shelters in Japan. If you want to survive, you have to provide your own defense. People of noble virtue, and people who . . . have overcome hardships and privations, and who possess karma, will survive. We will see the creation of a world populated by a new race that surpasses the human race in its present form.

"You have to provide your own defense" – Kiyohide Hayakawa was hard at work doing exactly that. The Soldiers of White Love, Aum's commando unit, finished training at a deserted high school in the country and were brought to Mount Fuji to help prepare for war. Clear Stream Temple had now produced over 10,000 core components for the AK-74 assault rifle, including breech blocks, sights, triggers, and cartridges. Since a prototype rifle was presented to the guru at New Year, another rifle had been completed, along with a number of handguns.

Hayakawa urgently needed more manpower to speed up the cult's firearms program. He also planned to build an entirely new factory – this one for explosives. To do this, he needed not just laborers, but also designers, engineers, metalworkers, and other specialists. So Hayakawa turned to another Aum front company he had set up the previous fall. The declared business activities of the World Unification Company were a curious combination of construction, detective services, and fortune-telling. The curtains of the company's eighth-floor office in central Tokyo were permanently drawn, and a constant stream of people entered and left the office, where they seemed to hold meetings with all the lights out.

Soon the World Unification Company approached a public employment office to ask for 105 staff. The request included thirty construction workers, five building designers, ten plumbers, twenty-five woodcraft workers, and ten welders – all skilled workers who were needed on the firearms and explosives projects. He also requested twenty private investigators, as well as people with a background in credit research, computerized fortune-telling, and entertainment. Fortune-tellers and entertainers would be useful in recruiting, while private eyes and credit researchers would easily find work inside a group so fond of extortion, abduction, and spying.

Aum's insatiable acquisition program pushed ahead on other fronts. In February, a battery company turned down a cult request for 530 gallons of dilute sulfuric acid, but front companies successfully bought large quantities of nitromethane and other chemicals. Through Aum's Manhattan branch, an order also went out for 400 gas masks from a military surplus wholesaler in the U.S. Paid for up front, the shipment was due to arrive in Japan by air freight on March 19.

Meanwhile, the buzz of activity at World Unification's Tokyo office continued. Almost every evening, a number of men, some in business suits, arrived to hold meetings late into the night. People in neighboring buildings often wondered what was going on. One clue to the activity inside was an odd sign at the company's entrance. It read: "The Japan Secret Nikoratesura Association."

"Nikoratesura": it sounded like another of Aum's poorly translated Sanskrit terms. In fact, the word represented yet another cult project to research weapons of the future – this time a device of almost biblical destructive power.

For Asahara, the Great Hanshin Earthquake was stunning proof of the coming apocalypse. Hideo Murai, however, did not believe the quake was an act of God. He was a scientist, after all, and scientists have rational explanations.

"There is a strong possibility that the Great Hanshin Earthquake was activated by electromagnetic power or some other device that exerts energy into the ground," Murai later told an assembly of international reporters. This device, he added, was possibly operated by the U.S. military. Murai's attempts to explain further were drowned out by derisive snorts from reporters. A device capable of triggering massive seismic movements sounded hopelessly sci-fi and far-fetched. But as it turned out, Aum wasn't the first to be fascinated by the idea.

"Nikoratesura" is the closest Japanese rendering of Nikola Tesla

(1856–1943), the brilliant Croatian-American who invented the AC motor and pioneered radio and remote control. Tesla studied the possibility of transmitting electric energy over long distances by taking advantage of electromagnetic waves emitted by the Earth – in effect, using the planet itself as a giant wireless conductor. In 1899 at Colorado Springs, Tesla lit hundreds of lamps about 25 miles away using a large induction coil, a device that produces an electric current by changing magnetic fields. He afterwards claimed that the same method could in theory be used to send a signal through the Earth which could be picked up on the other side.

Nikola Tesla's remarkable mind led him to a field we now know as telegeodynamics. Here his theories grew extraordinary. He believed that by manipulating the Earth's electromagnetic forces, one could dramatically affect both climate and seismic activity. Tesla warned that his discovery could split the planet in two – "split it as a boy would split an apple – and forever end the career of man."

Although many geologists dismiss this notion as comic-book nonsense, recent research has shown that earthquakes are preceded by unusual emissions of low-frequency electromagnetic waves, produced by small cracks in lower layers of plates in the Earth's crust. Tesla's ideas were in fact taken very seriously by both the U.S. and Soviet militaries. Portions of his papers, seized by the U.S. government after his death, remain classified even today. Some U.S. experts reportedly believe the Soviets used a "seismic weapon" to trigger an earthquake in Beijing in 1977.

An earthquake machine! It is not hard to imagine how much the idea excited Hideo Murai. He wanted to know more, and that's where the six members of the Japan Secret Nikola Tesla Association came in. A month after the Kobe quake, the members began a series of trips to the Tesla museum in Belgrade, Serbia, where many of the inventor's papers are kept. There they searched for data on seismology and electromagnetism. Meanwhile, the cult's New York office contacted the International Tesla Society in the U.S., asking for information on Tesla's inventions, patents, and writings. The Kobe tremor may have been an act of God. Hideo Murai was determined that Japan's next earthquake would be an act of Aum.

By now over a month had passed since news of the Mount Fuji sarin residue. Yet the Japanese police had still done nothing to stop the cult. While police scratched their heads, 23-year-old Mika (a pseudonym) was trying to hack her way out of a cargo container behind Satian 6.

Mika's nightmare had begun in December 1994, when she visited Mount Fuji to see two former classmates who had joined the cult. When it was time to leave, she was restrained and then confined.

Two weeks later, she tried to escape, but was knocked out with sodium thiopental and locked up in a windowless cubicle inside Satian 6. She was soon after moved to a cargo container so small that she couldn't even sit up straight. She was given one meal a day of bread, a cookie, a banana, and a steamed bun. On one of her rare chaperoned trips to the shower room, Mika saw a screwdriver and quietly slipped it into her clothing. Back in the container, she took out every screw in the walls, floor, and ceiling. Still the prison held fast. After weeks of desperate effort, Mika managed to peel away part of the floor, only to find that a steel sheet had been placed beneath the container to foil just such an escape attempt.

From then on until her rescue in mid-March, Mika sat curled up in the darkness, clutching the screwdriver, thinking constantly of suicide. Only one thing stopped her from taking her own life – the other life growing inside her. Mika was at least four months pregnant.

Mika's fate was sealed by news of the sarin residue in January. There was no way the cult would release her into the glare of media attention. But she was still fortunate compared to Aum's other victims. Since the previous fall, cult doctors had invented a brutally effective method of making wayward followers keep their mouths shut. It was called the Initiation of an Apple Crowned with Thorns, or, more simply, the Datsura Experiment. ("Datsura" was supposedly derived from the Tibetan for "poisonous apple.")

One follower who underwent this "initiation" was the former Japanese soldier who had been abducted in Osaka the previous December. He was first confined, then injected repeatedly with what Aum's doctors called "new narco" – apparently amylobarbitone, a highly addictive hypnotic drug which suppresses vital REM sleep and kills willpower. Because of such side effects, professional doctors prescribed amylobarbitone less and less. But it suited the needs of Aum's physicians perfectly.

Between massive shots of "new narco," the ex-soldier was interrogated and went for days without sleep or food. Over the next four months, he was also given scalding baths, electric shocks, and over 120 injections. He began to lose track of time, to forget where he was. On one occasion, a doctor shook him awake and threatened, "You won't have many lives left to live if you stay like this." On the wall the ex-soldier noticed a poster of a bearded man in purple robes.

The Datsura Experiment, it was declared, would remove the man's bad karma. What it actually did was remove his memory. When Aum's doctors were done, the ex-soldier suffered almost complete amnesia. He was a vegetable. He had lost 66 pounds and the right side of his body was paralyzed. On the rare occasions he spoke, he used baby talk. The Datsura Experiment was no "initiation." It was an unconscionably cruel kind of mental slate-wiper – brainwashing in its most literal form.

The ex-soldier was just one of many men and women who underwent this narco-lobotomy. By now, Aum's prisons were packed with the living dead. Some fifty followers were in dazed, incoherent, or emaciated states. Many were unconscious or too weak to stand. The ones who could muster the strength to walk moved like zombies.

These victims were tortured, confined, and forgotten about. This left time to pursue other runaways, other "betrayers of the guru's love." In late February, a 62-year-old follower sneaked out of Aum's Tokyo HQ and went into hiding. Since joining Aum through a yoga class, the woman had poured over $600,000 into cult coffers.

Furious, Asahara ordered a cultist to find the woman and bring her back. Much to the guru's irritation, the cultist failed. So Asahara gave another order: Get spy chief Yoshihiro Inoue to take care of it. And Inoue took care of it.

A few days later, a smart 68-year-old called Kiyoshi Kariya was walking home from his job at a Tokyo notary public office. Kariya was no doubt deep in thought that afternoon. He was worried about his sister, the follower who had fled the cult's Tokyo branch. He knew they would come for her.

There had been a call the night before. "Tell us where your sister is," the voice had demanded. Kariya refused, knowing his sister was hiding with a friend. Afterwards, he wrote a note to leave for his son. It read: "If I disappear, I was abducted by the Aum Supreme Truth sect."

Kiyoshi Kariya was too preoccupied to notice the rental van pull up alongside him. It wouldn't have helped if he had. Four robust men burst from the van doors and, as bewildered passers-by looked on, the elderly man was plucked like a feather from the pavement and bundled into the back of the van.

As the van raced out of Tokyo, Yoshihiro Inoue sat emotionless in the passenger seat. There were muffled cries and thumps from the back, as Inoue's thugs beat the old man senseless. Then there was silence. Kariya had been tranquilized by Asahara's personal physician, Tomomasa Nakagawa – the same Nakagawa who, six years before, had plunged fatal syringes of potassium chloride into lawyer Tsutsumi Sakamoto, his wife and baby son.

Within hours, the van arrived at Mount Fuji. The bloodstains were wiped from the van's interior with disinfectant, and a groggy Kariya was delivered to a windowless room deep inside Satian 2. Inoue and Nakagawa were there. With them was Ikuo Hayashi, the surgeon.

The doctors got to work. A needle was plunged into Kariya's arm and attached to an intravenous drip of thiopental, the cult's favorite truth serum. When Kariya's body went limp, Inoue began the interrogation. It went on for hours – Where's your sister? Where are you hiding her? – but Kiyoshi Kariya said nothing.

Inoue was frustrated. The guru's orders had been simple. "Pump him for information about his sister," he said, "then let him go after washing out his memory with drugs." But nothing was going according to plan. The stubborn old man wouldn't talk.

"We can't let him go on like this," said Nakagawa. "I think we'll use the potassium chloride. I'm going to see the guru at 10 a.m.," he told Dr. Hayashi. "Will you look after him until then?"

What happened next is unclear. Kariya either went into shock after another shot of thiopental the following morning, or he slipped into a merciful coma overnight. Whatever happened – and whoever did it – the result was the same. The next day, Kiyoshi Kariya was dead.

Kariya's corpse was put into a large trash bag and lugged down to the cult crematorium in the basement of Satian 2. The floor of the room was now littered with similar trash bags. The cadaver was microwaved for two days, then broken down further with nitric acid. Dr. Nakagawa dumped what was left into Lake Motosu, the deepest of the five lakes around Mount Fuji and a popular spot for watersports.

But Kiyoshi Kariya would rise to haunt the cult. By now, the authorities had any number of reasons to probe Aum's activities aggressively. The National Police Agency had already received more than a hundred complaints concerning the cult, including allegations of land fraud, wiretapping, and abduction. When the story of Kariya's disappearance broke, there was hardly a soul in Japan who did not believe Aum was behind it. The police could shuffle their feet no longer.

Shoko Asahara perhaps realized this. The abduction of a notary public in the nation's capital in broad daylight was a direct challenge to Tokyo police. After Kariya's kidnap, the guru gave an hour-long sermon to over a hundred followers. He spoke quietly and kept his eyes closed throughout. "Do not be afraid to sacrifice yourselves," he said. "You must fight as one. Although I will be captured, I shall surely return." It was the last time Asahara appeared in person before his flock.

32

THE WAR BEGINS

The national investigation of Aum Supreme Truth fell to the Tokyo Metropolitan Police Department. The 45,000-strong TMPD is widely considered the elite of Japanese law enforcement. While its primary role is to serve the capital's core population of 8 million, the department's vast resources and crime-fighting expertise are often called upon to crack major cases nationwide. The case against Aum was one of them.

TMPD headquarters are located in Kasumigaseki in the bureaucratic heartland of central Tokyo. A gleaming high-rise topped by an extraordinary array of communications gear, the TMPD building became the nerve center of the growing investigation into Aum. It also became the primary target in the cult's latest scheme. Aum would cripple the investigation by striking a devastating pre-emptive blow against TMPD headquarters. And they would use a laser to do it.

Locals at Mount Fuji had already witnessed one of Aum's laser experiments. But cult scientists were no closer to constructing the guru's beloved "death ray." Even with the right technical know-how, a high-energy vaporizing laser is enormously expensive to build and requires huge amounts of power to run. It would also be prohibitively bulky; the equipment needed to operate a single such laser could fill a four-engine cargo plane. As well as producing great heat, a laser cannon is hardly a weapon of stealth. One expert compared it to the blast of field artillery going off.

And so Aum's scientists changed tack. They would build a cheaper, lower-energy laser gun that could do its job in absolute silence. This weapon would not vaporize cops; it would just blind them. A laser gun can temporarily dazzle a victim, or cause flash blindness that leaves the victim sightless for hours. A stronger beam can bore agonizingly through the retina of the eye, rendering the victim permanently blind. It all depends on the power of the beam, the proximity of the target, and the ethics of the user.

By the end of February Hideo Murai's team at the Clear Stream Temple laboratory claimed to have perfected a laser gun. The weapon was not powerful enough to slice the Tokyo Metropolitan Police Department building in half, but it might penetrate windows and blind police officers working inside. The laser gun was mounted in a customized truck, and an attack was scheduled for early March.

But something went wrong – the sensitive, power-hungry equipment apparently broke down. While Murai's scientists were sent back to the drawing board to redesign the laser, Aum USA tried to buy one. A cultist in New York contacted a California company called Hobart Laser Products with an urgent request to buy a three-kilowatt industrial laser. The cultist said Aum USA was willing to pay the $450,000 price in cash. Hobart's reps explained that the firm's lasers are custom-built and take weeks to finish. Then there was the time-consuming process of passing strict export requirements. The purchase never went through. Cult leaders returned to Aum's diverse arsenal to explore alternative ways to thwart the police investigation.

Near midnight on March 5, strange fumes swept through a train in Yokohama outside Tokyo. Commuters began spluttering and choking, and eleven people were hospitalized with eye irritation, respiratory problems, nausea, and fever. Rail officials were baffled. What could have caused such a debilitating odor? Weeks later, the mystery would solve itself. Aum had been rehearsing for its next attack.

While the guru's men plotted murder, two members of Asahara's large family were plotting escape. "Horrifying incidents will continue to occur until the year 2000," Asahara had predicted in his latest book, and his wife Tomoko Matsumoto took this seriously. A day after the Yokohama incident, she and Asahara's favored third daughter, Aajadi, applied to a local government office for passports.

Four days later, an Aum clinic had its own brush with officialdom. The Public Health Department of Mount Fuji's Yamanashi Prefecture warned the cult that the clinic was violating health regulations by operating without a license. The cult hurriedly applied for one. While Aum doctors ran human experiments, dispensed hallucinogens, and imprisoned patients in drug-induced delirium, the Yamanashi authorities obligingly issued the license, obviously without inspecting the facility.

Meanwhile, the cult began exploring other ways of crippling the police investigation. An assault with AK-74 rifles was out of the question. Firearms production at Clear Stream Temple was still hampered by technical problems and lack of staff. The goal of producing a thousand rifles and a million bullets would take another six months to achieve. Aum's conventional armory did offer other choices; for example, a half-ton truck stuffed with TNT would make quite a dent in the TMPD building. But this low-tech option was not explored.

Then there was Aum's chemical arsenal. The sarin stockpile had been destroyed, but there was still mustard gas, cyanide, and VX. Cult leaders chose not to use these weapons, however, possibly because chemical agents were so much in the news in those days. Early plans to spray Tokyo with an incapacitant like LSD had also hit a snag: cult engineers had smashed up their drone helicopters and couldn't get the Russian-made MIL Mi-17 chopper to work. They had tinkered unsuccessfully with the Mi-17 since its arrival from Azerbaijan, but it now sat exposed to the elements behind a tarpaulin screen near Mount Fuji.

No, the attack would not use chemical weapons, nor conventional arms. There was no alternative: it would have to be biological.

An invitation to Shoko Asahara's banquets was an offer that cultists couldn't refuse. Aum's gourmet guru had thrown several feasts for "special guests" at the Mount Fuji HQ in recent months. But while the food was delicious and plentiful, it wasn't always easy to stomach. Afterwards some of Asahara's guests developed skin rashes or lost their voices. Others fell ill and disappeared. This had nothing to do with the food, guests were told. It was just another terrible symptom of the U.S. Air Force's chemical attacks.

The real reason was that the guru's sushi platters were laced with microorganisms cultured in sect biolabs. This was bad catering, but good science; cult biologist Seiichi Endo learned much about the effects of various toxins on human beings. After his many failures with bioweapons attacks, these feasts suggested that Endo had at last achieved success.

Using dinner guests as guinea pigs was a macabre idea, but perhaps Endo found it easy to justify. The cult was at war, after all, Endo soberly explained on Aum's regular Radio Moscow broadcast. Ebola virus, smallpox, yellow fever, plague – he noted that all these could be deployed as bioweapons against the cult. In fact, the biologist was giving a fairly accurate assessment of the threat Aum's own sizable bio-arsenal now posed. The agents in Endo's laboratory included at least three agents – anthrax, botulism, Q fever – and possibly others. But still he wanted more, as he suggested on his broadcast:

> At the time of the Korean War, bacterial weapons were not powerful enough. However, some viruses have now been invented that are effective and can kill people at a 90 percent rate ... Many countries are modifying viruses and bacteria to make them more toxic. There is a possibility that new bacterial substances are being used which have been created by biotechnology.

Biotechnology was Endo's dream. This rapidly expanding field allowed scientists to modify the genetic characteristics of cells or organisms at the molecular level. Bioengineering techniques have a variety of applications that are beneficial to humanity, like creating new vaccines. This had once interested Endo, but no longer. For him, advances in biotechnology heralded a much more useful invention: genetic weapons.

Biotech methods can be used to make biological agents easier to handle, cheaper to produce, harder to detect, and almost impossible to cure. For example, it is possible to create chemical mutagens that play havoc with the human genetic code, diseases that are resistant to antibiotics or vaccines (except, that is, to a vaccine genetically created at the same time), even agents that could scramble the enzyme systems in one racial group, but leave another unaffected. "Supertoxic chemicals and toxins will undoubtedly be feasible soon," wrote Charles Piller and Keith Yamamoto in their seminal book *Gene Wars*. "Nerve gas ... is mere perfume compared with some agents on the drawing board."

Bioengineering techniques rely on computer-controlled equipment that uses advanced molecular-design software. Little of this is sold in Japan. So, in January 1995, Aum's New York office bought software from an Oregon-based company which would allow Endo to experiment with synthesizing compounds on his computer screen. Over the next two months, Aum USA contacted two other American companies – Biosym Technologies in San Diego and Tripos in St. Louis – to acquire even more advanced molecular software.

Biosym sold Aum a computer hardware system for $47,000 and, on a trial basis, gave the cult twenty programs. The Tripos software, valued at $400,000, was installed at Aum's Manhattan office on a sophisticated Silicon Graphics workstation, the type used by professional scientists.

Tripos found their new client exceptionally eager. The St. Louis company's sales cycles typically lasted six to nine months; it usually took that long for the customer to master the software. But Aum USA said they were willing to buy the product within one month of installation. They wouldn't disclose the nature of their work, but that wasn't unusual – companies in the competitive world of biotechnology are notoriously tight-lipped.

While Tripos and Biosym gave Aum the benefit of the doubt, the cult was desperately trying to rip off their software. The cult shipped Biosym's disk drive to Japan, where its Mount Fuji scientists tried to pirate the software. When their attempt at copying Tripos's software also failed, Aum USA prepared to ship that overseas too.

Aum's aborted attempt to steal biotech software forced Seiichi Endo to shelve his research into genetic weapons. In one respect, the failure didn't matter. Biotechnology's immediate threat lies in its ability to make existing bio-agents easier to produce, store, and handle. And those agents were already deadly enough for Aum's purposes. For now, Endo would have to be satisfied with plain, genetically undoctored agents – like botulinus toxin.

By early March, the cult had hatched a new plan: botulism would be the weapon deployed in the next attempted strike against the state. The target this time was Kasumigaseki Station, a major subway intersection used by countless commuters every day – including those at the headquarters for both Tokyo police and the National Police Agency. Kasumigaseki was also the capital's bureaucratic center, work place of the thousands of officials who rule over the lives of 120 million Japanese. For the cult, Kasumigaseki was the embodiment of the state, now its greatest enemy.

Aum wasn't the first group to see the subway as the perfect target for a biochemical attack. In 1966, the U.S. Army had launched a simulated biological attack on the New York subway system. Agents secretly released trillions of supposedly benign bacteria called *Bacillus subtilis* into the midtown subway during rush hour. Light bulbs, each filled with some 87 trillion bacilli, were tossed onto the underground roadbeds or shattered on ventilation grills on the streets above.

The army's findings were alarming. The movement of the trains spread the germs into all but one station of the entire Eighth Avenue and Seventh Avenue lines. The bacilli persisted in the air for an hour, floating not only through stations but into trains, too. The army's final report concluded that "a large portion of the working population in downtown New York City would be exposed to disease if one or more pathogenic agents were disseminated covertly in several subway lines at a period of peak traffic." Defending against such an eventuality, the report added, was almost impossible.

Also in the mid-1960s, the U.S. Army used five aerosol generators in specially built suitcases to spray bacteria on travelers at National Airport, Washington, D.C. This experiment was considered a success, too; biological agents, the test report said, "can be disseminated with covert-type devices." The CIA conducted similar tests with rigged suitcases.

Perhaps unwittingly, Aum combined the ideas for its botulism delivery system. On Hideo Murai's orders, cult scientists began constructing a prototype dispenser which fitted into briefcases. The bacillus was held in solution in vinyl tubes, which were mounted on a small ceramic diaphragm. Powered by dry batteries, this device turned the solution into steam, which was then blown from the briefcase by a small electric fan. The whole system was ultrasonic. The vibration of a passing train was enough to trigger the mechanism and release a fine spray of botulinus toxin. This is perhaps why Aum was so keen on buying hundreds of electric fans and batteries from the U.S.

Borne on the air currents of passing trains, the toxin would then float through the subway's labyrinth of tunnels and stairwells. It would take eighteen to thirty-six hours to do its slow and deadly work, giving morning commuters a case of botulism from which they would never recover. Thousands would probably succumb to bouts of diarrhea and vomiting, swelling eyelids and creeping paralysis, until their heart or lungs ceased to work.

On March 15, under spy chief Inoue's direction, an unknown cultist slipped into the surging crowds at Kasumigaseki Station and placed briefcases at three ticket gates, then headed back up to the streets. Items considered lost property do not lie around for long in Tokyo's subway. All three cases were soon found by stationmasters. Even when they were picked up, two of the devices failed to activate. The third worked, and began to emit a cloud of steam.

Over the next twenty-four hours, the cult waited anxiously for results. But nothing happened. There were no alarming reports of mass poisoning – in fact, not even one case of botulism was reported. Seiichi Endo must have been bitterly disappointed. It was his fourth attempt at waging biological war, and each one had failed. He had been sure his toxins were now ready to kill.

The reason for this latest failure was soon discovered. None of the cases had contained the toxin; the one that went off blew out only harmless steam. The follower who deposited the cases had been struck by that rarest of feelings within Aum – a guilty conscience – and decided not to arm the devices.

The fate of the disobedient cultist is unknown. But his was the last humanitarian gesture that Aum would show. Disturbing news was filtering down from Aum's spies in law enforcement. On March 21, there would be a massive police raid on cult facilities across the country. Aum had twice failed to disrupt the police investigation. They could not afford to fail a third time.

Endo returned to his lab. There, on March 18, he received a delivery of three pounds of a final sarin precursor. The chemical had been unearthed from a site near Satian 6, where physician Nakagawa had buried it two months before. Hideo Murai visited Endo's lab and told him to make a large fresh batch of sarin.

Endo asked Murai what the nerve agent would be used for.

Murai's reply was terse. "It will be used inside subway trains," he said, and left Endo to his task.

33

STALKING THE SUBWAY

March 18, 1995. Saturday. There were four of them, the old man remembered, and they were sitting right next to him near the doors of a subway car on Tokyo's Hibiya line. They wore identical beige jackets, navy pants, sunglasses, and gauze flu-masks which covered the nose and mouth. One of them wore an absurd white wig. He seemed to be giving orders to the others.

The old man watched them closely. He noticed that each time the subway-car doors opened, two of the men checked their watches and two others scribbled something in notebooks. The old man leaned over to sneak a look at one of the notebooks. He saw a page criss-crossed with lines marked with the names of various Tokyo subway stations. Subway employees, the old man thought, and got off the train soon after.

From then on, Yoshihiro Inoue – the one in the white wig – and the three other disguised cultists apparently went unnoticed by Tokyo's commuters. The Aum spy chief and his men got on with their work. They noted what time different trains arrived and departed, which car doors opened nearest which exits, how long the doors stayed open. At Kasumigaseki, the stop nearest the TMPD police headquarters, Inoue recorded the locations of the huge station's numerous exits in his notebook.

Above ground, the TMPD was preparing a massive assault against Aum Supreme Truth. The plan was to launch simultaneous raids on cult facilities across the country, using the suspected abduction of Tokyo notary Kiyoshi Kariya as a legal pretext. The police clearly had some idea what they were up against. A few days before, the TMPD had contacted the Japanese army with a highly unusual request. They wanted to borrow chemical-warfare gear, including 500 gas masks. The raids were to begin as early as Monday, March 20, just two days away – the same date that Aum had chosen to strike a crippling blow against the police.

On the evening of the 18th, at around 11:30 p.m., Shoko Asahara's car pulled up outside an Aum-run vegetarian restaurant in Tokyo. Flanked by nervous bodyguards, the guru climbed out and walked slowly inside. His key lieutenants were already there, among them Murai and Tomomitsu Niimi. Inoue probably attended too, since the information he gathered earlier that day was vital. By the time the guru's car sped away again two hours later, the final details of the attack had been hammered out.

The target again was Kasumigaseki subway station, but this time the weapon was sarin. The cult would hit three of Tokyo's busiest subway lines: the Hibiya, Marunouchi, and Chiyoda. Two attackers would release the sarin on each line, one going in each direction. All three lines intersected at Kasumigaseki. The nerve agent would be spread in subway cars nearest to the exits used by police from the TMPD and National Police Agency.

The operation depended on precision timing, but here Aum was fortunate. It was attacking the world's most efficient subway system. Tokyo's subways carry 2.7 billion passengers a year, about twice the number of New York's underground and almost four times that of London. In a single day, the city's trains carry 5 million people and cover 470,000 miles, yet delays are remarkably rare. Aum could rely on all six trains converging at Kasumigaseki station between 8:09 a.m. and 8:13 a.m., the height of rush hour. At 8:30, police personnel changed shifts at the TMPD, and NPA staff began work. The trains would be packed with cops.

The attack was scheduled for Monday, the eve of a national holiday marking the first day of spring. Unfortunately, that meant fewer commuters, but delaying the attack might give police the advantage. And anyway, the subways would still be crowded enough. Hundreds, possibly thousands, would be killed. Asahara and his lieutenants believed it would be enough to stop the police investigation.

Kiyohide Hayakawa was apparently the only top cultist who saw the plan for what it was: complete madness. "Asahara surprised me so many times with his instructions, and the subway attack was one of them," the construction chief later told police. Hayakawa had been conspicuously absent from the restaurant meeting. Earlier that month, the guru had ordered him to visit Russia to fetch supplies of ergotamine, a substance used for producing LSD. On March 17, as his colleagues plotted mass murder, Hayakawa grabbed his chance and flew off on a five-day trip to Moscow.

This left his bitter rival Hideo Murai to get on with business. After leaving the restaurant, the restless scientist returned to Mount Fuji to hold a predawn meeting with Seiichi Endo. For the last twenty-four hours Endo had worked without rest to synthesize enough sarin for the attack. Now he and Murai had to decide how the sarin would be released.

This time, there would be no bulky heater-and-fan systems, no James Bond suitcases. Aum's hit squad would simply carry bags of sarin onto the trains and puncture them. The sarin would leak out slowly and evaporate into a ground-hugging killer mist. It was simple, it was low-tech, and it was fool-proof. Or so Murai and Endo hoped.

March 19, Sunday. The warning to cult disciples nationwide was posted on the Internet at 10:07 a.m. "From several sources, we have obtained information to the effect that raids against Aum Supreme Truth will be conducted within several days," read the message to Shimin Forum, a computer bulletin board which deals with citizens' movements and social problems. The sender was Ashura, an on-line pseudonym for Aum central command. Shoko Asahara was alerting his flock to be ready for war.

Warnings were also disseminated by more traditional methods. That day, a cultist in his twenties was seen handing out leaflets in the classy Tokyo shopping district of Ginza. The flyers advertised Asahara's latest book with the alarming line, "The Great Hanshin Earthquake is a mere prologue to the many terrors and tragedies that will strike Japan one after another." They also posed a question – "What will hit Japan next?" – and provided a clue to the answer. The handbills featured a map of the Tokyo subway system.

Meanwhile, Tokyo's police finalized their plans. The effectiveness of the upcoming raids on Aum depended upon meticulous planning, proper training, and simultaneous execution. That Sunday, an undisclosed number of police officers secretly trained with gas masks and chemical gear at a nearby military camp. Unfortunately, they weren't prepared for the shocking news from Osaka.

On Sunday evening, police had burst into Aum's Osaka chapter and arrested four cultists on suspicion of abducting a university student from his parent's home. Investigators at the Tokyo Metropolitan Police Department were stunned. "What is Osaka doing?" one officer was heard to moan. The Osaka raid had robbed the upcoming assault on Aum of any element of surprise, police chiefs concluded.

Then, to compound the poor timing, they made a critical misjudgment. The nationwide raids on Aum were postponed.

The hit squad drove out of Mount Fuji at sunset. There were five of them – one doctor and four vice ministers in the Science and Technology Ministry. The men chosen to unleash terror in the heart of Tokyo were among Aum's, and Japan's, brightest minds.

The first was Dr. Ikuo Hayashi. As the brains behind Aum's clinics, he had coldly presided over the wholesale doping, torture, and death of many followers. Still, he found it hard crossing the line from gross medical malpractice to mass murder, if later reports are to be believed. "I didn't know why I was chosen for the attack," Dr. Hayashi said. "I wanted to refuse, but the atmosphere didn't allow it."

Less likely to refuse the mission was the squad's second member, Yasuo Hayashi. The doctor's namesake was a six-foot-tall ethnic Korean who had grown up in Tokyo. He was a mean-looking 37-year-old with neanderthal brows and a rash of acne on each cheek. His qualifications included an electrical-engineering degree and a criminal record for substance abuse. His fascination with the supernatural had led him to India, then to drugs, and then to Aum. He became a monk in 1988, and proved adept at abduction, wire-tapping, and intimidation. The subway attack would earn him a new nickname from Japan's media: "Killer Hayashi."

The next man, thirty-year-old Kenichi Hirose, had graduated top of his class in applied physics from Waseda University in 1987. He turned down a job offer at a big electronics firm to join the cult, but often returned to the university to question his professor about laser research. The professor was baffled by Hirose's choice. "Floating in the air violates the law of inertia," he once said. "Why would a student of physics believe such an outrageous thing?" Hirose replied firmly: "Because I saw it."

Masato Yokoyama, thirty-one, was another graduate in applied physics. His classmates at Tokai University outside Tokyo remember him as a quiet student who dressed in preppy clothes and enjoyed bowling. On graduation he joined an electronic parts maker, and secretly attended Aum yoga classes. Then one day Yokoyama presented his boss with a cult book. "Please read this and study," he said. On the last page of the book, he had scribbled, "Those who handle this book carelessly will pay for it." Soon after, Yokoyama quit work and joined Aum – "to save mankind," he told his protesting family.

The fifth and final attacker was twenty-seven-year-old Toru Toyoda. He studied particle physics as a graduate student at Tokyo University, where his copious note-taking made him popular among classmates. Toyoda was relatively outgoing. Before joining the cult, he entertained his fellow lab rats with a mean impersonation of Shoko Asahara during Aum's 1990 election campaign. The guru had the last laugh. Toyoda was converted to Aum by another Tokyo University student and, in spring 1992, signed up.

Toru Toyoda came from a family proud of tradition. The Toyodas went back for generations in Hyogo, a prefecture famous for Kobe beef and high-school baseball. Every morning and evening, Toyoda's 79-year-old grandfather rang a bell in a nearby temple, then clasped his hands together to give thanks for the family's prosperity. Before long, the Toyoda family's neighbors would notice something strange. The temple bell had stopped ringing.

While the hit squad drove towards Mount Fuji, Yoshihiro Inoue was taking care of some other Sunday-evening business. With him at the Tokyo hideout was Sergeant Takahisa Shirai of the 1st Airborne Brigade. Inoue had more dirty work for Shirai to do. He wanted him to firebomb Aum's Tokyo headquarters.

Inoue's thinking was this: attacking Aum's building would boost the cult's image as victim and make them less likely suspects after the sarin attack the next day. But that's not quite what the spy chief told a meeting of Shirai and three other cultists.

"The police are going to raid our headquarters at any moment," Inoue said. "It's a shame, but we must stage an attack on our own headquarters to win sympathy from the public." He explained to Shirai that the "virtue" of the attack was to "save this society." Then he handed out maps which showed where each cultist would stand lookout. Shirai, who had operated howitzers and other large weapons, would not be shy of a Molotov cocktail. And he had the muscles to throw it.

The five piled into a car and set off. On the way, Inoue constructed a Molotov cocktail in the passenger seat. The Aum HQ was based in a relatively new building on a lesser-used intersection, and had a sales outlet for Mahaposya computers on the ground floor. Inoue handed the bomb to Shirai, then the team took their positions at different corners of the street.

There was a crash of glass and a brief *whump!* of igniting petrol as
Shirai lobbed the firebomb into the Aum building. Then the sound of
running feet, a car roaring off.

Either by design or sheer luck, the firebomb caused only minor
damage and no injuries. Locals who rushed out found the road
littered with leaflets – Inoue's final diversionary touch. The leaflets
read: "Death to Shoko Asahara. We will not forgive Aum, a group of
criminals. From the Science of Happiness." Inoue had used the name
of a rival Japanese cult which had recently been making loudspeaker
announcements across central Tokyo, claiming Aum was responsible
for a host of crimes. Just the day before, Aum had slapped the Science
of Happiness with a $100,000 law suit for damaging its reputation.

Inoue's team broke up. Sergeant Shirai returned to his barracks
outside the capital. Inoue went back to the Tokyo hideout, where he
met the subway hit squad at around 9 p.m. and went over the details
of the attack again. Each scientist was assigned a subway line, told the
time of the train he should board, and which car he should sit in. Just
before 8 a.m., as the train pulled into a designated station several stops
from Kasumigaseki, the attackers should puncture the sarin bags, leave
the train immediately, and then rendezvous with their driver at a
designated spot near the station. As the train continued on to
Kasumigaseki, the nerve gas would leak out, evaporate and do its job.

At around 10 p.m., the cultists went with their drivers to check
out the respective stations where the attacks were to take place, and to
decide on a post-attack meeting point. Then, at around 1:30 a.m., the
call came from Mount Fuji. It was Murai. The hit squad must quickly
return to Satian 7, he told them, for the holy task was complete. The
sarin was ready.

Inoue and the cultists climbed into two cars and set off for Mount
Fuji some 70 miles away. On the way, the cars stopped while Inoue
dashed into an all-night convenience store. He emerged carrying seven
plastic umbrellas. Then the convoy continued into the night.

Working without sleep, Seiichi Endo had produced nearly two gallons
of a solution of about 30 percent sarin. On that Sunday night he
visited Shoko Asahara in his quarters.

"It's done," Endo told the guru. "But it's still not pure."

"That's okay," Asahara replied. The attack would go ahead as
planned.

Back in Satian 7, Endo began work on the plastic bags. Helping
him was the guru's physician, Tomomasa Nakagawa. Murai gave the

two men a sheet of toxic-resistant polythene. In Endo's laboratory, it was cut into three-inch-square sheets, then crimped into bags using a thermal sealing machine. Endo and Nakagawa poured about 20 ounces of the sarin solution into each bag and sealed them. Then they placed these sarin pouches into larger bags, which were also sealed.

There were supposed to be twelve bags of sarin, two for each subway line. But for some reason – a shortage of sarin, sheer carelessness – Nakagawa and Endo made only eleven. Hideo Murai decided against using a single bag on one line; it would not be effective. Instead, the plan was changed to concentrate their attack on five subway lines. One of the killers would have to carry three bags. Endo also made five bags containing only water for the team to use in their rehearsals, while Nakagawa fetched five pills of pyridine aldozime methioxide, or PAM, a sarin antidote. Around 3 a.m., the bags were taken to Satian 7, where the hit squad was now waiting.

Inoue gave the umbrellas to another scientist, who used a lathe machine to sharpen their tips. Then, before an image of Shiva, Murai gave his final briefing. The attackers were to remove the outer bags before boarding the trains. They should place the inner bag on the subway floor, puncture it with the umbrella tip, then get off immediately. In the getaway car, the umbrella should be inserted into a soft-drink bottle to prevent any hazard from the sarin residue on its tip.

Then it was time to practice. It was an absurd scene – five earnest men puncturing water bags with cheap umbrellas – but the intent was deadly serious. A hard stab might send a stream of sarin shooting into the attacker's face. A gentle prod might fail to puncture the bag. "Mind training is essential," Murai told them. "If you don't want to do it, call it quits now." Nobody spoke.

Endo gave the team their antidote pills. These should be swallowed two hours beforehand, he said. As an extra precaution, each scientist was given a syringe of atropine to administer in the event of exposure to sarin. They then decided who would release the extra bag of sarin: Yasuo "Killer" Hayashi.

The hit squad left the compound in a convoy of cars, Mount Fuji brooding massively in the darkness. The sarin bags rocked gently in Toru Toyoda's knapsack as the cars sped towards the capital. Once back at the Tokyo hideout, each scientist took their bags of sarin, pills, and an umbrella, and waited.

Then dawn broke, and it was time.

34

SHIVA THE DESTROYER

Killer Hayashi was the first to leave. On the way to Ueno station in northern Tokyo, his driver stopped to buy a pair of scissors, some adhesive tape, and the morning edition of the *Yomiuri* newspaper. In the car, Hayashi took out his supply of sarin and carefully cut away the outer plastic bag. Then he wrapped the inner bags in the newspaper, and fastened the package with tape.

His driver, a thirty-year-old cultist called Sugimoto, was nervous as hell.

"We're doing this to confuse the police investigation," Hayashi reminded him.

"Doing this will just attract the attention of the police," Sugimoto replied.

Killer Hayashi shrugged. "There's nothing we can do," he said.

Soon after 7 a.m., Hayashi was pushing through the morning crowds at Ueno station. He bought a ticket for the Hibiya line and boarded an eight-car train heading for Kasumigaseki. The train made its first stop minutes later. Hayashi waited. When the doors closed, Hayashi calmly placed the package on the floor.

Announcements crackled through the car as the train pulled into the next station. As it slowed to a halt, Hayashi leaned forward, stabbed the package repeatedly with his plastic umbrella, and elbowed his way off the subway car. Then the doors closed again and the train pulled off. A dark stain began to spread across the newsprint.

At the other end of the Hibiya line, Toru Toyoda was trying to keep his mind on the details: first car, train number B711T, seat near the door. The particle physicist sat down and immediately began fidgeting with the package on his lap. Commuters would later accurately describe Toyoda to police, right down to the anchor design on his coat buttons. The gauze mask obscuring his mouth and nose was common enough during Tokyo's hay-fever season. The elbow-length plastic gloves were not. And, on this fine Monday morning, Toru Toyoda was clutching an umbrella.

At 8:01 a.m., four stops from Kasumigaseki, commuters watched as Toyoda placed the package on the floor. They saw him plunge an umbrella into the newspaper before dashing off the train. Minutes later, a video surveillance camera near the wickets captured Toyoda on film for ten seconds. He looks around nervously, spots the camera, turns quickly away. Then he is gone.

Back on the train, a retired cobbler called Shunkichi Watanabe was slumped in a seat near Toru Toyoda's package. He was ninety-five years old. The old man was sleeping. Soon he would be dying.

Meanwhile, Aum's third attacker was locked in a station toilet at one end of the Marunouchi line. Kenichi Hirose, the bright young physicist, spread a colorful tabloid newspaper on the toilet seat and placed his bags of nerve agent on top. Then he wrapped the bags up and put the package gingerly inside his shoulder bag.

By 7:59 a.m., Hirose was wedged into a packed train heading for Kasumigaseki. He was panicking. His station was coming up, but he couldn't free his knapsack from the crush of commuters. Jammed up against the door, Hirose finally managed to release his knapsack. But as he pulled out the package, the newspaper slipped off and the bags of nerve agent tumbled to the floor.

Horrified, Hirose nudged the packets toward a nearby seat with his toe. Then he reached over and pierced them with the umbrella tip. The train doors opened and Hirose darted thankfully into the crowd. Kasumigaseki was five stops away.

Aum's other applied physicist, Masato Yokoyama, sat anxiously at the other end of the Marunouchi line. His package was wrapped in Japan's leading financial daily. Yokoyama counted the stations until the train approached the third stop from Kasumigaseki. Then he laid the package on the floor and began poking it with his umbrella. He managed to puncture only one bag before leaving the train. It would be enough.

The last cultist, Dr. Hayashi, was standing at his designated spot on a Chiyoda-line platform. The doctor was having a last-minute fit of morals. He looked around and saw a young girl waiting in line behind him. *Go away*, he thought. *If you get on here, you'll die.*

The train pulled up. Dr. Hayashi boarded the first car, as instructed, and sat close to the door. He caught the eye of a woman in her thirties, and quickly looked away. *You too will be dead soon*, he thought. His sarin package was wrapped in two newspapers: *Red Flag*, the Japanese Communist Party daily, and *Seikyo Shimbun*, published by a rival religious group whose leader Aum nearly assassinated. Dr. Hayashi hoped the choice of reading matter would later throw police off the scent.

His station was announced over the intercom and the train slowed with a lurch of brakes. Kasumigaseki was now four stops away. Dr. Hayashi placed the package at his feet and stuck the umbrella in several times. He felt one of the bags rupture, but wasn't sure about the second one. He wasn't waiting around to find out.

By 8:10 a.m., Dr. Hayashi and the four other cultists were back at street level, looking for their drivers. Soon after, the getaway cars were nudging through Tokyo's morning traffic, heading back to the hideout. In the tunnels below, eleven bags of nerve agent on five subway cars thundered towards the city center, along with thousands of unlucky commuters.

Killer Hayashi's three bags of sarin were leaking rapidly as the Hibiya-line train pulled off without him. A puddle of dirty liquid was forming near the car door. Trampled down by the feet of a hundred commuters, the evaporation process was accelerated. Fumes began spreading.

Yoshio Saito, a forty-year-old hospital worker, saw the pool of liquid. Then he noticed the stench. "I can't describe the smell but when I inhaled I started coughing. I didn't have a cold but my nose started running." Saito moved away and opened a window. The foul odor blew in the opposite direction.

Within minutes, the air was thick with choking, invisible fumes. Pure sarin is odorless, but Aum's batch was a cocktail of stinking impurities. One man was snapped out of a light doze by a sharp smell he compared to mustard. Another woman recalled the stench of burning rubber. By 8:02, as the train arrived at the next stop, sarin had leaked across the floor, and nearby passengers were coughing and groaning with nausea.

The doors opened, and one man kicked the offensive package onto the platform. At that instant, a man and a woman collapsed on the ground, their bodies in spasm. Other passengers staggered from the cars, coughing and wheezing for breath. One dazed man saw scores of people crouching on the platform before his eyesight dimmed and his head crashed with pain.

But the Hibiya-line train did not stop. The doors closed a minute later and the train pulled out, bang on time. In the third car, passengers were dying. As the train arrived at the next station, a woman suddenly clung to a nearby passenger as her legs buckled and the life drained from her body. She was carried off to the station office, an ambulance was called, and the train pulled out yet again. Left behind were three passengers hunched in pain and bewilderment on the platform benches, holding their heads in their hands.

The train was leaving its next stop when the growing panic in car number three reached critical mass. Someone punched the emergency alarm button. Passengers were gagging and vomiting, clutching handkerchiefs across their faces. Confusion and hysteria swept through the train. A 23-year-old civil servant called Mieko Nakajima watched a middle-aged man lying on the wet floor. "I didn't know what had happened," she recalled. "I didn't know what to do. I started to feel suffocated."

At 8:10, a volley of contradictory announcements blared through the train. It was stopping because a passenger had fallen ill – no, because "an explosion has occurred at Tsukiji," the next station, four stops from Kasumigaseki. Then the stop was announced – "Coming up, Tsukiji, Tsukiji" – and a 59-year-old man called Minoru Shida stumbled towards the car doors. He looked down: he was standing in a pool of liquid. That was the last thing he remembered.

The doors opened, and passengers surged and tumbled from the train, gasping for breath. Five collapsed on the platform, foaming at the mouth. Three others lay inside the car, their bodies jerking violently. Tsukiji is a small station on a poorly ventilated subway line, and the sarin hung invisibly all around. Along the platform, commuters staggered towards the exits with fading vision and blinding headaches. An announcement echoed across the station: "Evacuate, evacuate, evacuate."

Above ground it was pandemonium. Hundreds of commuters streamed from subway exits into the bright morning sun. The pavements and soon the roads were blanketed with casualties lying where they had fallen, or clutching tissues to staunch blood flowing from their noses and mouths. It was an eerie kind of chaos. The commuters made little noise, since the nerve gas had crippled their lungs and stolen their voices. On this subway line alone, eight people would soon be dead, and nearly 2,500 injured.

Before long, the sound of ambulance sirens cut through the silence, and TV helicopters throbbed overhead, relaying the first horrific scenes to the nation. Even as police tried to work out what had happened at Tsukiji – a gas leak? an explosion? a terrorist attack?

– more reports were coming in. Another subway line had been hit . . . and another, and another.

In the first car of the Hibiya-line train, sarin began spreading across the floor almost as soon as cultist Toru Toyoda dashed out. At the next stop, David Pearson boarded the car behind. The 42-year-old banker from Sydney was one of many Westerners on the trains that morning. Clustered along the Hibiya subway line are many of Tokyo's expatriate communities, foreign company headquarters, and embassies.

As he stood in the crowded car, Pearson eavesdropped on two Americans nearby. "They were talking about how many people seemed to have colds and coughs, and I realized they were right," Pearson recalled. Still, nothing seemed amiss yet.

In the next car, the nerve agent was kicking in. Commuters were coughing and choking and throwing open the car's windows. Others squatted on the floor – a sensible precaution during a house fire, but the worst place to avoid a ground-hugging mist of nerve agent. Passengers began to twitch and stagger.

At the stop before Kasumigaseki, full-scale panic erupted. "It's gas!" someone yelled, as people tumbled off the cars. Nobuo Serizawa, a photographer, saw people collapse on the platform or fall to their knees; one man was "thrashing around on the floor like a fish out of water." Others vomited repeatedly.

One car away, David Pearson noticed an odor around him. "It was a very, very faint, sickly smell," he said. "I don't know whether it was intuition or just caution, but I decided to get off." Then Pearson began to feel nauseous. His eyes wouldn't focus and he felt as if he would pass out. Struggling to stay conscious, he joined the scores of commuters now blundering up the steps with pinhole vision.

Once outside, Pearson tottered along the pavement like a drunkard. Disoriented and half-blind, he couldn't distinguish taxis from the blur of traffic passing by. He threw his hand out anyway. Eventually a taxi stopped and took him to his bank's headquarters.

Down below, Tokyo's brutally efficient network continued to run virtually unsupervised. Several unconscious passengers lying on the car floor were ferried out, among them the retired cobbler Shunkichi Watanabe, now comatose. Ambulances were called, and nauseous commuters in car number one were moved to other cars. The train pulled out seven minutes behind schedule and reached Kasumigaseki two minutes later.

Only then did the gravity of the situation sink in. Passengers were asked to leave the station calmly and service was halted. The same stench passengers complained of in the tunnels could now be smelled as they passed through the ticket gates near street level. As station exits across central Tokyo turned into emergency zones, more reports flooded in. At one station on the Marunouchi line, staff rushed to help two passengers who began foaming at the mouth and convulsing. At the next stop, a woman on car number three fell unconscious and began twitching in her seat like a rag doll. Foam bubbled at her lips.

Assistant stationmaster Shizuka Nagayama discovered two plastic bags on the floor. One was empty; the other dripped with liquid as Nagayama wrapped it in newspaper. He deposited the package in a plastic bag held by another stationmaster. Soon both men would be terribly ill. The train continued on, carrying the fumes through station after station. By the time the service had stopped, one person was dead and hundreds were injured.

On the Chiyoda line – Dr. Hayashi's target – passengers were complaining about a strange package on a train at Kasumigaseki leaking liquid and spreading fumes. Stationmaster Tsuneo Hishinuma, wearing the pristine white gloves of Tokyo subway workers, entered the first car and picked up the package. There was no mop around, so Hishinuma wiped the remaining liquid off the floor with nearby newspapers. Then, with the help of a colleague, he put the package in a plastic bag and took it to the station office about 50 yards away. The train left Kasumigaseki two minutes behind schedule.

Hishinuma phoned a superior to report the package. He also said he didn't feel well. The superior arrived at the station office soon after. He found Hishinuma and his colleague lying unconscious on the floor, red bubbles foaming at their mouths. Their hearts had stopped and they would soon be dead.

Hishinuma's action undoubtedly saved many lives. But fumes still swept the Chiyoda-line train, and it was stopped and evacuated at the next station. By now, across central Tokyo, people were emerging like zombies from subway exits. Makeshift signs were posted outside stations, announcing they had been closed "owing to a terrorist attack," while the injured were rushed to over thirty hospitals across the city. St. Luke's hospital near Tsukiji station admitted 500 patients in the first hour and its fleet of ambulances worked non-stop. The hospital's 100 or so doctors canceled all routine surgery and, along with 300 nurses and volunteers from a nearby nursing college, administered I/V drips and oxygen to the injured.

The doctors were perplexed. The first emergency call at 8:16 had reported a gas explosion on the subway. Hospital staff were told to brace themselves for victims of burns and carbon monoxide poisoning. But these people weren't burnt or asphyxiated by CO gas. Doctors watched while their patients' pupils shrank to the size of pinpricks. Some were unable to write their own names on admission forms; their motor control had failed when the nerve agent scrambled their nervous systems. As the hours passed, the condition of many patients only grew worse.

As doctors tried to isolate the medical cause of this deluge of casualties, two plastic bags of sarin placed by physicist Kenichi Hirose had yet to be discovered. They were lying in the fifth car of a Marunouchi train, hemorrhaging nerve agent along the entire line. The train not only passed through Kasumigaseki and reached its terminus; astoundingly, it then turned around and passed through Kasumigaseki again. At one stop, a stationmaster with a broom and dustpan removed a package from the fifth car, and the train went on. It would eventually pass three times through Kasumigaseki, killing two passengers and injuring hundreds of others, before grinding to a halt at 9:27 near the Diet building.

The wave after wave of victims flooding Tokyo's hospitals now included police and firefighters. Medical staff were still perplexed by the symptoms, unsure of how to treat the blind, vomiting, disoriented commuters who filled every available space in the emergency rooms. Early reports were coming through: passengers might have been poisoned by acetylnitrile, which indeed the cult had added to the sarin solution to accelerate the evaporation process.

It wasn't until 10:30 a.m. that a military doctor tentatively made an almost inconceivable diagnosis: their patients were dying of exposure to sarin, a nerve gas. Doctors around the city immediately began prescribing the sarin antidote, PAM. At St Luke's, handwritten memos circulated to update staff. Tokyo doctors also phoned the hospital in Matsumoto that had treated victims from Aum's last sarin attack.

Medics already knew they were dealing with an extremely dangerous substance. Doctors and nurses who treated incoming patients were developing sore throats and eye irritations. At Jikei University Hospital, the severely injured were isolated in case they contaminated others. Patients were told to burn their clothes, since droplets of the toxin clung to material for hours. One man with only minor symptoms returned home and gave his suit to his wife to press. She later came down with the same nausea and headaches as her husband.

By 1:30 p.m., military experts clad in full chemical-warfare gear were dispatched, along with a hundred infantry. They descended into the subway system, the sound of their breathing apparatus eerily loud in the deserted tunnels and walkways. Meanwhile, casualty figures continued to escalate. Many passengers, like banker David Pearson, arrived at work in terrible shape, and were taken immediately to the hospital. Others were oblivious to what they had just survived until they saw harrowing television reports of the chaos on the subways. Before long, their vision would falter, or a knot of nausea would tighten inside them, and they too would be hospitalized. In all, 169 hospitals would report sarin cases over the next days and weeks.

By now the whole nation reeled at the news. Over 5,500 people were afflicted, many with appalling injuries. At least two passengers now slept eternally in vegetative comas. One woman was admitted to a hospital in agony after the nerve agent had fused her contact lenses to her eyeballs. She had both eyes surgically removed.

The death toll eventually climbed to twelve people. Aum's victims were neither meddling bureaucrats nor police. They were average citizens like Hajime Kojima, a 42-year-old engineer, and Eiji Wada, a 29-year-old employee of Japan Tobacco. Kojima was about to celebrate his daughter's acceptance to a respected university. Wada would not live to see his first child, born just a month later.

Aum's weary hit squad drove back to Mount Fuji that same afternoon. On the way, they burned their clothes on the banks of the Tama River in Tokyo's suburbs, then tossed the umbrellas into the water. At Mount Fuji, they were summoned by Asahara, who congratulated them. Afterwards, the guru's executioners were given money and told to lie low for a while.

By the evening, Dr. Hayashi had obviously put the day behind him. He was staying in a distant hotel, having sex with his mistress. Perhaps his guru's words that afternoon had reassured him.

Shoko Asahara had urged his followers not to mourn those who died in agony on the subways that day. The dead should be grateful, he explained, for the cult had given them the opportunity to reach a higher spiritual level.

"It is good," the guru said, "that the victims lost their souls to this holy leader, and to Shiva."

PART THREE

DAMNATION

35

CITY OF FEAR

The scenes of almost surreal horror on Tokyo's subways stunned the nation. A rare Nazi nerve gas cutting down innocent commuters in the very heart of orderly, secure Japan – it was too much for many to comprehend. As reports and rumors buzzed through the capital, shocked residents struggled to grasp the new terror in their midst: a silent, invisible killer that struck at random and without warning – and could strike again at any moment.

Tokyo's millions moved under a cloud of fear. Taxi drivers reported a surge in business as people avoided the subways. Commuters who had no alternative were seen sniffing subway cars before boarding. Fewer people dozed in their seats. The most common of sounds – a person coughing, a child's scream, a can rattling down the aisle – was enough to send ripples of alarm through the car. On the day after the attack, one subway line was stopped while a foul-smelling package was investigated. It contained fish.

The world's safest metropolis now felt like a city under siege. The Japanese military went on red alert to guard against further terrorist attacks. Sports stadiums and department stores hired extra staff to check customers' bags, and security was tightened at airports, corporate headquarters, and public facilities. The Tokyo Metropolitan Police Department again geared up to raid Aum, this time as the prime suspect in a mass murder. Police borrowed more gas masks and chemical gear from the military. Paratroopers stood by to decontaminate areas affected by poison gas and transport casualties of any Aum counterattack. However, the police refused openly to link the cult to the subway attack, insisting the raids were prompted by the abduction of notary public Kiyoshi Kariya.

To the public, the intense speculation on whether a religious group had gassed Tokyo's subways was almost as unbelievable as the attack itself. Police had never aired their suspicions about Aum, nor had the media investigated the true threat the cult posed. If people recalled Aum at all, it was as a cartoonish band of mystics in elephant masks during the 1990 elections. Now the cult had exploded back into public consciousness.

Aum took full advantage of the confusion to protest its innocence. "We carry out our religious activities on the basis of Buddhist doctrine, such as no killing, so it's impossible for us to have committed the incident," attorney Yoshinobu Aoyama told a packed press conference on the day after the attack. Aoyama pointed the finger again at a familiar target. "Sarin can only be made by experts, like those in the U.S. military."

Meanwhile, the cult began to cover its tracks. The Internet buzzed with coded warnings from Aum central command. Ashura forecast a "100 percent chance of rain" at 7 a.m. on Wednesday, March 22 – the time chosen by Japanese authorities to move on Aum's facilities nationwide.

The next forty-eight hours saw a surge of activity at Mount Fuji. Cultists carried boxes of documents and equipment into vehicles, and drove off in busy convoys. Several hundred pounds of mustard gas were destroyed, and bottles of hydrogen cyanide were buried on the banks of the Fuji River. At Clear Stream Temple, bullets were melted down and machines reprogrammed. Aum chapters across Japan hid membership lists and burned notebooks. Droves of followers fled to secret hideouts, among them a hundred core members of Aum's science division.

Early that morning, locals at Mount Fuji had seen a white Rolls-Royce and two other cars leave an Aum compound and head towards Tokyo at high speed. The Rolls was soon spotted again, this time in the underground parking lot of a classy Tokyo hotel, where guests claimed to have seen a bearded man in flowing robes. Police put the car under twenty-four-hour surveillance. They were soon joined by hordes of reporters. A few days later, the Rolls-Royce screeched from the parking lot with police and reporters in pursuit. Somehow, the pursuers lost sight of the Rolls – and with it, the last physical traces of Shoko Asahara for nearly two months.

But the guru's dark presence was felt. Only hours before the police raids began, a Radio Moscow broadcast was monitored from Vladivostok. Asahara was rousing the faithful for the final showdown:

> Your true nature will never be corrupted, for you are the pupils of my former life and you possess souls which are essentially different from others, because you have been born to help with salvation. I am

waiting for you to serve as my hands, my feet, my head, and to help with my salvation project. Let us proceed with salvation and meet death without regrets.

Death, the guru continued, was inevitable.

Whether you deceive yourself or not, you will certainly die . . . Glory to infinity! True glory to my beloved followers who have been slandered simply because they have received Aum Supreme Truth's teachings! Glory to those who have recently joined us!

It was like a prelude to the apocalypse which cultists had for so long cherished. Soon after dawn on March 22, a thousand police in riot gear and chemical-warfare suits marched across Mount Fuji's slopes towards Aum's desolate compounds. They carried electric saws, blowtorches, crowbars, and an age-old early-warning system for poison-gas emissions – caged canaries. Water cannons, armored trucks, and ambulances brought up the rear.

Searchlights swept over one facility as police drew near. "Aum Supreme Truth has nothing to hide!" a follower shouted into a megaphone. "This is an unjust search, but we will cooperate!" Then police broke through makeshift barricades and streamed into the compounds. At the same time, hundreds more cops burst into Aum offices and facilities across Japan.

For the next week, as a mesmerized nation watched live on television, police began unearthing a mammoth stockpile of chemicals at Mount Fuji. Sodium cyanide, hydrochloric acid, chloroform, phenylacetonitrile for stimulant production, glycerin for explosives, huge amounts of peptone for cultivating bacteria, sack after sack of sodium fluoride, 500 drums of phosphorus trichloride – the list grew longer and more frightening by the day. Police estimated that Aum's stockpile held more than 200 kinds of chemicals, including all the key ingredients for producing sarin.

As men in bulky chemical gear picked their way by flashlight through the compounds' dim interiors, the scale of Aum's empire began to reveal itself. There were metalwork and print shops, a martial-arts training hall equipped with punch bags and weight-training equipment. There was a hospital stocked with powerful drugs like thiopental and PAM, and, in the Finance Ministry building, a safe stuffed with $7.9 million in cash and 22 pounds of gold. And, as police quickly discovered, there were brainwashing chambers and prisons.

Investigators opened a prayer room to find about fifty emaciated followers. Some were so close to starvation, so severely dehydrated, that they barely responded as police arrived. Although many refused medical treatment, six followers – two of them in critical condition – were carried on stretchers to awaiting ambulances. Other cultists looked on and wept.

Police began checking cargo containers lying outside, and found they had been separated into tiny cells with hatches for handing in food and removing waste. In one container they found the crouched figure of Mika, the pregnant woman who had tried to hack her way to freedom with a screwdriver. Another victim, the subject of Aum's electrode surgery, was freed as well. He had lost 66 pounds and could barely speak. Police also found a drug-addled victim of the Datsura Experiment. He was completely incoherent; a doctor said the man was lucky to have survived at all.

"It won't be long before we start finding dead bodies," one police officer confidently told reporters. But the cops were too late to find even corpses. Apart from the living dead, investigators discovered a funeral urn containing the bones of a woman and an infant, possibly a mother and child. And in the basement of Satian 2, there was a microwave generator and eighty blackened metal drums. The walls and ceiling were covered with soot – the only traces left of the followers who had been cremated there. Authorities would soon investigate twenty murder cases linked to Aum without recovering a single body.

Police leaked many of these grisly finds to the media. But they refused to implicate the cult in the subway attack or arrest any suspects for murder. On day one of the raids, only four cultists, including three doctors, were arrested, all on suspicion of illegal confinement.

The following morning, they arrested a follower carrying notebooks labeled "War with Police." Amid constant references to massacres and mayhem, the notebooks described basic methods for germ cultivation, as well as a warning to "cover your ears and open your mouth during a nuclear explosion."

By now, Mount Fuji's army of police and reporters had been joined by desperate parents from all over Japan. "I have come to kill myself if my son and other followers commit mass suicide," said one woman, who had traveled from western Japan. "My daughter is being deceived! I want to take her home!" shouted a Kobe woman after police prevented her from entering a cult compound.

Police still seemed not to comprehend the full scope of Aum's horror. One ex-follower came with a court order to retrieve his children. He entered a compound and, in the confusion, managed to guide them out. It was a happy reunion: the man had not seen his children for months. But as he was leading them back to his car, the police approached – and promptly arrested him for illegal entry. As the father was taken away for questioning, cultists led his children back into the compound. It would be many weeks before he would see them again.

The raids continued. Inside Satian 7, the Styrofoam sculpture of Buddha was chipped away to reveal the latticework of pipes and filters, chemical reactors, and computer-controlled equipment. Outside the death factory, police dwarfed by mammoth ventilation pipes found plastic tubs stenciled with "Ministry of Science," and added them to a haul of some 1,200 drums of toxic chemicals.

By day six, a murder inquiry had been officially opened. Investigators now believed that Aum was capable of producing enough sarin to kill over 4 million people.

Aum's response to the stunning allegations was shamelessly direct: deny everything. The stockpile of chemicals was for producing semiconductors, plastics, fertilizers, and pottery, cult leaders insisted, while bacteria cultures were vital to manufacturing foodstuffs and drinks. Attorney Yoshinobu Aoyama slammed the police probe as persecution by a fascist government and, in an act of extraordinary legal chutzpah, filed suit against the city of Tokyo for $300,000 in damages for the raids.

Cult leaders were advised directly by the guru, who kept a mobile phone nearby at all times. Asahara also joined the media campaign. Four days after the subway attack, he appeared in a poor-quality video message broadcast on national television. "I am seriously sick," he said. "About 50 percent of my 1,700 pupils are troubled with sickness as we have been sprayed with poisonous gases such as sarin and mustard gas . . . The gas was unmistakably sprayed by U.S. troops."

Asahara's video address was received by a confused and fearful populace. The massive raids had reassured few. Police had not arrested a single cultist in connection with the subway sarin attack, although the cult was popularly believed to be the culprit. Indeed, it would be many weeks before the attack was formally pinned to Aum. In contrast to the cult's loud declarations of innocence, Japanese authorities seemed intent on keeping the public in the dark. The people of Tokyo knew only two things for sure: the perpetrators were still out there, and so was the threat of further terrorist attacks.

Meanwhile, the media advised the nation how to survive sarin attacks, including the advice to "flee in the direction you see fewest bodies." One mother told reporters she and her family now always carried a wet towel with them "in case of a gas attack." Tokyo's bookstores took Aum publications from the shelves and replaced them with guides to "protection, rescue, and recovery from destructive cults." There were strong sales of a novel called *Deadly Perfume*, in which terrorists plot an anthrax attack on London and Paris subways.

When the Dalai Lama visited Japan at the end of March, he found a country wracked with Aum fever. The Tibetan holy leader was on a scheduled tour, but was predictably swamped by questions about Aum. He expressed shock at the subway attack and denied any "special relationship" with Asahara, although he said he had met him four or five times. "I consider him as my friend," the Dalai Lama said, "but not necessarily a perfect one."

The Dalai Lama's imperfect friend had disappeared. And with him had fled some of the cult's most dangerous men.

One of Japan's most wanted was Takeshi Matsumoto, a 29-year-old loyalist who joined Aum after telling his parents he had seen hell. Matsumoto had driven the car used to kidnap Kiyoshi Kariya. He had also left his fingerprints on the rental-shop receipt where the car had been hired. After going on the run, Matsumoto finally took refuge at a remote cottage near the Sea of Japan. He was joined there by Dr. Hayashi and his wife Rira, an anesthesiologist. They had orders to remove Matsumoto's fingerprints, and soon the young cultist experienced hell for a second time.

First Rira Hayashi gave Matsumoto a general anesthetic. When Matsumoto was under, Ikuo put his scalpel to work. Taking each of Matsumoto's fingers in turn, he sliced away a thick layer of skin from the top joints to the tips. Then he did the same with the thumbs. Once all Matsumoto's fingerprints were removed, Dr. Hayashi apparently performed some abortive surgery on the cultist's jawbone and eyelids. When Matsumoto finally came round, his pain was excruciating. Soon, he was on the run again.

Police who later raided the cottage were met with a gruesome sight. Matsumoto was gone, but fragments of his bones and discs of curling skin clung to bloodied cotton batting on the floor. Surgical equipment and notes on operative procedure lay nearby.

Investigators believed that up to six cultists used the cottage as a safe house, leaving behind an airline timetable, road maps, and code books for contacting fellow fugitives. Even in a relatively small and densely populated country like Japan, tracking down Aum suspects was a tough task. In March alone, the cult reportedly amassed around $2 million dollars in donations, which it used as a "war fund" to harbor followers at as many as forty secret locations.

Spy chief Yoshihiro Inoue was holed up at one of Aum's Tokyo hideouts. With him was Toru Toyoda, one of the subway attackers, and a handful of other fugitives. Inoue had orders to disrupt the police investigation and prevent the arrest of the guru at any cost. Luckily for him, fleeing members had carried with them a small armory of deadly substances, including sodium cyanide, hydrochloric acid, RDX explosive, and – buried secretly by Yasuo "Killer" Hayashi – VX nerve agent.

As the police raids on Aum's facilities continued, Inoue's men were hard at work. First they hollowed out a book. Then they began working on ways to pack the cavity with RDX explosive and a triggering device. A new campaign of terror was just beginning.

The official head of the Aum investigation was Takaji Kunimatsu, chief of the National Police Agency. Japan's top cop was a stickler for routine, and the morning of March 30 began like every other.

Kunimatsu lived in an apartment in an upmarket condominium complex by Tokyo's Sumida River. A heavy drizzle was falling when, soon after 8 a.m., a chauffeur-driven car arrived to take the police chief downtown to NPA headquarters. An aide greeted Kunimatsu in the lobby, then held an umbrella over his boss's head as they walked out to the car.

The shots came from behind. Gunfire boomed between the apartment buildings as a hollow-point bullet slammed into Kunimatsu's body. The aide was still clutching the umbrella as the police chief began crumpling to the ground. Even as Kunimatsu fell, three more shots ripped through his leg, chest, and abdomen.

Kunimatsu was taken to hospital with three bullets lodged in his body; the fourth had apparently passed straight through. The bullets were removed after six hours of surgery. The police chief was stabilizing in intensive care as his men tried to piece together what had happened.

Police believed the revolver that shot Kunimatsu was a U.S. made .357-caliber Colt Magnum, probably a double-action model,

loaded with cartridges that expand on impact. The shots were fired
near a utility pole some 30 yards away. Police knew that the gunman
was a pro. In poor visibility, he had hit a moving target four times
from afar with a revolver that kicked like a mule. Only a few people in
Japan could achieve such accuracy, like a marksman in the police or
military. Or possibly someone trained by experts overseas – experts in
Russia, for instance.

Kunimatsu's condo might have been staked out from an
adjacent apartment; seven cigarette butts were found on the first floor.
The gunman had fled the scene on a bicycle, a seemingly absurd
choice of getaway vehicle, but actually the fastest way of escaping
through narrow lanes to one of twelve train stations within a mile's
radius.

Who was the hit man? Witnesses had spotted one cyclist aged
around forty, wearing a dark coat and pants, an alpine hat, and a
hay-fever mask. Police found a North Korean military badge and coin
at the scene, but suspected they were placed there to mislead
investigators. Some observers believed the shooting was perpetrated
by a member of Japan's underworld, who had decided to use the
hysteria over Aum as a cover, but few who knew the *yakuza* thought
that likely. The cult claimed innocence yet again. A spokesman
insisted an unknown group had committed the crime to "put more
pressure on Aum."

But less than two hours after Kunimatsu was hit, a Japanese
television network received an anonymous call. The message was
brief: if the investigation into Aum was not stopped, the voice warned,
then more cops would die – starting with the head of the Tokyo
Metropolitan Police. The voice would later be identified as that of a
28-year-old cultist from Aum's Construction Ministry. A car belonging to the ministry's chief, Kiyohide Hayakawa, was also spotted close
to Kunimatsu's residence. Police would eventually investigate the
possibility that more than seven cultists were involved in the
attempted hit.

Until then, however, Kunimatsu's shooting remained the subject
of speculation. The NPA ordered beefed-up security for VIPs,
important facilities and crowded areas, and the raids at Mount Fuji
went on. Hundreds of police entering Clear Stream Temple scuffled
with followers. As mantras blared through loudspeakers, it dawned on
the cops there that Aum attempted to mass-produce machine guns as
well as biochemical weapons.

The cult's war of words escalated. Aum leaders appeared on so many TV shows that they were now household names in Japan. Among them was chief scientist Hideo Murai, who lent his calm and confident manner to countless protests of the cult's innocence. Nothing seemed to faze him, not even the laughter of foreign reporters as he explained how the Americans had caused the Kobe earthquake with a seismic weapon.

On April 5, Murai gave an interview to the UPI news agency and explained the reason behind the cult's vast chemical supplies.

"We are stocking many chemicals in our compound to prepare for life after the end," he said in his oddly inflected English. "The Japanese state wants its subjects to remain unthinking and loyal. People of higher intelligence sympathize with our Buddhist approach. That is why we are being singled out as a suspect."

So who really gassed the Tokyo subway?

"I do not know," he replied. "But whoever they were, they must have had highly developed facilities."

Hideo Murai had only eighteen days to live.

36

DAY OF DOOM

The Tokyo subway attack and its startling aftermath sent tremors around the globe. The scenario that security experts had warned of for so long – urban terrorism using chemical weapons – had finally happened for real. And of all places, it had happened in Tokyo, a city renowned for its law and order.

Mass transit systems in London, San Francisco, and Barcelona tightened security, while police in Seoul probed possible Aum activities in South Korea. Tensions were particularly high in the U.S. In New York, a jet spent ten hours on the runway at John F. Kennedy airport while the FBI checked out a threat that poison gas was aboard the flight.

Two days after the subway attack, Aum's office in Manhattan issued a press release accusing the Japanese government of plotting to murder cult members and "making it appear like a mass suicide." "Of course, we know nothing of this incident in Tokyo," said Yumiko "Subha" Hiraoka, Aum's New York chief. "We are Buddhists . . . We cannot kill any sentient being, not even the insects." Subha's explanation failed to convince most of Aum's hundred or so New York members, who quickly disappeared, leaving only a dispirited core of die-hard followers.

As cultists cleared the New York office of all documents and records, FBI and Customs Service agents began investigating Aum's U.S. activities. They checked into followers' backgrounds and traced purchasing routes to find out whether the sect had exported sensitive technology or dangerous materials. Most of all, U.S. authorities wanted to know whether the cultists still posed any terrorist threat. For one frightening moment, it seemed they did.

Over the busy Easter holiday weekend, Disneyland in Los Angeles received a videotape. It showed a man from the chest down wearing rubber gloves and mixing chemicals. "Guests will die," the voice said. A massive deployment of FBI and army personnel found the threat to be a hoax – but not before Aum was mistakenly identified by the U.S. press as the perpetrator. Coincidentally, four cultists had arrived in Los Angeles that weekend on a mission to recruit American scientists sympathetic to the sect. Two were held and interrogated by Immigration and FBI agents, then released under surveillance.

In the weeks that followed, FBI officials grew increasingly frustrated by the lack of cooperation from Japanese authorities. As the FBI saw it, Aum was a global terrorist group with a major base of operations in New York City and a declared hatred of Americans. The implied threat in the cult's comment about Bill Clinton being a "one-term president" was enough to prompt a special alert by the U.S. Secret Service. Yet Japanese police refused to hand over lists of known members or front companies. "We found out more from the morning paper than from our briefings by the Japanese," one American official complained.

It was an old story with the Tokyo authorities. Like open markets, the international trade in police intelligence between the U.S. and Japan was largely a one-way street. Dealing with Japanese police on criminal matters was like "pulling teeth," said one top American cop. With the Aum case, the frustration of FBI agents soon turned to fury. The situation was eventually smoothed over, but only after the U.S. almost took the unprecedented step of issuing a *démarche*, a formal diplomatic protest usually reserved for nations harboring terrorists, building nuclear bombs, or starting wars.

Australian and German authorities, each trying to investigate Aum in their countries, were also angered by the lack of Japanese cooperation. The Australians in particular had many questions. In the days following the Tokyo subway attack, companies in Sydney had received typed letters reading, "The subways was a try . . . Japanese airlines and businesses in Australia will be next." The senders identified themselves only as "the Team." Australian Federal Police had also received strange news from the current owners of the remote Banjawarn Station, formerly Aum's outback test site, and went to investigate.

Police found the remains of twenty-nine dead sheep at Banjawarn. They were unshorn and still wore ID tags. Curiously, the carcasses were arranged in a semi-circle. The cause of death was unknown, but the cops had their suspicions. Investigators took wool and bone samples, and brought in a United Nations consultant who had researched Iraq's nerve-gas attacks on its Kurdish population.

The samples contained traces of methylphosphonic acid, a residue from the last stage in the decomposition of sarin.

Politics was also interfering in the Russian investigation of Aum, but in a different way. Five days before the subway attack, the cult's assets were frozen by a Moscow court after the Youth Salvation Committee, a group of Russian parents, had filed a civil suit claiming Aum had brainwashed and kidnapped dozens of followers. On the same day, police raided the cult's northern Moscow branch and found a cache of white powder, later believed to be narcotics.

After the subway attack, Aum launched the usual media offensive, claiming Russian followers had also suffered symptoms of poisoning. "They say in Japan that Aum has spread poison gas, but that's far from being true," said Fumihiro Joyu, Aum's Moscow chief. Shoko Asahara also released a hysterical message to his Russian followers: "If you hear anything about suicide, then know that we have been killed – that is, physically destroyed by the organs of state oppression."

On the surface, Russia's crackdown on the cult seemed swift. Aum's assets had already been frozen and, a week after the subway attack, its legal registration was canceled and its Moscow headquarters sealed. Even so, the cult had plenty of time to cover its tracks. Cultists destroyed documents and fled to Moscow hideouts. Barrels of unidentified chemicals were spirited away in cars from at least two of Aum's Moscow branches. According to Alexandr Dikov, a prosecutor quoted in a leading Russian newspaper, witnesses said some of the cars bore number plates belonging to Russian military intelligence. Six days after the subway attack, a fire broke out at the Russia–Japan University (RJU) building on Petrovka Street, conveniently gutting Aum's office on the third floor before police could search it.

Russian authorities not only failed to gather crucial evidence, but also missed the chance to question key Aum officials. On March 22, construction chief Kiyohide Hayakawa and two other cultists left Russia after a five-day visit. They carried with them cookie tins containing eleven pounds of ergotamine, the substance used in LSD production. Hayakawa's movements during the previous five days were as mysterious as ever. The Japanese and Russian media later concurred that Hayakawa traveled to the Caucasus city of Vladikavkaz, where Aum tried to charter two aircraft to carry weapons to Vladivostok. Investigators in Moscow neither confirmed nor denied these reports.

Within a week of Hayakawa's departure, Joyu also returned to Japan before he could be questioned. Russian police eventually arrested Joyu's deputy, Toshiyasu Ouchi, a grinning naïf described by one academic as "knowing as much about Russia as the farthest star." How much he knew of Aum's sinister activities remained to be seen.

By early April, Aum was officially banned in Russia, and was later ordered to pay $4 million in compensation to the Youth Salvation Committee, the anti-Aum parents group. Followers reportedly left Moscow in droves to establish cells in remote corners of the Russian Federation such as the Tatarstan capital of Kazan, where an Aum leader was later arrested. Radio Moscow and the 2×2 television network stopped broadcasting cult programs. President Boris Yeltsin ordered an investigation into the sect, but this seemed to move with sloth and secrecy. While Russian and Japanese reporters made extraordinary revelations about Aum's influence-buying and weapons acquisition, Russian investigators refused to comment or report on their progress.

Equally uncooperative were the powerful men now being tagged as Aum's supporters. Former Supreme Soviet member Ruslan Khasbulatov denied acting as a go-between on Aum's MIL Mi-17 helicopter deal. Russian military officials issued a stream of indignant statements. The air force's supreme command denied that three cultists had received helicopter training in 1994, and the head of Russia's biochemical defense troops dismissed reports of Aum's military ties as the product of "a very rich imagination."

And what of Oleg Ivanovich Lobov, the chairman of the Russian Security Council and RJU president? Press reports were alleging Lobov was the Russian godfather of a Japanese killer cult, which he denied.

"There were many articles in various newspapers and most of them are made up," he told one Russian reporter.

"So you're suggesting your links with Aum and Asahara are also fabricated?" asked the reporter.

"I did meet Asahara," said Lobov. "But what is the significance of this? It's nothing. When I was in Japan, I met more than 150 people . . ."

"But from those 150 people, only Asahara came here," the interviewer remarked.

Lobov's patience ran out. "That's not true," he snapped. "Many journalists come to me, yet you expect me to tell you everything?"

Lobov then stressed that he could hardly be blamed for meeting

Asahara, since he had received no prior warning from Russia's foreign ministry or intelligence services, nor from the Japanese authorities. And that was Oleg Lobov's final word on the Aum affair – although his press secretary did add that anyone who believed Russian media allegations was "a peasant." Within months, President Yeltsin appointed Lobov as his envoy to the troubled republic of Chechnya, where he narrowly avoided an assassination attempt.

Japanese police were still unsure about the ultimate target of Aum's subway attack. But the shooting of NPA chief Takaji Kunimatsu was a clear declaration of war on the police, and the cops finally responded in kind.

The faces of Aum members now peered from wanted posters plastered across Japan. Thousands of officers manned twenty-four-hour roadblocks in a nationwide dragnet for cult fugitives. Investigators worked round the clock sifting through mountains of evidence, including 100,000 train tickets bought on the day of the subway attack. One lawyer visited a police station to report the date rape of a client, only to be told that officers were "too busy with the nerve-gas incident."

This intense activity did little to assuage public fear and confusion. With the subway attack, Japanese watched their hard-earned peace and security seemingly crumble overnight. The shooting of Kunimatsu also exploded the myth that Japan's authorities were in control of the situation. And despite day after day of raids, investigators apparently did not have evidence to pin the subway attack on Aum.

Nor did police seem any closer to finding Shoko Asahara – who, in any case, was still wanted only for questioning, not on suspicion of murder. He was last seen in public on March 3 buying a slide and swing set in a provincial toy store. In early April, police waited in vain for Asahara to turn up at Tokyo's international airport, after a booking had been made in his name for a flight to Moscow. Six hundred officers and a helicopter also went on a wild-goose chase after a service station employee claimed to have spotted a bearded man in purple robes speeding past in a car.

But the nationwide dragnet soon began to pay off. Dr. Ikuo Hayashi was arrested in early April. He told police he would fast for ten days. Within twenty-four hours, he was eating three meals a day. Then Aum's hit man Tomomitsu Niimi was picked up near the Imperial Palace. In custody, Niimi refused to answer any questions.

"This is a good opportunity for me to practice," he said, smiling at police, then assumed the lotus position. Niimi would have plenty more time to meditate.

Niimi was soon joined by Kiyohide Nakada, the former member of the mighty Yamaguchi-gumi crime syndicate. The day after Nakada's arrest, the Yamaguchi-gumi's Kobe headquarters ordered bosses of all affiliated gangs to weed out Aum believers in their ranks. Apparently, not even Japan's most ruthless criminal group wanted any association with the cult. Next, police nabbed Kiyohide Hayakawa. He appeared live on a TV show to deny Aum had produced guns or sarin. As soon as he took off his microphone, he was handcuffed and led away.

More than a hundred cultists were now behind bars. Still, none had been arrested on sarin-related charges. Niimi and Dr. Hayashi were arrested for confining followers, Nakada for blackmailing, and Hayakawa for trespassing. Many other followers were picked up on minor charges such as riding an unregistered bicycle, adapting a greenhouse without permission and – in the case of one 35-year-old cultist – performing back rubs in violation of the Massage and Shiatsu Practitioners Law.

Behind this bizarre rap sheet was a police force anxious to get as many Aum members as possible off the streets. Police can detain a suspect for up to three weeks without a lawyer present. During this time, they put enormous pressure on suspects to confess. With Aum, police hoped to convince cultists in custody to confess to more heinous crimes, or implicate their colleagues, including the guru.

Despite criticism from civil-liberties watchdogs, this strategy had popular support and would eventually pay off. Niimi, Hayashi, Hayakawa, and others would soon all be indicted for murder. And, as the weeks passed, the list of charges began to reflect more accurately the full range of Aum's criminality. Cultists would be arrested on suspicion of kidnapping, illegal confinement, extortion, forgery, and the production of firearms, biochemical agents, and explosives.

The hunt continued for the guru. Police in Taiwan increased border surveillance after reports that Asahara intended to take refuge on the island. Cult leaders said Asahara would not appear in public until the situation had "cooled down." In fact, the situation was about to heat up to critical levels.

Asahara had written a new book called *The Pity of a Ruinous Country – Japan*. In it the guru explained how he was suffering from heart disease and cerebral thrombosis. "I am now leading a life of fighting against illness," he claimed. After expressing "pity" for the police, Asahara warned that if the government "oppresses a prophet, the people should suffer a national disaster."

It was the usual dire blend of self-pity and apocalypse – except for one prophecy. Asahara warned that a disaster would soon befall Tokyo that "would make the Kobe earthquake seem as minor as a fly landing on one's cheek." The content of the prediction was vague, but the date was precise. Something "horrible" would happen in the capital on Saturday, April 15, 1995.

The Japanese authorities immediately entered a state of emergency. Another 10,000 police were deployed across Tokyo and, on the eve of Asahara's "Day of Doom," the biggest raids yet were launched against the cult at 120 locations nationwide. Police hoped to uncover supplies of sarin or other deadly agents the cult might hold. They found nothing, except for a disquieting note. It read, "If police ever enter the place where Master Asahara is hiding, we will throw sarin at them and die together."

The authorities also decided to rescue the children. Amid cries of "Kidnappers!" and "Give our children back!," police entered Mount Fuji's Satian 10 facility and took fifty-three children into protective custody. They ranged from toddlers to teenagers, and most wore electrode caps. Eight children seemed malnourished and were taken to hospitals. The others were bussed to a child welfare center nearby, where they tried to readjust to life outside the cult. A nine-year-old girl said that she never played outside because "the air is full of poison gas." A five-year-old girl told a social worker, "The war will start soon. We have to fight back, otherwise I won't live until my sixth birthday."

By now, too, police had found Endo's biolab, which was reportedly lined with test tubes filled with unknown cultures. The lab was immediately sealed, and a directive issued forbidding anyone to enter. It would still be shut tight months later, along with the mouths of any investigators on the case.

Tokyo was bracing itself for a more immediate threat. As the guru's April 15 prophecy approached, rumors flashed around the city. Aum intended to poison the water supply, said one report, prompting some residents to store water in their bathtubs. When another rumor claimed that sarin would be released in Tokyo's crowded shopping district of Shinjuku, stores in the area increased security or closed completely. A chemical-warfare unit was put on red alert at a nearby army base, and local hospitals stocked up on nerve-

gas antidotes. Across the city, armored police buses guarded public
buildings and helicopters thrummed constantly overhead. While
many Japanese canceled planned trips to Tokyo, over 500 cultists left
the city for Mount Fuji. "Tokyo is dangerous according to our
leader's predictions," one follower explained.

During these anxious days, Tokyo learned a painful lesson in the
tactics of modern terrorism. Once the terrorist has displayed the
dreadful destruction he is capable of, there is no need to launch
another attack to disrupt a city and hold its population ransom. As
one journalist noted, the mere threat of another attack "paralyzed
Tokyo almost as effectively as nerve gas itself." It was Shoko
Asahara's finest hour. The guru had spoken, and an entire metropolis
sat up, listened – and trembled.

Saturday, April 15 came. Shinjuku's shops and subways were
abnormally quiet. Shoppers were outnumbered by police in bulletproof vests, and by hordes of cameramen half hoping for the worst.
But nothing happened, not in Shinjuku, nor elsewhere in the capital.
The guru's day of doom passed without incident, and Tokyo breathed
a sigh of relief – prematurely, as it turned out.

Four days later, choking fumes swept through Yokohama station
outside Tokyo. In a scene eerily reminiscent of the Tokyo sarin attack
only a month before, police and chemical troops rushed to the station
along with a fleet of ambulances. Nearly 600 commuters were
hospitalized with sore throats and eyes.

Aum's attorney insisted the cult had nothing to do with the
incident. For once, he was right: a small-time gangster later confessed
to spraying Mace at Yokohama station because of "personal
problems." The Yokohama incident might have stolen world
headlines had the worst terrorism incident in American history not
occurred on the same day. On April 19, a powerful bomb ripped
through the Federal Building in Oklahoma, killing 169 people and
injuring 500. Emergency personnel were still combing the rubble
when, two days later, another mysterious gas emission in Yokohama
sent twenty-four shoppers to the hospital. To many Japanese, it
seemed as if the world was spinning out of control.

All this heaped pressure on Japanese investigators. Police had
now determined beyond doubt that Aum had manufactured nerve
agents, but had still to charge a single cultist with the Tokyo sarin
attack. By comparison, within twenty-four hours of the Oklahoma

blast, U.S. authorities had arrested an anti-government extremist called Timothy McVeigh.

Police chiefs across Japan were urged to redouble their efforts and speed up the Aum investigation. "A new kind of indiscriminate terrorism has become possible," said one anonymous senior officer. "If we don't solve this case at any cost, legal order will collapse."

37

JUDAS

Media coverage of the cult had reached fever pitch. The Aum affair seemed to dominate every page of newsprint, every hour of broadcasting. While the police probe continued with almost feudal secrecy, ratings-obsessed networks fought to interview the cult's media-savvy leaders, who grabbed the chance to issue denials and proselytize on prime time. Aum was winning the propaganda war hands down.

The undisputed darling of the media was Fumihiro Joyu, the former chief of Aum's Moscow operation. With his telegenic good looks, turquoise pajamas, and fluent English, Joyu was looked upon by most Japanese as a dangerously glib and slippery operator with the ability to lie in two languages. To some young women, however, he was irresistible. Women's magazines ran articles about Joyu's slender figure and doe-eyed beauty with headlines like, "Ain't he neat?" Fans known as "Joyu gals" sent Joyu love letters and had Joyu dreams. "He took me to a strange basement room," confessed one student, "and then we made love."

Giggling flocks of girls waiting for a glimpse of their idol added to the crowds outside Aum's Tokyo headquarters. An army of reporters and cameramen, some with gas masks, were permanently encamped on the pavement there. Staff from local restaurants threaded through police lines to deliver take-out meals. Right-wing groups thundered past in sound trucks, denouncing the sect and shouting pro-Emperor slogans. Families on outings stopped to pose for photographs.

On the morning of April 23, a man called Hiroyuki Jo stepped into this carnival atmosphere. Nobody noticed Jo, a 29-year-old Korean whose real name was So Yu Haeng. He was a well-built man with short, tightly curled hair, and his patterned sweater would later be easy to spot in the background of many TV reports that day.

The Korean had a curious employment history. He once ran his own promotions company until it went bust with debts of over $200,000. After a spell as a truck driver, he began delivering prostitutes and collecting debts for the Hane-gumi, a small gang set up in Ise City in western Japan and affiliated with the Yamaguchi-gumi crime syndicate. As he stood in the crowd outside the Aum building that morning, he was just about to make another career move: from small-time punk to big-time killer.

The day before, Jo had bought a butcher's knife with an eight-inch blade. Then he had spent the night in a Tokyo love hotel with his regular hooker, and arrived at the Aum HQ by 11 a.m.

Soon after, Jo watched as Fumihiro Joyu and his aides pushed their way into the building through a forest of microphones. Three hours later, the Korean saw cult attorney Yoshinobu Aoyama run the media gauntlet to enter the HQ. Afterwards, Jo went for a bowl of noodles in a nearby restaurant. Then, in the late afternoon, he returned to the Aum building, and waited.

Around 8:30 p.m., another cult car pulled up. Chief scientist Hideo Murai climbed out and was immediately engulfed by a sea of journalists. As camera lights snapped on to relay pictures live to the nation, Murai's aides beat a path through the crowds. Murai had almost reached the door when it happened.

Hiroyuki Jo burst through a wall of cameramen and thrust the butcher's knife into Murai's belly with rapid stabs. Murai doubled up in pain, then stood upright. For a second, he stared with surprise at some blood on his wrist. Then his face contorted, his legs crumpled, and he collapsed into the crowd.

As mayhem broke out, Hiroyuki Jo threw the bloody knife on the ground and stood a few paces away with a nervous orbit of cameramen around him. "Isn't anybody going to arrest me?" he asked the crowd. It was a full minute and a half before a plain-clothes police officer approached him. Soon after, Jo was handcuffed and led away.

Hysterical cultists pushed back a surge of reporters and cameramen to let Murai's stretcher through. By the time the ambulance sped off, the scientist had lost a huge amount of blood. Jo's knife had pierced his abdomen and arm, creating a five-inch-wide wound that had lacerated a kidney and sliced through a major vein. Murai died of blood loss six hours later.

One magazine described it as "the most public assassination since Jack Ruby killed Lee Harvey Oswald." The murder of Murai was also one of the most mysterious. At first, Jo claimed he had

stabbed the scientist on his own initiative. "I got angry after watching
TV," he told investigators. "They are bad guys. We've got to do
something."

Soon, however, Jo changed his story. He claimed in court that
Kenji Kamimine, a key figure in the Hane-gumi gang, ordered him to
kill a high-ranking cultist – Murai, Joyu, or Aoyama would do. "Do it
for the gang," Kamimine allegedly told Jo. When Kamimine was
then arrested on murder charges, he admitted knowing Jo and
meeting him twice before, but claimed he had nothing to do with
Murai's killing.

And there the trail ended and the guessing began. Jo claimed he
had been ordered to kill any high-ranking cultist. Why then did he
wait while both Joyu and Aoyama passed by? Jo was almost certainly
a contract assassin, but who had hired him? One media theory held
that Japanese gangsters wanted Murai dead to prevent him from
revealing underworld links to stimulant production.

But the most furious speculation surrounded the cult itself. Aum
leaders knew that police were about to bring in Murai for questioning.
Were they scared the scientist might say too much? Despite its united
front, the cult leadership was apparently riven with factionalism; Joyu
and Murai were barely on speaking terms. There were other
tantalizing clues that Aum was behind the killing. On the way to
hospital, ambulance workers said Murai had repeatedly mumbled the
word "Judas" – code, perhaps, that he had been betrayed. Another
report claimed that Murai muttered, "Jews, Jews." Joyu tearfully
remembered the scientist's last words as "I am innocent."

The killing remained a mystery, and the enigma of Hideo Murai
died with him. Behind Murai's genteel public façade was a cold-
hearted fanatic with a hand in almost every murder the cult
committed. As the father of Aum's weapons' program, he had loyally
provided a religious despot with the means of venting an unholy rage
upon the world. Murai was posthumously indicted on charges of
murder and attempted murder in connection with the subway attack
and Matsumoto gassing. Police later dropped the charges.

The prime-time execution of Murai punched a mile-wide hole in the
police probe. Few leaders had known more about the cult's dark
secrets than the guru's science chief and right-hand man. Was a
faction within Aum's increasingly divided ranks now killing off key
followers before police could arrest them? Fumihiro Joyu for one was
taking no chances. Aum's dashing spokesman now wore a riot helmet

and bulletproof vest over his turquoise robes, and was shadowed everywhere by bodyguards.

The nation, too, was numbed by Murai's assassination. For many, it seemed as if the Aum saga would never end. What would happen next? A new word had been coined to capture the pervasive mood of apprehension: "sarinoia." A broken saké bottle leaking on one Tokyo train was enough to delay service. When thirty weather balloons fell to earth in western Japan, police in gas masks were dispatched and a nearby kindergarten evacuated. Osaka City Hall received a call from a self-proclaimed Aum member threatening to plant a bomb on the city's subways.

For Japanese children, the missing guru was the new bogeyman. The city of Atsugi closed all school swimming pools after a letter signed by "an Aum follower" warned that someone would "throw poison into a school pool." The word "sarin," previously barely known outside chemical warfare circles, now tripped easily from the lips of every high-school kid. In another sign of the times, a best-selling manual of dangerous substances included sarin under the heading "Everyday Poisons."

Three days after Murai's murder, police made yet more raids on ninety Aum facilities in and around Tokyo. The Mount Fuji compound of Satian 2 had been searched almost every day for a month now. But this time police discovered a secret basement not shown on any plan of the facility. And in the basement, they found the alchemists of Armageddon – Masami Tsuchiya and Seiichi Endo. They were arrested on suspicion of harboring suspects.

Tsuchiya wore a faint smile as police led him out of Satian 2. Once in custody, he refused to talk, saying only, "I belong to the chemical unit." Soon, however, he began to point the finger. "I report to Asahara about everything I do. Ask him." The arrest of Tsuchiya and Endo was considered a major break in the Aum case. Tomiichi Murayama, Japan's ineffectual prime minister, declared to the nation, "I believe the investigation is entering the final stage."

The premier's words meant little to the many people who were still counting the human cost of the subway attack. At least three passengers were still hospitalized. Two were in vegetative comas, the third suffered from acute amnesia. One victim of the attack aborted her baby rather than risk the effects of the nerve agent on her unborn child.

St. Luke's Hospital was treating seven passengers for insomnia, intense headaches, and flashbacks of fear – all classic symptoms of post-traumatic stress disorder, a syndrome usually associated with war veterans. And the bereaved were inconsolable. "I just want my daughter back," said the mother of one victim. "She did nothing wrong. I want to throw sarin at the people who killed her."

About a hundred children of Aum were eventually taken into protective custody. Only eleven were claimed by parents or relatives in the first few months. One by one, the children at the welfare center took off their electrode caps. Soon they were watching cartoons and playing games, and behaving much like other kids their age – almost. One teacher found the children had scribbled on a blackboard the phrases "Master Asahara" and "Let's keep up with training."

Japan's temples and churches had begun the task of helping adult followers break their emotional ties to Aum. Many people had now left the sect, but their slow return to society was typically accompanied by anger, fear, and confusion. One ex-believer who ran an Aum victims group kept bursting involuntarily into Aum songs while cycling home. There were worrying reports that former followers were still being sent letters pressuring them to return to the cult. A public telephone was incongruously erected at a Mount Fuji roadside to allow followers to phone home.

Many cultists preferred to live on in delusion. They believed Aum had been framed, and had no intention of leaving. A believer in his thirties said, "The only thing I am afraid of is that if Asahara disappears from this world, I won't be able to attain enlightenment." Another follower, a doctoral candidate at Tokyo University, believed the allegations against the cult were false. "To ignore the rumors and accept hardship – that's my latest training," he said.

The cult continued to declare its innocence and sue its loudest critics. Aum filed suit against a Japanese daily for $100,000 in damages for linking the cult with the Matsumoto sarin incident. Two Aum-run restaurants added their own protest. Their menu now offered "Armageddon bowl," a spring roll with egg and soy sauce on a bed of rice. A dish called "Poa curry" took its name from a cult word now almost synonymous with "kill" or "murder." The promising-sounding "Trumped-up lunch set" was a simple fried tofu patty and croquette.

By the end of April, about 150 cultists had been arrested, some on serious charges like kidnapping. But six weeks after the subway attack, there had still been no arrests for sarin-related crimes. The investigation progressed with the same secrecy, with police leaking information to selected reporters instead of issuing statements or holding news conferences. By now, even Aum officials were loudly demanding a progress report. Police responded with another series of raids on Aum's Mount Fuji facilities.

One man they had yet to find was young spymaster Yoshihiro Inoue. "I will never be caught," Inoue once boasted. He claimed his "higher state of enlightenment" allowed him to anticipate where police would look for him. In his Tokyo hideout, Inoue was planning a terror campaign to prevent his guru's arrest. With him were Tomomasa Nakagawa, Asahara's personal doctor, and particle physicist Toru Toyoda.

Inoue's team took stock of what weapons the cult could still wield. They worked feverishly at developing letter bombs, but had yet to complete one. However, they had perfected another inventive device, and were ready to try it out on Tokyo.

38

I AM THE GURU

May 5 was Children's Day, one of the national holidays making up Japan's frenetic Golden Week. With record numbers of Japanese leaving on vacation, an extra 60,000 police had been deployed in shopping precincts and tourist spots nationwide. In Tokyo, trains and subways were packed to bursting.

One of the busiest stations in the capital was Shinjuku. The station is a city within a city, an enormous underground network of shops and restaurants linked by passageways clogged with a constant stream of people. Every day, Shinjuku's trains are used by 1.6 million commuters – the equivalent of over half the population of Rome.

At around 7:40 p.m., a bag left in a Shinjuku restroom burst spontaneously into flames. When station staff doused the burning bag with water, it began spewing choking fumes. Fire department staff in breathing apparatus finally extinguished the fire, and nobody was seriously injured. Only later did police realize just how lucky Shinjuku's commuters had been that evening.

Investigators found the remains of two condoms attached to the bag. One contained granulated sodium cyanide, the other dilute sulfuric acid. The condoms were part of an ingenious ignition system. Whoever built the device knew the sulfuric acid in the first condom would eat through the rubber and mix with the sodium cyanide, producing hydrogen cyanide gas.

Hydrogen cyanide is infamous as Zyklon B, used by the Nazis to murder millions in Auschwitz and other World War II death camps. It kills by entering the bloodstream through the lungs and blocking the body's ability to absorb oxygen. Once a lethal dose is inhaled, death is painful and rapid. The compound is so volatile that it is lethal only in confined areas, like subway stations or gas chambers. It was developed by the French during World War I and has a faint smell of bitter almonds.

A later police simulation at Shinjuku found that the gas would

SULPHURIC ACID + SODIUM CYANIDE = HYDROGEN CYANIDE GAS.

have been sucked from the restroom by the ventilation system, then pumped onto the heads of passengers waiting on a nearby platform. If the device had not been extinguished, police believed, the chemicals could have mixed to produce enough gas to kill up to 20,000 people.

Tokyo's residents greeted this news with dazed resignation. Public confidence in the Aum investigation sank to a new low. Tokyo police now believed Aum no longer possessed "a large amount of sarin," the media reported. But this was hardly reassuring, and even less so when the cult clearly still had other killer compounds, like hydrogen cyanide.

Ten days after the foiled attack on Shinjuku station, Yoshihiro Inoue's powers of enlightenment finally failed him. He was spotted in a Tokyo suburb and arrested. The car he was driving contained several nitrate compounds for manufacturing high explosives. With Inoue's arrest, most of the cult's most dangerous members were now behind bars. But the nation would remain on edge until the police had caught the most dangerous cultist of all: Shoko Asahara.

As if stage-managing a great drama, police had apparently known the guru's whereabouts for weeks. He was right under their noses, in the Mount Fuji compound of Satian 6. Spokesman Fumihiro Joyu often entered and left the facility, and cultists had been spotted carrying in melons, the guru's favorite fruit. Police knew where to arrest Asahara. The question now was when they would do it. Clearly, they had decided not to move until they had gathered enough evidence to arrest Asahara on murder charges that would stick.

On May 14, a large floodlight was set up to illuminate Satian 6. Electric rumors shot through the assembled reporters and camera-men, and a huge media mobilization began. One network deployed twenty-four vehicles, seventy cameras, 700 people, and three helicop-ters to cover what promised to be the biggest event of the year. The police had finally decided. It was time to get the guru.

May 16, 1995. A dense mist rolled over Mount Fuji's flanks, obliterating everything beyond a few feet away. Dawn made barely a dent on the murky twilight. Soon, hundreds of ghostly figures began emerging from the fog – police in riot gear, backed up by armored personnel carriers and water cannons. As helicopters hovered somewhere overhead, police marched into the yard at Satian 6. It was day 56 of the raids.

Investigators talked briefly to a follower at the compound's back

TO KILL 20 000 PEOPLE

door. Then the cultist closed the door and locked it. Half an hour passed. Then police armed with blowtorches and circular saws cut through the door's hinges in a cascade of orange sparks. The door was pried open with crowbars, and the police poured in.

While hundreds of reporters waited outside, police with flashlights moved cautiously through the labyrinth of Satian 6. The electricity had been cut off, so the narrow passageways were pitch black. The cops began breaking the locks on dozens of tiny compartments, and ferreted out more than fifty followers.

For the next four hours, Japanese were riveted to TV reports. Live pictures flashed up on giant TV screens on buildings across Tokyo. Trading stopped on the Tokyo Stock Exchange. In the U.S., CNN interrupted its blanket coverage of the O. J. Simpson murder trial to report live from Mount Fuji.

At around 9:30 a.m., police found a tiny chamber hidden between the building's second and third floors. They forced open the hatch and peered in. Inside was a figure sitting cross-legged in the gloom.

"Are you Asahara?" police asked.

"Yes, I am the guru," the voice replied.

Asahara was dressed in his usual purple with white pants. At his side was a cassette player, some medicine, and over $100,000 in cash. There was also, said some reports, an AK-74 assault rifle nearby. Asahara was told he was under arrest for murder as the mastermind behind the sarin attack on Tokyo's subways. Then police tried to lead him away.

"Don't touch me," he said. "I don't even let my disciples touch me."

But Asahara leaned wearily on investigators as he walked down to the ground floor. He said he had been meditating in the chamber for two or three days. It was probably much longer. His beard was matted and greasy, and he was surrounded by an unholy aura of rancid body odor. Yet, for all his claims of terminal illness, a doctor pronounced him in good health.

At 10:35, riot police held back a great surge of reporters and cameramen to let a blue police van out of the compound. A blinding strobe of camera flashbulbs gave the public the first glimpse of Shoko Asahara in months: a smudge of purple, the puffy, bearded face, the eyes slitted in contemplation.

The van sped towards Tokyo along Route 139, flanked by police cars with flashing lights. A cavalcade of cars, motorcycles, and helicopters followed. In a scene reminiscent of O. J. Simpson's dash for freedom along the freeways of Los Angeles, crowds massed at the roadside and on overhead bridges to watch the procession go past. An hour later, Shoko Asahara was behind bars.

Fumihiro Joyu denounced the guru's arrest. "But followers took it calmly," he said, "like Buddhists."

That evening, a secretary for Tokyo governor Yukio Aoshima was opening his boss's mail at City Hall. Only a few hours before, the governor had announced his intention to revoke Aum's religious status. The secretary picked up a package the size of a video cassette, and looked at the back. The sender was listed as a prominent Tokyo assemblyman. As the secretary began to open it, the package exploded in his face, ripping the fingers off his left hand. Inoue's letter bomb had finally reached its destination.

In 1986, Shoko Asahara walked into the Himalayan mountains as a con artist, and emerged as a self-proclaimed messiah. In 1995, he came down from the mountains again, this time as one of the century's most notorious mass murderers – as the prophet of hi-tech terrorism.

Asahara himself would not admit to such a description. In fact, Asahara would not admit to anything at all. "How could I, a blind man, have possibly done such a thing?" he said when accused of the Tokyo sarin attack. Over the following weeks of police interrogation, the fallen messiah seemed unclear whether to defend his flock or blame them. "Please believe me," he said through a lawyer. "It is not true that my disciples made sarin, and I never ordered them to." At another time, he said, "I have so many followers, it's impossible for me to know what everyone is doing."

Asahara fasted in his detention cell at first. Soon, however, he began to eat and bathe. The color returned to his cheeks and his figure plumped out beneath the white tracksuit he now wore. He claimed to have regained his eyesight, and urged followers, "Wait for my return." Before long, police questioning hit a brick wall. Shoko Asahara's invincible arrogance had returned. "A samurai warrior never justifies himself," he told his captors.

Many arrested cultists were less reticent, and used their court appearances to express years of pent-up rage towards the guru. "Asahara kept his hands clean and turned almost 200 followers into criminals," sneered Dr. Ikuo Hayashi's wife Rira. An ex-nurse added, "He is so cruel, it is difficult to believe he has the warm blood of a human being." One of Asahara's bodyguards told the court, "Aum is a devilish group. Please put Asahara to death."

But other followers remained silent, still tormented by Asahara's malevolent spirit. As one cultist was about to confess his crimes, an Aum lawyer warned him, "The guru will come and you will go to hell." One jailed nurse suffered terrible nightmares of being buried up to the neck in sand, watching the tide come in to drown her. Or she would dream that an Aum leader had handed her a bomb to use in an attack, and would wake up screaming. For those in custody, the ordeal was far from over.

Nor did Japan's year of living dangerously end with Asahara's arrest. A month later, an All Nippon Airways jumbo jet with 365 passengers on board was hijacked over Japan by a self-declared Aum member. He held a bag of clear liquid, which he claimed was sarin, and threatened to pierce it with a screwdriver. "I'm doing this for the guru," he told a flight attendant. After a fifteen-hour stand-off on the runway, police stormed the jet and rescued all on board. The hijacker turned out to be a 53-year-old bank employee on prolonged sick leave who "just wanted to attract attention." The bag contained water.

Aum's entire leadership was now in jail. Yet, like a headless corpse, the cult stumbled on. During one twenty-four-hour period in July, there were four more failed gas attacks on Tokyo's subway. Two involved condom devices capable of producing enough hydrogen cyanide to kill thousands. Neither worked, and no one was injured. Acting on tips from jailed cultists, police unearthed caches of sodium cyanide and sarin components at two mountain hideaways. Cultists admitted the caches were to be used to launch new chemical attacks.

And so the nation's relief at Asahara's arrest was tempered with caution. The cult had preyed upon public vulnerability too many times. The media continued to reveal an organization of unimaginable evil – heavily armed, fanatical, inhumane. For many Japanese, life had not yet reverted to normal. Perhaps it never would.

A state of vigilant calm returned to Tokyo's subway system, which carried the city's millions to their jobs and homes with typical efficiency. The world's busiest underground railway now had a more historic claim to fame: as the target of the first civilian act of chemical terror in a world capital.

At Ginza, one of the stations badly affected by the sarin attack, it was apparently business as usual. Over three months had passed since that horrific March day, and subway staff were gearing up for another rush hour. Equipped with wireless microphones, Ginza's stationmasters announced incoming trains and politely reminded passengers of closing doors over the public-address system.

At around 4 p.m. that day, the microphones suddenly stopped working. Something was jamming the frequency. As staff shouted uselessly into their mikes, a song began to play at deafening volume through the station speakers. It sounded like a hymn, but of the strangest kind. Booming across the platforms, echoing up through the tunnels and stairways, one word now droned over and over again:

"Guru, guru, guru, guru, guru, guru . . ."

EPILOGUE

By February 1996, Shoko Asahara had been served with ten indictments, including twenty-three counts of murder. Represented by twelve lawyers – an unprecedented number for a single Japanese defendant – he was expected to plead innocent to all charges. But given Japan's 99 percent conviction rate and confessions by his top lieutenants, Asahara is unlikely ever to be a free man again. He may well face the death penalty, although repeated appeals could keep him from the hangman's noose for many years. Asahara has urged bright young cultists to study law and join his legal team.

Aum's heart-throb Fumihiro Joyu was arrested in October on perjury charges. Attorney Yoshinobu Aoyama was arrested for libel. Takeshi Matsumoto, the Aum fugitive who had his fingerprints surgically removed, was apprehended in Tokyo three days after his guru. He was identified by his palm prints. As of February 1996, Yasuo "Killer" Hayashi remained at large.

By the end of 1995, over 350 followers had been detained. About half of them were later released. Of the rest, the majority were charged with serious crimes like kidnapping and murder, while others faced further questioning. The first wave of more than a hundred Aum cases flooded Tokyo District Court in September. Most suspects pleaded guilty, and announced their intention to leave the cult. Japanese courts, which reward contrition, handed down suspended or moderate sentences.

The trials of high-ranking cultists began in 1996. Asahara and his lieutenants faced charges of murder, attempted murder, kidnapping, and drug production, to name the most serious crimes. For men who claimed to live for the next life, Aum's leaders now showed a remarkable eagerness to save their own skin. Of the leading cultists – Hayakawa, Dr. Hayashi, Inoue, Niimi, Nakagawa, Tsuchiya, and Endo – several asked to be spared the death penalty in return for confessions. Their fates are as gloomy as that of their guru.

*

Few embers of Aum activity remain in the U.S., Germany, and Australia. Workers at Aum's Sri Lankan factory filed a complaint with local police for unpaid wages, but their Japanese bosses had fled.

In Moscow, the media linked the cult ever more deeply with members of Russia's political, military, and intelligence communities. But the state investigation appeared to have largely petered out. Worsening matters was the untimely death of Vitaly Savitsky, head of a state Duma investigation that looked into Aum and other sects. Savitsky died in a suspicious car accident in St. Petersburg in December 1995. The full reach of Aum in post-Soviet Russia may never be known.

The music of the Chyren orchestra was broadcast in Red Square during the Victory Day parade on May 9. To the pride of flutist Evdokimov and conductor Koudria, the orchestra played Prokofiev, Shostakovich, Tchaikovsky – the works of Russian greats, not Japanese gurus.

The number of followers living at Mount Fuji dropped to new lows. It was unclear how many had left the cult, how many had fled, and how many were missing. By early 1996, police were still trying to find some forty members who disappeared in dubious circumstances.

Anticipating legal action against Aum itself, cult officials began transferring the group's huge assets to over 300 bank accounts held by affiliated companies. The Tokyo District Court subsequently stripped Aum of its religious status and ordered its assets seized. In December 1995, the Justice Ministry followed with controversial plans to ban Aum entirely, under the nation's rarely-used 1952 Antisubversive Activities Law.

Compensation suits were filed against the cult by sarin victims in Matsumoto and Tokyo, villagers at Mount Fuji, and others who had suffered by Aum's hand. The cult's dwindling band of devotees were ordered to help shoulder legal costs by taking jobs at construction sites, security firms, and snack bars. Eleven "Satian" shops opened across Japan to recruit more followers and sell a variety of products – guru T-shirts, Joyu dolls, cookies stamped with Aum's Sanskrit insignia.

Also cashing in was the anonymous creator of a new computer game called Kasumigaseki. The goal of the game is to kill people with sarin on five Tokyo subway lines.

The full extent of Aum's killing fields remained hard to judge. The sarin attacks on Tokyo and Matsumoto, together with other cult murders, claimed the lives of at least twenty-seven people. That death toll could eventually double, considering the number of followers who disappeared or died in suspicious circumstances in Japan and Russia. But Aum's path of destruction is not only littered with corpses. The cult's insanity injured nearly 6,000 people, destroyed countless families, robbed and impoverished scores of victims, and left hundreds of young men and women with mental and physical scars they will bear for life.

Almost a year after the sarin attack in Matsumoto, police in the Japan Alps town "absolved" Yoshiyuki Kono, whom they had falsely accused of causing the incident. "I feel like I've won an innocent verdict at a trial," Kono said. Every day, the machinery salesman still visited his comatose wife Sumiko to play her music. "When I'm alone, I think of my wife and cry," Kono reflected. "But I have to appreciate the fact that she's alive. I can't die before she does because only I can protect her."

National Police Agency chief Takaji Kunimatsu recovered from his bullet wounds and returned to head the Aum investigation. He admitted that branding Kono a suspect in the Matsumoto attack was an "inconvenient" aspect of the case, but defended his officers against public criticism that police had botched the Aum investigation. Not until the February 1995 kidnapping of Kiyoshi Kariya did police have the "confidence" to pursue Aum, Kunimatsu insisted.

Kiyoshi Kariya was laid to rest in a modest ceremony at a Tokyo shrine. There was no body in the coffin. All it contained was a spare pair of Kariya's eyeglasses and some earth taken from the spot near Lake Motosu, where Aum had scattered his remains after murdering him.

The City Hall secretary injured by the letter bomb returned to work. He had lost the use of his left hand. Five cultists were later indicted for planning the attack, including spy chief Inoue, physicist Toru Toyoda, and a medical graduate of Tokyo University.

In September, acting on tips from jailed Aum leaders, police began digging holes at three desolate mountain spots. They were searching for the remains of Yokohama lawyer Tsutsumi Sakamoto, his wife Satoko and their one-year-old son Tatsuhiko, whom the cult had murdered and buried in 1989.

Tsutsumi Sakamoto was identified by the last scraps of skin clinging to the fingers of his skeleton; his wife was discovered soon after. Police labored for five more days in knee-deep mud before they unearthed the right palm of a small child – all that was left of little Tatsuhiko. A small cross was erected on the spot.

Over 25,000 people later filed into a Yokohama stadium to pay their last respects to the Sakamotos. A huge photo of the smiling family was erected behind a bank of white flowers. A local choir joined with the Japan Philharmonic Orchestra to perform the couple's favorite piece, Sibelius's "Finlandia." Then, almost six years after their brutal murder, the Sakamoto family was finally laid to rest.

AFTERWORD

A psychopathic band of brilliant scientists, bent on indiscriminate murder and the world's end – Aum's story seems more at home in the world of science-fiction novels and TV thrillers. Yet it happened in real life. More frightening still, it will happen again.

"We've definitely crossed a threshold," warns terrorism expert Bruce Hoffman. "This is the cutting edge of hi-tech terrorism for the year 2000 and beyond. It's the nightmare scenario that people have quietly talked about for years coming true."

In the weeks following Aum's subway attack, terrorists in Chile and the Philippines threatened to unleash their own chemical arms. In America, Ohio traffic cops pulled over an outspoken white supremacist and found in his car three vials of the bacteria that cause bubonic plague. Meanwhile, two members of the Minnesota Patriots Council – one of scores of heavily armed U.S. militia groups – were convicted of planning to use ricin, a biological toxin, to kill federal agents. The trial was a sign of the times: the men were the first convicted under a 1989 U.S. law, the Biological Weapons Anti-Terrorism Act.

It would be easy to dismiss Aum as a peculiarly Japanese case, and indeed, there are conditions in Japan that shaped the cult's unique character. The straitjacket schools and workplaces, the absentee fathers and alienated youth no doubt helped fuel Shoko Asahara's rise to power. But to suggest that what happened in Japan could not happen elsewhere would be a dangerous mistake. Ineffective and bungling police, fanatic sects, and disaffected scientists are hardly limited to the Japanese.

Aum's forays into conventional weapons – its explosives and AK-74s – were alarming enough, as were the cult's eerie experiments with electrodes, drugs, and mind control. But where Asahara and his mad scientists charted new ground was in their pursuit of the weapons of mass destruction. This, unfortunately, will prove Aum Supreme Truth's lasting legacy: to be the first independent group, without state patronage or protection, to produce biochemical weapons on a large scale. Never before had a sub-national group gained access to so deadly an arsenal.

As the Cold War recedes into history, we leave behind a strange stability from the balance of terror that once existed. It was a time of mutually assured destruction, when communist and capitalist super-powers divided the world neatly into two well-controlled camps. Terrorism was by and large state-sponsored and politically motivated. Now, as the new millennium approaches, we face another kind of threat, one of unrestrained killers and renegade states armed with the deadliest substances on Earth.

The word is out. A college education, some basic lab equipment, recipes downloaded from the Internet – for the first time, ordinary people can create extraordinary weapons. Technology and training have simply become too widespread, too decentralized to stop a coming era of do-it-yourself machines for mass murder. We are reaching a new stage in terror, in which the most fanatic and unstable among us can acquire the most powerful weapons.

In late 1995, the U.S. Senate Permanent Subcommittee on Investigations took a hard look at Aum's remarkable record. The subcommittee staff, known for its hard-hitting probes into organized crime and terrorism came away worried and amazed.

"Although the findings may initially sound far-fetched and nearly science fictional . . ." concludes the group's report, "Aum was merely one example – a case study – of what may be the most dominant, emerging threat to our national security." In the hearings that followed, Senator Sam Nunn called the cult "a warning to us all." Nunn, one of the leading defense experts in Congress, put the matter bluntly: "I believe this attack signals the world has entered a new era."

Nearly every expert agrees. "It would be foolish to think that this couldn't happen in London, Paris, or New York," warns Kyle Olson, who studied Aum's attacks for the Chemical and Biological Arms Control Institute. "It breaks a taboo," says Brian Jenkins of Kroll Associates, the investigative and security firm. "Others will ask whether such tactics should be adopted by them. It is now more likely that at least some will say yes."

The men who keep the poisons agree as well. "The operative question may not be whether biological agents will be used as terrorist weapons against the United States, but rather when they will be used," observes Lieutenant Colonel Edward Eitzen, a medical doctor and top official at Fort Detrick, the U.S. Army's chief biological-weapons lab. And when the attack comes, says Eitzen, it will be "potentially devastating."

Terrorism is changing. Groups like the Palestine Liberation Organization and the Irish Republican Army tended to hit high-profile but symbolic targets. Most political terrorists, says Jenkins, are not interested in mass murder – they are out to gain support for their cause. "Terrorists want a lot of people watching, not a lot of people dead," he writes. "Terrorists operate on the principle of the minimum force necessary."

The great exception to this are religious terrorists, who murder in the service of a higher calling. Responsible only to God and scripture, they feel absolved from the laws and values that govern the rest of us. In that sense, Aum belongs in the company of Islamic fundamentalists, apocalyptic Christians, and messianic Jews. Their violence transcends this world and becomes a sacramental rite, a divine duty. Such beliefs justify the act of mass murder.

The good news is that terrorism overall is down. The end of the Cold War helped cool the number of international terrorist attacks to a twenty-three year low in 1994, according to the U.S. State Department. The bad news is that the attacks are growing more violent and more fanatical. The numbers of those who believe in "holy terror" appear to be growing, and their actions promise to escalate.

Not every cult is capable of terrorism, of course. But as we head for the year 2000, the proliferation of apocalyptic sects should give everyone pause. The aptly named Millennial Prophecy Report claims to track 1,100 in the U.S. alone. The 1993 mass murders of the Branch Davidians in Waco, Texas, and, a year later, the Solar Temple in France, Quebec and Switzerland are but two extreme examples. As Aum demonstrates so well, these groups are hardly limited to the West. In 1995, a former cop called Vissarion drew Russian media attention by building a community of intellectuals in Siberia and declaring himself Christ. In China that year, authorities arrested fifteen members of a doomsday cult called Bei Li Wang. And in Thailand, police raided the headquarters of the Sri-ariya cult, whose guru claims to be the master of heaven in the "Millennium Kingdom." Followers greet each other with Nazi-style salutes and call themselves by the names of past Thai kings.

More worrisome, perhaps, are Islamic fundamentalists, who bring to bear their own form of apocalyptic judgment. These believers in *jihad*, or holy war, have proven again and again their willingness to kill and die for Allah. The fanatics who struck at New York's World Trade Center in 1993 clearly meant to commit mass murder. Guided by their own blind cleric, Sheik Omar Abdel-Rahman, the group exploded a powerful home-made bomb that killed six people, injured scores more, and caused $500 million in damage. Like Aum, the Sheik's men also held an interest in chemical weapons. To ensure the greatest possible carnage, the terrorists reportedly packed cyanide into their bomb, which ended up evaporating in the blast. The attack was to be the first in a worldwide campaign of terror, said to include plane bombings, assassinations, and the destruction of the UN, the Lincoln Tunnel, and other New York landmarks. "We have to thoroughly demoralize the enemies of God," read one member's notebook. "This is to be done by means of destroying and blowing up the towers that constitute the pillars of their civilization . . ."

America's militia movement brings a similarly evangelical and heavily armed response to the world. Dozens of these small grass-roots armies have arisen, with names like the Militia of Montana and the Hillsborough Troop of Dragoons in New Hampshire. They are a disturbing bunch, many of them consisting of white supremacists and survivalists, skinheads and anti-Semites. Most share a deep-seated, Christian fundamentalist view of the world, filled with the kind of intense paranoia that infected Aum so deeply.

According to their own literature, these people are afraid of bar codes on manufactured goods (the codes denote routes for UN invasion troops); the U.S. government (riddled with agents of the New World Order, who have rewritten the Bill of Rights and the Constitution); gun control (an international plot to enslave freedom-loving Americans); and, at one time or another, all of the following: Jews, Blacks, Democrats, Republicans, bankers, the CIA, foreigners, tax auditors, and environmentalists.

The fanatics of the Arab Mideast and American Midwest, at least, are known quantities. Less familiar, but possibly of far more consequence, are those from the republics of the former Soviet Union. Not only is the region fertile ground for cults and extremists, but its role as a supermarket for weapons and technology will make it a favorite target of every madman intent on death and destruction. At his hearings on Aum and proliferation, Senator Sam Nunn put the matter well: "Never before has an empire collapsed leaving some 30,000 nuclear weapons, hundreds of tons of fissile material, at least 40,000 tons of chemical weapons, advanced biological weapons, huge stores of sophisticated conventional weapons, and thousands of scientists with the knowledge to make all of the above."

One can take some solace, perhaps, from the fact that many of Aum's plans ended in failure. Despite its vast resources, fanatical scientists, and years of work, the cult was unable to wreak havoc on a larger scale. Its exotic plans to build nuclear bombs, laser guns, and electromagnetic weapons came to naught. In the end, Aum probably killed as many people by strangling and injection as it did by biochemical attack.

But make no mistake: we are lucky. Impurities in the cult's sarin kept hundreds, perhaps thousands of people from dying in Tokyo. Instead, the cult's home-made weapons that day killed "only" twelve and sent over 5,500 to the hospital. Aum's attacks, using anthrax, botulism and cyanide gas appear to have failed, largely because of problems with the delivery systems. Had the cult not spun out of control – had Aum not begun killing and kidnapping at will in 1994 – Asahara's scientists probably would have had time to perfect their biochemical weapons. In the end, Aum's greatest enemy was itself.

The performance of Japanese police, so abysmal as to defy belief, is now part of the historical record. Those who wonder how not to conduct an investigation of a terrorist or criminal organization need only consult the six years of mistakes, mismanagement, and missed opportunities by that nation's once proud police force.

Since the sarin attacks, Japan has tightened up its laws on toxic agents and religious groups, promised to set up units to investigate new types of crime, and considered letting police do undercover work and electronic surveillance. Such measures would certainly have helped stop Aum, but that was not the core of the problem. In the end, the fault in Japan lies not so much with laws as with leadership.

However poorly the Japanese cops performed, they weren't the only ones who missed Aum. The CIA, which boasts a forty-five-year presence in Japan, never saw the cult coming, despite Aum's rampant anti-Americanism, nerve-gas attacks, arms shopping, and threats against President Clinton. In their review of the cult, U.S. Senate investigators were incredulous. "How does a fanatic, intent on creating Armageddon, with relatively unlimited funds and a world-wide network of operatives, escape notice of Western intelligence and law-enforcement agencies outside of Japan?" they asked.

The answer was as direct as it was alarming. "They simply were not on anybody's radar screen," replied a top U.S. counter-terrorism officer.

Not on anybody's radar screen? Apparently we need new radar. The sarin attack on Matsumoto was the world's first nonmilitary use of nerve gas. For days, it was the biggest news story in Japan, the world's second biggest economy. Obviously, foreign intelligence agencies can't investigate every intriguing lead, but perhaps the CIA and other agents are too worried about the balance of trade and industrial spying these days. By then, Aum had accumulated as much as $1 billion, ran offices in six countries on four continents, and virtually declared war on the United States. But with Matsumoto seen as a domestic issue, there was hardly any follow-up by either foreign governments or the large foreign press corps in Japan. Those concerned by the attack waited for Japanese authorities to act, until one day the world awoke to find the Tokyo subways filled with nerve gas.

Aum was not the only terrorist group failing to blip on those radar screens. Unlike Japanese police, American law enforcement has access to state-of-the-art investigative tools. Yet since 1993, U.S. officials have been unable to stop two of the deadliest attacks in history. Three years before the World Trade Center bombing, authorities seized evidence pointing to the coming campaign of terror. But lacking Arabic translators and experts on fundamentalism, they didn't see the clues. Similarly, officials failed to prioritize surveillance of the now notorious militia movement, despite subtle threats aimed at everyone from local judges to the president. The result: the 1995 bombing of a U.S. federal building in Oklahoma City, the worst terrorist incident in the nation's history. Both the New York and Oklahoma bombs were a decidedly low-tech mixture of diesel fuel and fertilizer. What will happen when these killers graduate to biochemical weapons?

A certain fatalism seems to accompany any discussion about terrorism and weapons of mass destruction. It is as if the movies have conditioned us to expect a James Bond to come to our rescue, defusing nuclear bombs and killing off terrorists by the dozen. Failing that, we simply sit back and cross our fingers, hoping that somebody somewhere does something.

Of course it doesn't work like that. To stop terrorists from gaining weapons of mass destruction will take plenty of hard work. It will require a concerned public, enlightened leaders, and more than a few dollars. Fortunately, there are a number of fairly obvious steps that can be taken.

The first is to address the problem. A world that spent trillions of dollars on nuclear and biochemical weapons must now find billions to stop their spread. Senator Richard Lugar, of the Senate Foreign Relations Committee, calls for action "that is as focused, serious, and vigorous as America's Cold War strategy." Lugar is concerned not only by terrorist groups but by the overall proliferation in weapons of mass destruction, which he calls the "greatest threat to our national security."

Certainly law-enforcement and intelligence agencies can do better – better training, better intelligence, more expertise. With the Cold War over, bringing the world's security agencies to bear on this challenge might prevent untold disasters. Until now, Western intelligence has focused largely on proliferation by nations, not by individuals or groups. Clearly this needs to change. A glaring need exists for a global strategy, particularly in close cooperation with former Soviet states. There needs to be better tracking of criminal and terrorist organizations, and of nuclear, chemical, and biological materials. In most nations, there are fewer controls on biological toxins than on marijuana.

Another difference could be made by the Chemical Weapons Convention, signed by over 150 nations since 1993. Despite support from world leaders, three years later the pact still awaited ratification by many governments, including the United States. Once its provisions are enforced, signatory states are bound to destroy their chemical-arms stockpiles, allow immediate inspections of suspect facilities, and ban shipments of key chemicals to nonsignatory states.

Other laws can no doubt be helpful, but the need for investigative powers will have to be balanced against the right to civil liberties. Antiterrorist measures in the world's democracies have stirred impassioned debate about the growing intrusion of security measures into our daily lives. It is an old but still critical dilemma: in our struggle to stop a dangerous foe, we endanger the very way of life we hope to defend. Airport metal detectors are one thing; widespread surveillance and military police are quite another. Ultimately, though, the right balance must be found. The risks are simply too great otherwise.

CAST OF CHARACTERS

Yoshinobu Aoyama
Aum's "Minister of Justice" or chief attorney. Aoyama, born in 1960, passed his bar examination before graduating from prestigious Kyoto University.

Shoko Asahara
Aum's "Holy Monk Emperor" – otherwise known as Chizuo Matsumoto, the cult's partially blind, bearded guru who founded Aum Supreme Truth in 1987. A native of southern Japan, Asahara was born in 1955.

Seiichi Endo
The cult's biological warfare expert or "Minister of Health and Welfare." Endo researched viruses at Kyoto University before joining Aum in his late twenties.

Kiyohide Hayakawa
Aum's "Minister of Construction" who oversaw the cult's expansion worldwide. A fast-talking Osaka native in his late forties, Hayakawa ran Aum's vast militarization program. He and Murai became Asahara's top two advisers.

Ikuo Hayashi
A middle-aged former cardiovascular surgeon who ran cult clinics and presided over human experimentation and drugging.

Yoshihiro Inoue
The guru's young spymaster or "Minister of Intelligence," responsible for gathering information, recruiting, and eliminating dissidents. Inoue was only eighteen when he joined the cult in 1988.

Fumihiro Joyu
Telecommunications graduate of elite Waseda University and former

employee of Japan's space agency. Born in 1962, Joyu ran Aum's Moscow office before becoming the cult's bilingual spokesman.

Kiyoshi Kariya
Tokyo notary public abducted by Aum in 1995.

Yoshiyuki Kono
Machinery salesman wrongly accused of releasing sarin in the Japan Alps town of Matsumoto in 1994.

Oleg Lobov
Chairman of Russia's powerful Security Council and close aide to President Boris Yeltsin. Lobov was widely tagged as Aum's influential supporter in Moscow.

Hideo Murai
The guru's devout "Minister of Science and Technology" and the dangerously brilliant architect of Aum's futuristic weapons program. Murai was born in 1958 and studied astrophysics at Osaka University's graduate school.

Tomomasa Nakagawa
The guru's personal physician and a top cult official. Nakagawa joined Aum before graduating from a Kyoto medical school.

Tomomitsu Niimi
Aum's "Minister of Internal Affairs" – in reality, the cult's security chief. Niimi was born in 1964 and graduated in law. His job included liquidating Aum's enemies.

Tsutsumi Sakamoto
Crusading Yokohama lawyer abducted by Aum in 1989 along with his wife and one-year-old son.

Masami Tsuchiya
Aum's workaholic chief chemist. Tsuchiya earned a Ph.D. in organic chemistry from Tsukuba University in Japan's "science city." He was thirty when arrested.

NOTES ON SOURCES

Andrew Marshall's work on Aum began in January 1995, when he reported on the Matsumoto sarin attack for British *Esquire*. Following the subway attack in March, David Kaplan began work with Nippon Television tracking Aum's activities overseas. The authors then teamed up to launch six months of intensive research for this book.

To piece together Aum's story, the authors and their associates conducted scores of interviews with past and present cult members, law-enforcement officials, intelligence agents, diplomats, and others. This included work in Japan, Australia, Germany, Russia, and the United States.

Various law-enforcement reports were made available to us; these proved particularly helpful. Also valuable were prosecutors' indictments, accounts of cult members' confessions, and an October 1995 report by the U.S. Senate Permanent Subcommittee on Investigations, "Global Proliferation of Weapons of Mass Destruction: A Case Study on the Aum Shinrikyo."

Another key source was Aum itself. The cult left a rich record of materials dating back to 1987 that include books, videos, sermons, magazines, flyers, public statements and press releases. Official records on the cult, such as incorporation papers and property deeds, were also made use of.

Following the subway attack, Aum was reported on extensively by the news media. The authors examined thousands of newspaper stories, hundreds of magazine articles, and scores of TV reports in Japan. The most complete and colorful coverage was done by the nation's often sensational weekly magazine press. Here we relied on a handful of the most dependable magazines: *Aera, Shukan Bunshun, Shukan Asahi,* and *Sunday Mainichi*. Articles in the monthly *Bungei Shunju* were of great help as well. Thorough searches were also done of news reports in Australia, Germany, Russia, and the United States.

Publishers in Japan have churned out some thirty books on Aum. Most are heavy on speculation, rumors, and second-hand reports, but a handful proved of particular value. The most dogged and impressive reporting was done by journalist Shoko Egawa, who

offers the best account of Asahara's life and Aum's early days in her
Kyu Seishu no Yabou (Ambitions of a Messiah), published by Kyoiku
Shiryo Shuppankai, 1991. Other books we found useful were Egawa's
Aum Shinrikyo Tsuiseki Nisen Nihyaku Nichi (The 2,200-Day Pursuit of
Aum Supreme Truth), from Bungei Shunju, 1995; Susumu Shimazo-
no's *Aum Shinrikyo no Kiseki* (The Tracks of Aum Supreme Truth), from
Iwanami Shoten, 1995; Yoshifu Arita's *Oitsumeru Aum Shinrikyo*
(Cornering Aum Supreme Truth), from KK Besuto Seraazu, 1995;
and Shoichi Fujita's *Aum Shinrikyo Jiken* (The Aum Supreme Truth
Case), by Asahi Shimbunsha, 1995. These provided important
background on cult rituals, daily life, and early history. Fujita's work
was also useful on Aum's weapons plans.

Much of the material for the four Russia chapters was drawn
from a fall 1995 trip to Moscow by Andrew Marshall, and from
research by our associate Vladimir Galin. In addition to numerous
interviews, the authors were aided considerably by information from
the Youth Salvation Committee and a state Duma investigation into
Aum. Russia's diverse press was also useful, especially *Izvestia*,
Moskovski Komsomolets, and *Komsomolskaya Pravda*.

On the proliferation of weapons of mass destruction, work by
two committees of the U.S. Congress proved invaluable. From the
Senate Permanent Subcommittee on Investigations came two sets of
hearings: "International Organized Crime and its Impact on the
United States," May 25, 1994; and "Global Proliferation of Weapons
of Mass Destruction," October 31 and November 1, 1995. And from
the House of Representatives Committee on Armed Services, a
February 1993 report, "Countering the Chemical and Biological
Weapons Threat in the Post-Soviet World."

Background on the various weapons systems discussed came
from many sources. The following books were of particular help:
Brian Beckett's *Weapons of Tomorrow* (Plenum Press, 1983), Bengt
Anderberg and Myron Wolbarsht's *Laser Weapons* (Plenum Press,
1992), and, on conventional weapons, the various Jane's guides.

On chemical weapons, we made use of Edward M. Spiers's
Chemical Weaponry (Macmillan, 1989); on biological weapons, Leonard
A. Cole's *Clouds of Secrecy: The Army's Germ Warfare Tests over Populated
Areas* (Rowman & Littlefield, 1988), and Charles Piller and Keith
Yamamoto's *Gene Wars: Military Control over the New Genetic Technologies*
(William Morrow, 1988). On terrorism and biochemical weapons,
research by the Rand Corporation was quite useful, particularly
reports by Jeffrey D. Simon, Brian Jenkins, Bruce Hoffman, David

Ronfeldt, and William Sater. Also helpful were Richard Clutterbuck's *Terrorism in an Unstable World* (Routledge, 1994) and *America the Vulnerable* by Joseph D. Douglass, Jr. and Neil C. Livingstone (Lexington Books, 1987).

On the effects of drugs and biochemical weapons, the authors consulted several medical manuals, including the *Merck Manual of Diagnosis and Therapy*, *Brain's Diseases of the Nervous System*, and the *Physicians' Desk Reference*.

ABOUT THE AUTHORS

DAVID E. KAPLAN is an investigative reporter and editor who specializes in Asia and the Pacific. He is co-author of *Yakuza* (1986), regarded as the standard work on Japanese organized crime, and author of *Fires of the Dragon* (1992), on the murder of Chinese-American journalist Henry Liu. He is also an editor of three books, among them *Paper Trails: A Guide to Public Records in California* (1990). In 1993, Mr. Kaplan left as news editor at the Center for Investigative Reporting, where his work was honored with more than a dozen awards, including the Investigative Reporters and Editors Award, a Gavel Award from the American Bar Association, and two International Journalism Awards from the World Affairs Council.

ANDREW MARSHALL is chief Asian contributor to British *Esquire*. His Aum feature for the magazine drew international attention for predicting the March 1995 nerve gas attack on Tokyo. Mr. Marshall began his journalistic career at the *Daily Telegraph*, Britain's largest quality daily newspaper, where he wrote features and edited science and youth supplements. He moved to Japan in 1991 to become deputy editor of *Tokyo Journal*, the city's premier English-language monthly, and is now a contributor to major newspapers and magazines worldwide.

INDEX

fever, 151, 213, 233;
recruiting Russian experts,
76; research into genetic
weapons, 232–4; sarin nerve
gas production, 85–6, 97–8,
108, 121–5, 131–3, 139, 140,
149, 150, 212–13; shopping
in Russia, 106–12; Time
Tunnel rail gun, 220–1; VX
nerve agent, 211, 214
wiretapping, 188
World Unification Company,
Tokyo, 223–4
X-Day to seize Tokyo, 154
Australian operation, 126–33, 265–6

Banjawarn Station, Western Australia,
126, 128–31, 133, 265–6
Aum purchase of, 127
Basov, Nikolai, 74, 207
Bei Li Wang cult, China, 291
Bihar visit, 67
biological warfare worldwide, 54–8, 76,
95, 122–3
Biosym Technologies, San Diego,
approached by Aum, 233,
234
Bonn European HQ of Aum, 45–6, 67,
103
Brookhaven National Laboratory, New
York, 102
Brosnan, Neville, 129–30, 131
Brosnan, Phyllis, 131
Büchler, Hans, 45
Buddhism, 10

Cairo visit, 14
Caplan, Alexander, 74
Central Intelligence Agency (CIA), 58,
191, 192, 235
shortcomings, 293–4
Chechnya, 268
arms purchases by Aum, 109–10
Chemical and Biological Arms Control
Institute, USA, 290
Chemical Weapons Convention, 295
Clinton, Bill, 219, 220, 293
Cuban missile crisis, 151

Dalai Lama, 67
friendship with Asahara, 13–14,
260
visits Japan, 260
Dallas, 123
Dharmsala, 13–14
Diet, Japanese, failed botulism attack by
Aum, 58–9, 92
Dikov, Alexandr, 266

Ebola virus, 96–7
Egawa, Shoko, 27–8, 181, 185
Aum attempt to silence, 185–6,
198, 211
author: *Ambitions of a Messiah*, 158,
185; *The 2,200-Day Pursuit of
Aum Supreme Truth*, 175; *The
Kidnapping of a Yokohama
Lawyer*, 185
Einstein, Albert, 207
Eitzen, Edward, 290
Enderlein, Hinrich, 45
Endo, Seiichi (Aum microbiologist and
bioweapons specialist), 28,
85, 93, 94, 97, 102, 127, 128,
270
anthrax failure, 95–6
arrest, 276
botulism toxin project, 52–3, 57,
59, 150–1
drugs production, 163
Ebola virus, 96
Minister of Health and Welfare for
Aum, 157
produces sarin gas for subway
attack, 236, 239, 242–3
Q fever culturing, 151
research into genetic weapons,
232–4
studies germ warfare in Russia, 107,
108
Evdokimov, Sergei, 199, 200, 201–2,
203, 204–5, 286

Forbes magazine, 89
Fort Detrick, USA, 291
Frankfurt, 191
Fujinomiya, 21

Gates, Robert, 76
Gavanti (Asahara disciple), 18
German expansion of Aum, 45–6
Gibson, William: *Neuromancer*, 183